# Someone to Remember

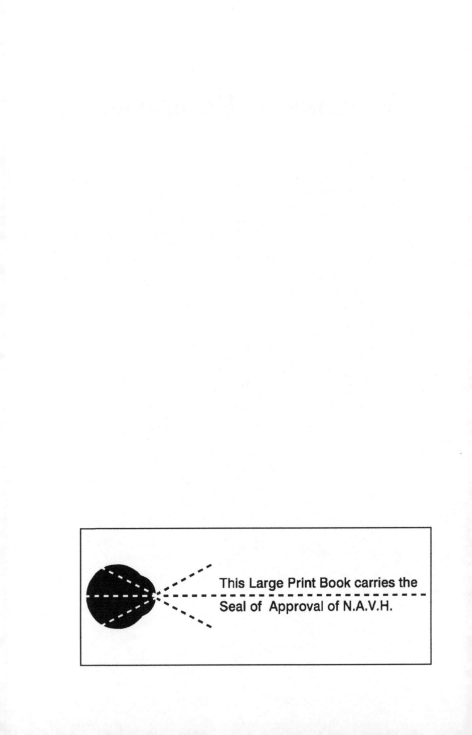

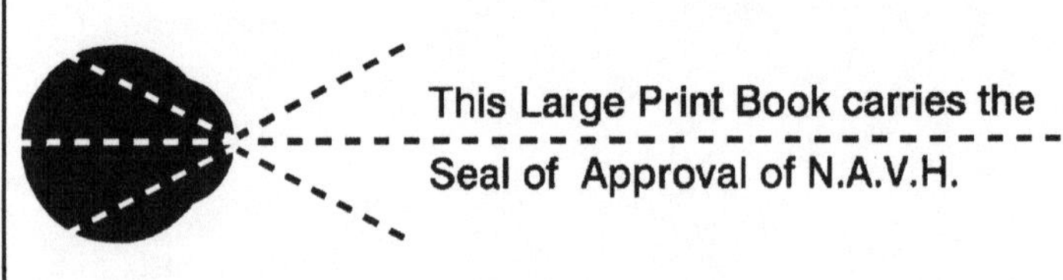
This Large Print Book carries the
Seal of Approval of N.A.V.H.

A WESTCOTT NOVEL



# Someone to Remember

Mary Balogh

**THORNDIKE PRESS**
A part of Gale, a Cengage Company

A Westcott Novel.
Thorndike Press, a part of Gale, a Cengage Company.


Thorndike Press® Large Print Core.
The text of this Large Print edition is unabridged.
Other aspects of the book may vary from the original edition.
Set in 16 pt. Plantin.

**LIBRARY OF CONGRESS CIP DATA ON FILE.
CATALOGUING IN PUBLICATION FOR THIS BOOK
IS AVAILABLE FROM THE LIBRARY OF CONGRESS**

ISBN-13: 978-1-4328-7352-3 (hardcover alk. paper)

Published in 2020 by arrangement with Berkley, an imprint of Penguin Publishing Group, a division of Penguin Random House, LLC

Printed in Mexico
Print Number: 01 Print Year: 2020

Dear Reader,
Welcome to the Regency world of the Westcott family.

Whether this story is your first venture into the series or you are an old friend who has read all or some of the six books that preceded it, I am delighted you have decided to read this novella. It was not part of the original plan for the series, but it caught my imagination anyway and insisted upon being written! I am thoroughly enjoying bringing this whole family to life by telling the love story of one of its members in each book.

The Westcott series was born in my mind with the idea of a crisis situation. What if the head of a family — an earl, no less — had entered into a bigamous marriage when he was a young man, tempted to it because he was in dire financial straits and needed a wealthy wife? What if he justified it, in his own mind, anyway, by the fact that the wife he had married secretly a few years before was dying of consumption?

Would anyone know? There was a daughter from that first marriage, but she was still an infant at the time. He decided that if she was put into an orphanage, no one would ever know who she was.

What if he got away with the bigamy until after his own death more than twenty years later, when his widowed countess sent her lawyer to find and pay off the orphan — presumably a love child from an illicit affair — she secretly knew her husband had been supporting?

What if the countess's son, the new earl, lost his title and fortune after the shocking discovery was made that he was illegitimate?

His sisters would also lose their titles and social status.

The larger family, thrown into turmoil, would somehow have to learn to cope with a new reality. A cousin who had never expected or wanted to inherit the title would find it foisted upon him anyway.

And there would be the added complication of the only legitimate daughter of the late earl discovering who she was at the same time as the family discovered it.

Would the family open — or close — its ranks to her? Would she want to be a part of it?

*Someone to Love,* the first book of the Westcott series, deals with just such a catastrophe. Specifically it is the love story of Anna Snow, in reality Lady Anastasia Westcott, the firstborn child of the earl, and Avery Archer, Duke of Netherby, guardian of Harry Westcott, the newly dispossessed young Earl of Riverdale. What would happen if that newly titled orphan fell in love with the man honor bound to protect the dispossessed heir? What if he fell in love with her?

My plan for the series was to write eight books — for Anna; for Harry and his sisters, Camille and Abigail, and their mother, Viola, the bigamously married Countess of Riverdale; for Alexander, the new Earl of Riverdale, and his sister, Elizabeth; and for Jessica Archer, cousin and best friend of Abigail. Most of them are young people. The eldest is Viola, who is forty-two when her story is being told in *Someone to Care.*

*Someone to Remember,* this additional and originally unplanned- for novella, is different from the others in that its heroine, Lady Matilda Westcott, is in her mid-fifties, considerably older than any other heroine I have ever created. But her story was begging to be told, and I know there are readers who want romances about older heroes and heroines. I have to admit, I absolutely adored writing this story. I do hope you will enjoy it too.

This story is special to me because of how it called to my imagination. It all started with Matilda, the spinster daughter of a former Earl of Riverdale, who appears in each of the Westcott novels. She is the one who remained single to devote herself to her mother's care, while her younger brother and two sisters married. In all the previous books, she came alive on the page as an overly fussy character, constantly irritating the dowager countess by wrapping shawls about her shoulders and otherwise protecting her from drafts and other hostile elements. She presses smelling salts upon her at the slightest hint of an upset. Uninvited and often unwanted, she always seems to be the one who heads family committees to deal with the crises that arise from time to time within the family. While she and her sisters are planning a grand society wedding for Anna and Avery in *Someone to Love,* for example, Avery whisks Anna off to a small, obscure church one afternoon and marries her privately. At that point, early in the series, Matilda certainly did not seem like a potential heroine.

That began to change, however, in *Someone to Trust,* book 5, Elizabeth's story. The change became irrevocable in *Someone to Honor,* book 6, Abigail's story. What happened was that Matilda started to become a real person to me, and suddenly she was precious.

She was far more than just an aging spinster daughter or sister or aunt to the other characters. She was more than just a fussy woman whose world revolved around her mother and the wider Westcott family. She was a *person.*

I started to see that she genuinely loved her family and wanted the very best for them all. She was a romantic at heart, as shown in her reactions when some of the family members chose mates the rest of the family found less than ideal. She was happy for Elizabeth and spoke out in her defense when Elizabeth made the shocking announcement that she was going to marry a man nine years her junior. She was happy for Abigail after Abigail married a man who had begun life as the illegitimate son of a village washerwoman.

By this time in the series, I realized I felt very tenderly toward Matilda and wanted her to have her own chance for romance and happiness. I also wanted to *know* her fully (this, by the way, is how all my main characters begin and grow — through the stories I write for them). What was the story behind her spinsterhood and her fussiness? Had she always been the same? Wasn't she ever interested in marrying? What was her truth? Since she had no reality beyond my imagination, only I could answer those questions — by writing her story.

I had decided after finishing *Someone to Honor* at the end of last summer that I would do something I had not done before, since I started writing in the 1980s, and take off the whole winter before starting on Jessica's story in the spring. However, I had organized a four-day writing retreat with a group of writer friends in November. I *love* those retreats, both for the concentrated writing time and for the camaraderie, and hated not to go. But if I did go, I couldn't spend the days twiddling my thumbs while all about me friends were happily tapping away on their keyboards. But what was I to write?

The question soon found an answer, of course. I would write a novella — a long story, a short novel — for Matilda. I thought at first it would be published just as an e-book. I jumped in with enthusiasm and had produced a third of the story by the end of the retreat. It all came together with relative ease despite the looming Christmas season. The hero had already obligingly identified himself in *Someone to Honor.* It was simply a matter, then, of bringing these two lonely souls together in a warm, romantic love story. Perhaps the imminence of Christmas actually helped me, even though it is not set at Christmastime.

As soon as I finished, I sent the story off to Claire Zion, my editor. After reading the finished novella, Claire liked it so much that she felt it had to be brought out for all the Westcott fans, and not just the e-book readers. Hence, you now hold in your hand the print edition (or maybe you're reading the e-book edition, which we also did).

As I'm sure you have noticed, this book is less expensive than my full-length novels. That's only because it's shorter, not because it's any less important to me than the novels. Matilda is a full member of my beloved family now! I have grown very fond of her and am glad as many readers as possible can find her story, regardless of their preferred reading format.

We have also included in this volume excerpts from all six of the Westcott novels already published. If by chance Matilda's story is the first of the series you have read, perhaps the excerpts will entice you to enrich your acquaintance with the family by reading the full stories of six of its members. The hope is that these excerpts will help you pick the next one to read.

If you have already read them, perhaps the excerpts will remind you of each separate story and send you back to reread them in their entirety. I asked on my Facebook page recently how many people are rereaders and was surprised that the overwhelming majority of those who answered are. So am I. There is something very comforting about meeting old friends again within the pages of a loved book. It's a bit like coming home.

But whether you are an old or new fan of the Westcott family, I offer you the below to help you navigate the series:

*Someone to Love,* book 1, involves the discovery soon after the death of the Earl of Riverdale, head of the Westcott family, that his marriage of more than twenty years was bigamous and that the son and two daughters of that marriage are therefore illegitimate. The secret, legitimate daughter of his first marriage, who grew up in an orphanage, unaware of her true identity, now inherits everything except the title itself and the entailed properties. That child, Anna Snow, now grown to adulthood, is the heroine of this book, which shows her as she copes with the staggering new realities of her life, not the least of which is the unexpected courtship of the very aristocratic Duke of Netherby, whose stepmother was a Westcott by birth.

*Someone to Hold,* book 2, is the story of Camille, one of the dispossessed daughters of the late earl. As well as losing her title and social status, Camille lost her aristocratic fiancé, who broke off their engagement as a result of the news. The proud, straitlaced, somewhat humorless Camille has to piece her life together somehow and takes the totally unexpected step of applying for the teaching job at the orphanage in Bath recently vacated by Anna, the half sister she at first deeply resents. There Camille meets Joel Cunningham, Anna's close friend and former suitor.

*Someone to Wed,* book 3, is the story of Alexander Westcott, suddenly and unwillingly the Earl of Riverdale after his second cousin Harry loses the title upon the discovery of his illegitimacy. Along with the title, Alexander has inherited the entailed mansion and estate that go with it, both of them neglected and shabby and in need of a huge influx of money — which he does not have. Resentfully but dutifully, Alexander turns his mind toward the search for a wealthy wife. At the same time, Wren Heyward, a reclusive neighbor who always wears a veil because of a disfiguring birthmark on one side of her face, decides to use the vast fortune she has recently inherited from an uncle to buy herself a husband and some sense of belonging.

*Someone to Care,* book 4, is the story of Viola, the forty-two-year-old former Countess of Riverdale, who reacted to the knowledge that her marriage had been bigamous and her children illegitimate first by running away to live with her brother and then by living quietly in the country with her younger daughter. She has suppressed her anger and her suffering for a few years. But her control finally snaps for no apparent reason at the christening of her grandchild in Bath, and she leaves alone to return home. On the way there, she encounters a man who once, years ago, tried to coax her into an illicit affair. She refused then, but now when he suggests that she run away with him for a brief romantic fling with no strings attached, she asks herself, why not? She does it — she runs off with Marcel Lamarr. As it turns out, however, there are many strings attached to that impulsive decision — for both Viola and Marcel. For each of them has a family that cares.

*Someone to Trust,* book 5, is the story of Elizabeth, Lady Overfield, the new earl, Alexander's, widowed sister, who left her abusive husband a year before his death. Now she has decided that she wants to marry again, but not for love this time. She wants a marriage of mutual respect and quiet contentment. However, at a Christmas family gathering in the country, she spends time with Colin, Lord Hodges, whose sister is married to her brother. There is an unexpected chemistry between them, but any thought of romance is out of the question, for Colin is nine years younger than Elizabeth and he too is in search of a bride among the young debutantes of the coming Season. I loved the challenge of dealing with the older woman / younger man dilemma. I also loved creating Colin's mother, the super-narcissistic villain, who first appeared in *Someone to Wed.*

*Someone to Honor* (make that *Honour* if you have the British edition!) is the story of Abigail, who is still grappling with the way her life completely changed after it was discovered that she was illegitimate. She still does not know quite who she is or what she wants out of life. Then she meets Lieutenant Colonel Gil Bennington, a friend and colleague of her brother's. Gil is a military officer and seems to be a gentleman, but in reality he is the illegitimate son of a village washerwoman and grew up as a gutter rat, to use his own words. He has acquired some wealth and a home in the country, but he is desperate to recover his young daughter from her maternal grandparents, who took her away when his wife died while he was away fighting in the Battle of Waterloo. His lawyer warns him that his best chance of winning the upcoming lawsuit is to marry again so he has a mother, as well as himself, to offer his child.

I do hope you enjoy the new story, *Someone to Remember.* I hope you will agree with me that Matilda is a precious person and deserving of her own happily-ever-after even though it has come late in life. And I hope you will agree that Charles is perfect for her and appreciates her as fully as she deserves. And expect to meet them again in future books — as well as Charles's children, including his first son, Gil Bennington, and, of course, Matilda's family, the Westcotts.

Please look for the next book in the series, book 7, Lady Jessica Archer's story, next year.

All the best to all of you,
Mary Balogh

# *The Westcott Family*

(Characters from the family tree who appear in *Someone to Remember* are shown in bold print.)

Stephen Westcott m. Eleanor Coke
Earl of Riverdale (1698–1761) — (1704–1759)

George Westcott m. **Eugenia Madson**
Earl of Riverdale (1724–1790) — (b. 1742)

Andrew Westcott m. Bertha Ames
(1726–1796) — (1736–1807)

**Matilda Westcott** (b. 1761)

Humphrey Westcott
Earl of Riverdale (1762–1811)
m. **Viola Kingsley** (b. 1772)
m. Alice Snow (1768–1789)

**Louise Westcott** (b. 1770) m. John Archer
Duke of Netherby (1755–1809)
m. Ava Cobham (1760–1790)

**Jessica Archer** (b. 1795)

**Mildred Westcott** (b. 1773) m. **Thomas Wayne**
**Baron Molenor** (b. 1769)

**Boris Wayne** (b. 1796) — Peter Wayne (b. 1798) — Ivan Wayne (b. 1799)

David Westcott (1756–1806) m. **Althea Radley** (b. 1762)

m. **Marcel Lamarr**

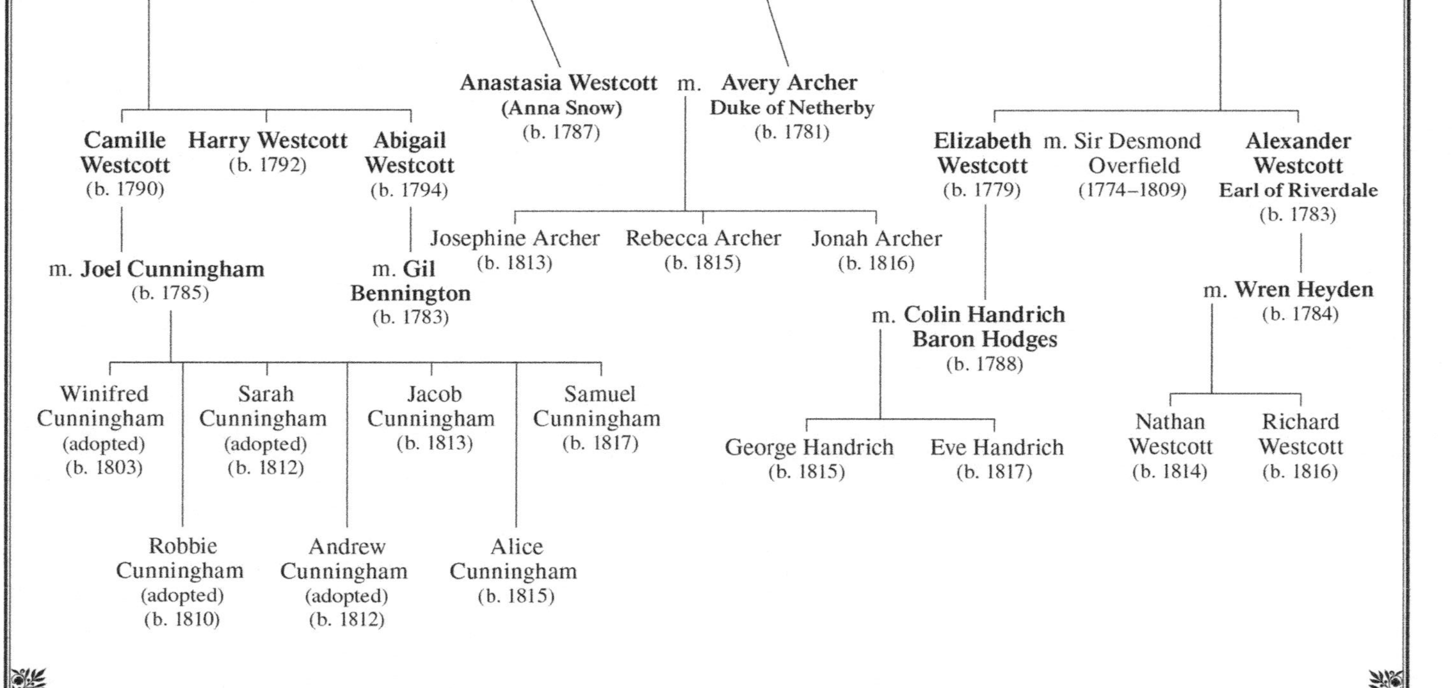
Anastasia Westcott (Anna Snow) (b. 1787)
m.
Avery Archer Duke of Netherby (b. 1781)
Camille Westcott (b. 1790)
Harry Westcott (b. 1792)
Abigail Westcott (b. 1794)
Elizabeth Westcott (b. 1779)
m. Sir Desmond Overfield (1774–1809)
Alexander Westcott Earl of Riverdale (b. 1783)
Josephine Archer (b. 1813)
Rebecca Archer (b. 1815)
Jonah Archer (b. 1816)
m. Joel Cunningham (b. 1785)
m. Gil Bennington (b. 1783)
m. Wren Heyden (b. 1784)
m. Colin Handrich Baron Hodges (b. 1788)
Winifred Cunningham (adopted) (b. 1803)
Sarah Cunningham (adopted) (b. 1812)
Jacob Cunningham (b. 1813)
Samuel Cunningham (b. 1817)
George Handrich (b. 1815)
Eve Handrich (b. 1817)
Nathan Westcott (b. 1814)
Richard Westcott (b. 1816)
Robbie Cunningham (adopted) (b. 1810)
Andrew Cunningham (adopted) (b. 1812)
Alice Cunningham (b. 1815)

# ONE

Lady Matilda Westcott's day had just taken a turn for the worse. She had not thought it possible, but she had been wrong.

She was sitting behind the tea tray in the drawing room, pouring for her mother and their visitors, whose unexpected arrival had cheered her at first. Alexander, Earl of Riverdale and head of the Westcott family, and Wren, his wife, were always welcome. They were an amiable, attractive young couple, and Matilda was extremely fond of them. Their conversation had followed predictable lines for several minutes — inquiries after the health of Matilda and her mother, and news of their young children and those of Elizabeth, Alexander's sister, and Colin, Lord Hodges, her husband, with all of whom they had enjoyed a picnic in Richmond Park the day before. But now they had changed the subject.

"Wren and I have decided that we really

ought to invite Viscount Dirkson to dine with us," Alexander said.

*"Ought?"* Matilda's mother, the Dowager Countess of Riverdale, asked sharply. Matilda meanwhile had gone still, the teapot poised over the third cup.

"As a sort of thank-you, Cousin Eugenia," Wren explained. "Not that any of us need to *thank* him, exactly. Gil is his son, after all. But Viscount Dirkson has had no dealings with Gil all his life and might easily have ignored that custody hearing a couple of weeks ago. His absence might have made no difference in the judge's decision, of course. On the other hand, perhaps it *did* make a difference. And we want him to know that we appreciate what he did. For Abigail's sake. And for Gil's and Katy's sakes. We have invited him for tomorrow, and he has accepted."

"But we would like it to be a *family* dinner," Alexander said. "Not all the Westcotts are in town, of course, but we hope those who are will join us." He smiled his very charming smile, first at Matilda's mother and then at Matilda herself.

Matilda scarcely noticed as she proceeded to pour the third cup of tea with a hand she held steady.

*She was invited too.*

She should have been delighted. While the last earl, Humphrey, her brother, was alive, the Westcotts had not been nearly as close a family as they were now. He had had little use for any of them, even his wife and son and daughters. And he had done terrible things during his life, the very worst of which was to marry twice. That was not a crime in itself, but in his case it was. His first, secret marriage, to Alice Snow, had produced one equally secret daughter, Anna. His second marriage, to Viola, his countess for twenty-three years, had produced three children — Camille, Harry, and Abigail. The criminal aspect of the second marriage was that it had overlapped with the first by a month or two before Alice died of consumption. As a result Viola and her offspring had ended up dispossessed while Anna, who had grown up in an orphanage, not knowing even who she was, had inherited a vast fortune, and the whole family had been thrown into turmoil, for the bigamous nature of Humphrey's second marriage had been unearthed only after his death.

*May he* not *rest in peace,* Matilda was often very tempted to think, even to say aloud. A very unsisterly sentiment, no doubt, not to mention unladylike. She often gave in to the temptation to think it nevertheless — as she did now.

She *should* have been delighted by the invitation, as Alexander was a far different sort of earl than Humphrey had been and had worked hard to draw the family together. However, the dinner was in honor of someone outside the family. Viscount Dirkson. *Charles.* A man Matilda would be very happy never to set eyes upon again for at least the rest of her life.

It had all started when Abigail Westcott, Humphrey's youngest daughter, had arrived unexpectedly in London a few weeks ago with an equally unexpected husband, whom she had married the day before. Lieutenant Colonel Gil Bennington had seemed a perfectly respectable young gentleman — he was a military friend of Harry, Abigail's brother. However, he had proceeded to reveal to Abigail's family that in reality he grew up as a gutter rat — his words — with his unmarried mother, who had scraped together a living as a village washerwoman. The family had been duly shocked. It really, truly *was* shocking, after all. Matilda had liked the young man anyway. He was tall and dark and handsome even if his face *was* marred by the scar of an old battle wound and even if he did tend to look upon the world with a dour expression. She had thought the sudden marriage wondrously romantic. She had fallen into shock only when Lieutenant Colonel Bennington had admitted, when pressed, that his father, with whom he had had no dealings all his life, was Viscount Dirkson.

He had been Charles Sawyer when Matilda had had an acquaintance with him ages ago, aeons ago. A lifetime. The title had come later, upon the death of his father.

But she had had a dealing with him since Gil's revelation — a secret, horribly scandalous dealing that would shock her family to the roots if they knew about it. The memory of it could still turn her cold enough to faint quite away — if she were the vaporish sort, which she was not. Well, it was not a secret from all of them. Young Bertrand Lamarr knew. He was Abigail's stepbrother, not a Westcott by birth but accepted by all of them as an honorary family member.

What had happened was that she, a single lady, had called upon Viscount Dirkson, a widowed gentleman, at his London home, with only young Bertrand as a companion to lend a semblance of respectability to what was in reality quite beyond the pale of it. She had screwed her courage to the sticking point, to quote someone in a Shakespeare play — Lady Macbeth? — though it might not be a strictly accurate quotation. Anyway, she had gone to persuade Charles to do something at last for his natural son, who was about to appear before a judge to plead for the return of his young daughter, who had been taken to the home of her maternal grandparents while Gil was away fighting at the Battle of Waterloo, and was never returned. It was the first time in thirty-six years she had come face-to-face with Charles or exchanged a word with him. After she had said her piece she had left with Bertrand, and she had comforted herself — *tried to,* at least — with the thought that *that* was the end of it. Finished. The end.

Now Alexander and Wren had invited him to a family dinner.

And she was a member of the family.

Charles Sawyer also happened to be the only man Matilda had ever loved. All of thirty-six years ago. More than half a biblical lifetime ago. She was fifty-six now.

All the cups had been filled, Matilda saw, and must be distributed before the tea in them turned cold. Her mother was talking.

"Viscount Dirkson is to be rewarded, then, for fathering a son out of wedlock and doing nothing for him in the more than thirty years since, until he spoke up on his son's behalf before a judge a few weeks ago?" she asked as Matilda set a cup of tea on the table beside her and made sure it was close enough for her to reach but not so close as to be knocked over by a careless elbow.

Wren came to take Alexander's and her cups from the tray and smiled her thanks to Matilda. "He did purchase his son's first commission some years ago, if you will recall, Cousin Eugenia," she said.

The dowager made a sound of derision and batted away her daughter's hand when Matilda tried to rearrange her shawl, which had slipped off one shoulder. "Don't fuss, Matilda."

"And that son is now married to Abigail and is therefore a member of our family," Alexander added, taking his cup and saucer from Wren's hand. "But even aside from purchasing the commission, what Dirkson did a couple of weeks ago was significant. Without his recommendation at the court hearing, Gil might very well not have regained custody of his daughter, and both he and Abigail would have been distraught. Dirkson would surely have attended the hearing for his own sake, of course, since Gil *is* his son. However, Wren and I feel an obligation to thank him on behalf of Abigail's family. Do say you will come too."

"It is nothing short of a miracle that Viscount Dirkson even found out about the custody hearing," Wren said.

But it had not happened by a miracle, Matilda thought as she picked up her own cup and sipped her tea. There was nothing miraculous about her.

"You are very quiet this afternoon, Matilda," Alexander said, smiling kindly at her. "What do *you* think? Will you come to our dinner? Will you persuade Cousin Eugenia to come too?"

Her opinion was rarely solicited. She was merely an appendage of her mother as she fussed over her, making sure she did not sit in a draft or overexert herself or get overexcited, though her mother resented her every attention. Sometimes, especially lately, Matilda wondered whether her mother needed her at all — or even loved her. It was a thought that depressed her horribly, for if the love and care she gave her mother were pointless, then what had been the purpose of her life? And why was she already thinking of it in the past tense?

"I think it is an admirable idea," she said. "You are a worthy Earl of Riverdale, Alexander. You take your responsibility as head of the family seriously. Inviting Viscount Dirkson to dine with as many of the family as are in London is a good way of showing him that we appreciate his speaking up for Gil. It will show him that we consider Gil one of us, that we value his happiness and Abigail's. And Katy's."

Katy was Gil's daughter — and Charles's granddaughter. That realization stabbed a little painfully at Matilda's heart every time her mind touched upon it. He had other grandchildren. Both of his daughters were married and both were mothers. His son, the youngest of his offspring, was as yet unwed. His wife of twenty years or so had died five years ago.

Alexander looked pleased at her praise. "You will come, then," he said. "Thank you."

Yes, she would go, though the very thought made her feel bilious. He was still so very handsome. Charles, that was. Whereas she . . . well, she was an aging spinster, perhaps even an *aged* one, and . . . Well.

"And will you invite Viscount Dirkson's family too?" her mother was asking. "His son and his daughters?"

"It is hardly likely they know of Gil's existence," Alexander said, frowning. "I doubt he would want them to know."

"Perhaps," Wren said, "we ought to inform Viscount Dirkson that he is welcome to bring his children if he wishes, Alexander. Let the decision be his."

"I will do that, my love," he said, nodding to Matilda, who was offering to pour him a second cup of tea. "Yes, thank you. You *will* come, Cousin Eugenia?"

"I will," she said. "Dirkson ran wild with Humphrey as a young man, you know, though he did not have the title in those days. His reputation became increasingly unsavory as time went on. He was not welcomed by the highest sticklers and perhaps still is not."

"I think we will not hold the past against him," Alexander said, a twinkle in his eye. "If he had not fathered an illegitimate child when he must have been a very young man, we would not even be planning this dinner, would we?"

"And Abigail would not have found the love of her life," Matilda said.

"Oh, I think you are right about that, Cousin Matilda," Wren said, beaming warmly at her. "I believe she and Gil are perfect for each other and perfect parents for Katy. No, no more tea for me, thank you. We must be on our way soon. We have taken enough of your time."

"But we have not told you our own very happy news," the dowager said.

"Oh," Wren said. "We must certainly hear that."

And Matilda was instantly reminded of why she had been feeling severely out of sorts even before Alexander and Wren arrived with their invitation.

"Edith is coming to live with us," her mother announced.

"Your sister, Cousin Eugenia, do you mean?" Alexander asked.

"Edith Monteith, yes," the dowager said. "I have been trying to persuade her to come ever since Douglas died a couple of years ago. She has neither chick nor child to keep her living in that drafty heap of a mansion all the way up as near to the Scottish border as makes no difference. It will be far better for her to come to me. She was always my favorite sister even though she is almost ten years younger than I."

"And she is coming to live permanently with you?" Wren asked. "That does indeed sound like good news." But she looked with a concerned frown at Matilda.

Her mother must have seen the look. "It is going to be wonderful for Matilda too," she said. "She will not be tied to the apron strings of an old woman any longer. She will have someone closer to her own age for companionship. Adelaide Boniface will be coming with Edith. She is a distant cousin of Douglas and quite indigent, poor thing. She has been Edith's companion for years."

Aunt Edith had suffered from low spirits since as far back as Matilda could remember, and Adelaide Boniface made good and certain they remained low. If the sun was shining, it was surely the harbinger of clouds and rain to come. If there was half a cake left on the plate for tea, then the fact that half of it was gone was cause for lamentation, for there would be none tomorrow. And she spoke habitually in a nasal whine while the offending nose was constantly being dabbed at and pushed from side to side with a balled-up handkerchief, the whole operation followed each time by a dry sniff. Matilda found the prospect of having her constant companionship, not to mention Aunt Edith's, quite intolerable. She really did not know how she was going to endure such an invasion of her home and her very life.

"I am very happy for you both, then," Alexander said, setting aside his cup and getting to his feet. "Are they coming soon?"

"After we go home to the country at the end of the Season," the dowager told him.

"We are certainly happy about it, are we not, Matilda?"

"It will be something new to look forward to," Matilda said, smiling determinedly as Wren hugged her and Alexander kissed her cheek and bent over her mother's chair after assuring her that she did not need to get to her feet.

"We will see you both tomorrow evening, then," he said.

Oh, Matilda thought after they had left, how was she going to *bear* it all? Coming face-to-face with Charles again tomorrow and spending a whole evening in his company. Going back to the country in one month's time to a home that would be home no longer. Could life possibly get any bleaker?

But how could spending an evening in Charles's company possibly matter after thirty-six years? One could not nurse a broken heart and blighted hopes that long. Or, if one did, one was a pathetic creature indeed.

Oh, but she had loved him . . .

All silliness.

"He is thirty-four years old," Charles Sawyer, Viscount Dirkson, was telling Adrian, at twenty-two the youngest of his offspring. "It happened long before I married your mother. Before I even knew her, in fact."

"Who was she?" Adrian asked after a pause, a frown creasing his brow, one hand clasping a leather-bound book he had taken at random from one of the bookshelves upon which he leaned. "Or perhaps I ought to have asked, Who *is* she?"

"Was," Charles said. "She died many years ago. She was the daughter of a prosperous blacksmith. I met her while staying with a friend at a house nearby. It was a brief liaison, but it had consequences."

"So all the time you were married to Mother," Adrian said, "you were seeing that woman and *him.* Your other family."

"Nothing like that," Charles assured him. "She would have nothing to do with me when she understood that I would not marry her even though her family had turned her out without a penny. She refused all support for herself and the child. She raised him on the money she made from taking in other people's washing until he went off with a recruiting sergeant at the age of fourteen to join the army. After she died I purchased a commission for him. But he stopped me and cut all ties with me later, after I had purchased a promotion for him. His mother raised a proud son."

"But he managed to rise to the rank of lieutenant colonel after you gave him a leg up into the officer ranks," Adrian said, opening the book briefly before snapping it shut without even looking at it. "And now he has married into the Westcott family. Bertrand Lamarr, that friend of mine from Oxford who came to call a few weeks ago, has a connection to them too. His father married one of them a few years ago. And the lady who came here with him was a Westcott. You took her to look at the garden while he and I were becoming reacquainted. Was it through her that you discovered your . . . *son* had married a Westcott and was in a court battle to regain custody of his daughter? Your *granddaughter*?" He laughed rather shakily and set the book flat on the shelf rather than slotting it into its appointed place.

"Yes," Charles said. "I went to the hearing and said a few words to the judge. Riverdale, head of the Westcott family, seems to believe that what I said made a difference and helped . . . Gil to win his case."

"Gil," his son said softly.

"Gilbert," Charles said. "She named him. His mother."

He had pondered telling his son after a second note had come from Riverdale following the initial invitation. Viscount Dirkson was quite welcome to bring his children and their spouses to the dinner too if he wished, the note had said. Charles most certainly did not wish any such thing. He did not even want to attend himself. Perish the thought. He could not see why the Westcott family felt somehow indebted to him. Gil was *his son,* after all. Katy, as Adrian had just pointed out, was *his* granddaughter. He had not attended that custody hearing for the sake of the Westcotts. He had done it for his son, whom he had never seen before that day but whom he had loved for thirty-four years. Yes. True.

Ah, but he had done it also at least partly for one of the Westcotts, had he not?

For Matilda?

He had rarely been more surprised — no, *shocked* — than he had been a few weeks ago when his butler had come to his dressing room to inform him that Lady Matilda Westcott was downstairs in the visitors' parlor with young Lamarr, Viscount Watley, who claimed to be a university friend of his lordship's son.

*Matilda.* Here in his own house. Wanting to speak with him. After . . . how long? Thirty years? Thirty-five? It must be the latter or even a bit longer. Gil was thirty-four, and all the drama with Matilda had been over before he was conceived. In fact there had been a connection. Charles would almost certainly not have engaged in that ill-considered affair with Gil's mother if he had not been raw with pain over Matilda's rejection when she had adamantly refused to stand up to her parents' disapproval of his suit. Within months or even weeks he had gone dashing into the arms of the first pretty woman to take his eye and respond to his flirtations. And he had taken none of the usual precautions when he lay with her. She had taken none either. Perhaps she had not even known such a thing was possible. Or perhaps she really believed he had promised to marry her, though he knew beyond all doubt that he had not.

He had got over Matilda years and years ago, though when they were both in London he had spotted her occasionally, growing ever older and more staid, wasting herself upon a mother who had denied her daughter's happiness and now did not seem to appreciate that daughter's attentions. He had felt irritated every time he set eyes upon Matilda Westcott — the only feeling he had had left for her.

Until, that was, he had stepped a few weeks ago into the visitors' parlor here in his own home and she had called him by his given name instead of his title, a woman of fifty-six who was a stranger and yet was not. He had found himself then remembering the pretty, vital, warmhearted young woman she had once been and had felt an irritation far more intense than usual — for her and perhaps for time itself for robbing her of youth and beauty. And maybe for himself for remembering not just facts but feelings too, most notably the depths of his youthful passion for her and the contrasting pain of his despair at losing her, not because she did not love him but because her parents did not think him worthy of her. And anger. That she had turned him out and there had been no way of getting her to see reason. And present anger that she had come to his home like this without a by-your-leave and with only young Lamarr's connection to Adrian as an excuse.

He had been angry that he could still remember those feelings. For it had all been a lifetime ago. And why should he remember? He had known scores of women both before and after her and even after his marriage.

Why should it annoy him that Matilda had grown old? No, not old. That was both inaccurate and unkind. Besides, she was almost the exact same age as he. She had grown middle-aged — to the shady side of middle age, to be more precise. She had never married. Why not, for God's sake? Had no one measured up to the expectations of dear Mama and Papa? Yet their two younger daughters had married well. Had Matilda been too valuable to them, then, as the family drudge? Had it pleased them to sap all the life and youth and passion out of her until she became as she was now?

But why should it annoy him, what had happened to Lady Matilda Westcott? A bruised heart did not remain bruised for very long. He had soon learned that. He had forgotten her before that summer was even over. Gil's mother had had successors. His reputation as a rake had been well earned.

"So," Adrian said, "is he going to be in your life now? As a semi-respectable member of the Westcott family? Is that what this dinner is all about?"

"The dinner," Charles explained, "is Riverdale's way of thanking me for appearing at the custody hearing and perhaps having some small part in enabling my . . . son to get his daughter back from her grandparents. He does not need to thank me. None of them do. I do not really want to go to the dinner, but it would seem the civil thing to do."

"And you want me to go with you," Adrian said.

Charles shrugged, picked up the quill pen from the desk before him to trim the nib, changed his mind, and set it back down. "I thought I ought to tell you at last," he said, "before word somehow leaks out, as it well might, and you learn the truth from someone else. The existence of my natural son makes no difference to my feelings for you and your sisters."

"I have a half brother twelve years my senior," Adrian said, as though he were only now understanding what Charles had told him several minutes ago. "Does he look like me?"

"No," Charles said.

"No." Adrian laughed. "How could he? I look like Mama. Does he look like you?"

"Yes," Charles said. "But he has a facial scar." With one finger he traced a line across one cheek and down over his chin.

"The crusading hero," Adrian said. "I suppose it makes him irresistible to women. And he is tall and dark like you, is he? I suppose you are going to grow close to him now."

"I very much doubt it," Charles said. "He

does not have a high opinion of me, and I cannot blame him."

"Do you have a high opinion of him?" his son asked.

Charles hesitated. "Yes," he said. He pushed his chair with the backs of his knees and got to his feet. "You may come to the dinner with me if you wish, Adrian. I will be pleased if you do. I will understand if you do not."

"Do you intend to tell my sisters?" Adrian asked.

Neither of them was in London at present. Barbara, the elder of the two, was in the country with her husband and children to celebrate the fortieth wedding anniversary of her parents-in-law. Jane had discovered herself to be with child just before the start of the Season and had remained in the country until she recovered from the bilious phase that had plagued her also with her first child.

"I do," Charles said. "In person when the opportunity arises." And for the same reason that had persuaded him to tell Adrian. The truth was bound to come out now that Gil had surfaced in his life, even though his son planned to live year-round in Gloucestershire. It was better that the news come from their father.

Adrian nodded and pushed away from the bookshelves. "I'll come," he said. "Bertrand will be there, you said?"

"Lamarr?" Charles said. "Viscount Watley? Very probably, since his father is married to the former Countess of Riverdale."

"Then I'll come," Adrian said again. "Just as long as your other son will not be there too."

"No," Charles said. "He has already taken his wife and daughter home to Gloucestershire."

"At your expense?" Adrian asked.

"No," Charles told him. "He is apparently independently wealthy. So is his wife."

"I have to go out," his son said abruptly, making his way toward the door. "I was supposed to be somewhere half an hour ago."

"Adrian." His son stopped, his hand on the doorknob, and looked back at him. "I adored you from the moment I first saw you all swaddled up in your mother's arms, your cheeks red and fat. I have not changed my affections since."

His son nodded again and was gone.

He was not good with words of affection, Charles thought. He had not been a good husband. They had not married for love, he and his wife, and they had lived very separate lives. They had always been polite to each other, but there had been no real warmth or affection between them.

It had been otherwise with his children. He had always loved them totally and unconditionally, and still did. He had spent time with them when they were young. He had taught them to ride and had taken Barbara hunting with him on several occasions. He had taken Jane and Adrian fishing. He had taken them all swimming and tree climbing — the latter when his wife was well out of sight. He had read to them before they could do it for themselves. Perhaps, he thought now, he had lavished upon his legitimate children all the time and affection Gil's mother had refused to allow him to lavish upon his firstborn.

He picked up the quill pen again, though he did not resume his seat, and turned it in his hand, brushing the feather across his palm.

He loved his firstborn son with a dull ache of longing. But he wished all this had not happened to churn up pointless emotions — Gil's sudden appearance in London with a wife, terrified that he might lose his daughter forever if the judge ruled against him; Charles seeing his son for the first time across that small courtroom where the hearing had been held, the Westcott family in their rows of chairs between them; the stiff, awkward breakfast meeting the following morning at Gil's hotel, arranged by Gil's wife; the almost certain knowledge that they would never see each other again.

Matilda.

He wished he did not feel angry with her, irritated with her for aging and making him want to lash out at someone or something for a reason he could not even fathom.

Passion was for young men. He resented the strong emotions that had been coming at him from all directions during the past few weeks. His life, at least for the previous ten years or so, had been on the placid side as he surrendered to middle age, prepared to enjoy his grandchildren, and rejoiced in how well his children were settling into meaningful lives. His relative contentment with life had included happiness for his firstborn, who had survived the unimaginable brutality of the Napoleonic wars.

He did not want strong emotions to erupt now at his age.

He did not want to have to look again into the wounded eyes of his younger son, who had just discovered the existence of an older half brother. He did not want to have to tell Barbara and Jane, and that was an understatement.

He did not want to go to this infernal dinner at Riverdale's house on South Audley Street. He did not want to have to talk about Gil with the Westcotts. He did not want to spend an evening in company with Matilda.

Especially that. In fact, without that, the dinner would be merely an inconvenience.

He had loved her . . .

But it was all foolishness.

# Two

Eighteen members of the Westcott family — though not all of them actually bore the name, or, in some cases, even the blood — were assembled in the drawing room at the house on South Audley Street where Alexander, Earl of Riverdale, had his town residence. They ranged downward in age from the dowager countess, who was in her middle seventies, to Boris Wayne, twenty-one years old, eldest son of Matilda's sister Mildred, newly down from Oxford and eager to cut a figure as a dashing young man about town, much to his mother's frequent consternation.

There were plenty of persons, in other words, among whom to hide. But they nevertheless seemed thin cover to Matilda as Alexander's butler announced Viscount Dirkson and Mr. Adrian Sawyer, his son, whom she had met very briefly a few weeks ago when she made her call upon his father.

She took up her accustomed position behind her mother's chair and busied herself with her usual tasks, checking to see that her mother was comfortable and in no danger of a draft from the opened door even though it was not the time of year when one was likely to take a chill from such exposure. She attempted to be invisible, to blend into the scenery.

Charles stepped into the room ahead of his son. He was a remarkably distinguished-looking man and was drawing all eyes his way. Well, of course he was. He was the newcomer, the guest of honor. He had just walked in among a crowd of people who all claimed some sort of kinship with one another. Nevertheless, he looked perfectly at ease as he smiled and bowed to Wren and shook Alexander by the hand. His hair was still thick and predominantly dark, though it was nicely silvered at the temples. Although he was not slim in the way a young man is slim, he had an excellent figure, the extra weight well distributed about his person. His evening clothes were expertly tailored.

All told, he was an extremely attractive man and Matilda dearly wished she had thought of some excuse not to come, though *what* excuse she did not know. She had always been notoriously healthy. She had never, all her life, laid claim to the vapors or heart palpitations or any of the other ailments many women trotted out anytime they wished to avoid an activity they considered tedious.

She *wished* her mind was not so full of buzzing bees.

She turned her attention toward Mr. Adrian Sawyer, several inches shorter than his father and fuller faced, fair-haired rather than dark — a pleasant-looking young man. He too was smiling as he bowed to Wren and said something that caused her to twinkle back at him. What reason had his father given him for their attendance at this family dinner? Had he told him the truth? Bertrand was making his way toward his former university friend, and the two shook hands warmly before Bertrand bore him off to introduce him to Estelle, his twin sister, and to an openly eager Boris.

Seeing Alexander begin to lead Charles about the room to make sure he knew everyone — though he surely did — Matilda stepped farther behind the chair and bent over the back of it to adjust her mother's shawl.

"Don't fuss, Matilda," her mother said just as the two men arrived before her chair.

"The Dowager Countess of Riverdale," Alexander said, "and Lady Matilda Westcott."

"I have an acquaintance with Viscount Dirkson," Matilda's mother said, her voice regal and a bit chilly, "though it has been a while since we last spoke. I did see you in the judge's chambers a couple of weeks ago but you did not remain after the proceedings were over. You used to be a friend of my son's."

"I did indeed, ma'am," he said, bowing to her. "The late Riverdale and I were acquaintances for a number of years. I also know Lady Matilda. How do you do, ma'am?"

He was looking very directly at her over her mother's head, and Matilda felt as flustered as a girl at her first *ton* party, her heart pounding hard enough in her bosom to rob her of breath, her brain spinning and fluttering with a thousand bees' wings so that no sensible answer presented itself immediately to her tongue and lips. No one was looking at her, she told herself. Not with any particular attention, anyway. And why should they? She was just Matilda. And why be so flustered? She had actually called upon him and stepped into his garden with him and spoken with him there less than a month ago. But that was half the trouble.

What must he have thought of her bold presumption?

"I am well, I thank you," her mother said in just the words Matilda ought to have uttered in the brief moment of hesitation that had followed his question.

His eyes remained on hers a moment longer before he looked down to acknowledge her mother's reply, and then he stepped away with Alexander to shake someone else by the hand.

Matilda leaned over the back of the chair again to adjust her mother's shawl, remembered that she had just been told not to fuss, and straightened. She, who never wept, even when there was good cause, wanted to weep now when there was none.

"It is easy to see where Gil got his height and his looks, is it not, Matilda?" her former sister-in-law, Viola, said, moving up to her side. "He and Abby and Katy arrived safely home in Gloucestershire. I had a letter today. Abby loves the house and the village and the countryside. I have rarely if ever had such an exuberant letter from her. I do believe she is going to be happy."

"I *know* she will be," Matilda said, patting Viola's arm. "She already is. They both are. He has a way of looking at her and she at him, and they have the child. And their cottage in the country with a garden full of roses."

"Now if I can just see Harry happily settled I will consider myself the most blessed of mothers," Viola said.

Her son, Harry, had very briefly been the Earl of Riverdale following his father's death — before it had been revealed that his birth was illegitimate.

"He will have his own happily-ever-after, never fear," Matilda assured her.

"You cannot be certain that anyone will be happy, Matilda," her mother said. "What do you know of marital bliss, never having been married yourself?"

Matilda did not wince, not outwardly at least.

"But Matilda knows a great deal about *love,* Mother," Viola protested, linking her arm through her erstwhile sister-in-law's. "I will take her word about Abby and Gil's future because I want to agree with her and actually do. And I agree about Harry."

Charles was bending his head to listen to the conversation of the small group to which he had been led. He was smiling, his eyes crinkling attractively at the corners.

He had fathered Gil very soon after she sent him away, even though he had sworn undying love and fidelity when he went. And for years afterward he had had what Matilda believed to be a well-deserved reputation as a rake and a gamester and a man who lived hard and behaved recklessly. He had perhaps mellowed with age. She could not know for sure. But surely her father had been right to refuse his consent to their marrying and her parents had been right to insist that she put an end to her acquaintance with him. *Acquaintance!* Ah, it had felt like far more than that. But surely she would have been miserable had she married him.

Wouldn't she?

Love would not have been enough.

Would it?

But they were pointless questions to ask herself. She could not know the answers. There was no going back to do things differently. There was no knowing how happy or unhappy their marriage would have been. There had been no marriage.

Dinner was being announced and Matilda entered the dining room with her mother. Fortunately she was able to sit halfway along the table, some distance from Charles, who was seated beside Wren at the foot. Unfortunately, perhaps, she had not thought to go to the other side of the table so that she would be on the same side as he and therefore unable to see him every time she looked up from her plate and turned her head that way. But it did not matter anyway. He was never looking back at her when she did inadvertently glance at him. He was always politely focusing his attention upon Wren to his left or Louise, Dowager Duchess of Netherby, Matilda's middle sister, to his right. Conversation was lively along both lengths of the table.

Matilda discovered without surprise that she had little appetite. She also felt like bawling for no good reason whatsoever — again. She sincerely hoped she was not about to develop into a watering pot at her advanced age.

It was a somewhat more pleasant evening than Charles had anticipated. For one thing Adrian was taken almost immediately under the wing of young Bertrand Lamarr, who introduced him to Lady Estelle, his twin sister; to Boris Wayne, Lord Molenor's son; and to Lady Jessica Archer, half sister of the Duke of Netherby, who was married to a Westcott. And since Adrian was a young man of generally even temper and easy manners, he appeared to be right at home with all of them and actually enjoying himself.

The dinner was excellent, the conversation pleasant. He had agreeable table companions. Only at the end of the meal was the subject of Gil raised when Riverdale got to his feet, a glass of wine in his hand.

"We Westcotts are always ready for an excuse to gather together," he said when everyone had fallen silent and turned his way. "We are happy this evening to have Viscount Dirkson and Mr. Sawyer with us too. Perhaps none of us needed to be present in the judge's chambers for the custody hearing a couple of weeks ago. Perhaps young Katy would have been released into Gil and Abigail's care even if we had all stayed away. But I am glad we went. Even if our presence did not weigh with the judge, at least we demonstrated to the newly married couple that we care, that we consider them family, that we will concern ourselves with their well-being and stand with them whenever it is threatened for any reason. It is what we Westcotts do for our own. It is what no doubt you do for your own, Viscount Dirkson. We are happy that your son came with you this evening. Shall we drink a toast to family — to all branches of it no matter how slight the connection?"

They drank, even Adrian, who looked steadily at his father as he did so.

The ladies withdrew to the drawing room after the toast, leaving the men to their port and their male conversation. In the drawing room later, the Marchioness of Dorchester, Gil's mother-in-law, came to sit beside Charles. She spoke of the difficulties her daughter had faced after the discovery that her father had married her mother bigamously. She spoke too of her conviction that her daughter's marriage to Gil would be a happy one for both of them.

"Ma'am," Charles said, "you do not have to convince me, if that is indeed what you are attempting to do. I agree with you." They smiled at each other, two parents linked by the marriage of their offspring.

He conversed with other members of the family too, even the Dowager Countess of Riverdale after she had beckoned to him, almost like a queen summoning her subject. He was not fond of that particular lady, though he had had no dealings whatsoever with her for many years and it would be foolish to hold a grudge for what she had done more than half a lifetime ago. But even this evening she had annoyed him. He had seen her as soon as he walked into the drawing room earlier, perhaps because Matilda had been standing behind her chair beside the fireplace, and Matilda was the Westcott he had least wanted to encounter this evening. But as he had approached with Riverdale to pay his respects, she had bent over the back of the chair to adjust her mother's shawl about her shoulders. The old lady had batted away her hands and admonished her not to fuss, a thinly disguised impatience in her voice, though she must have been aware that she might be overheard.

Or perhaps she had not been aware. Perhaps she was so accustomed to treating Matilda that way that it did not strike her as inappropriate behavior before a stranger. But then she had compounded her disregard for her daughter. Charles had acknowledged the older lady and turned his attention to Matilda and asked her how she did. But it was the mother who answered, leaving her daughter with nothing to say and perhaps feeling foolish. He had felt irritation with both of them, with the dowager for behaving as though her daughter did not even exist and could not possibly be the object of his inquiry, and with Matilda for meekly accepting it.

Was this the life for which she had renounced him all those years ago? But why should he care? It was all ancient history. Good God, he had had a full life since then.

Matilda was living the life she had chosen, as the spinster daughter who had remained at home, the prop and stay of her parent in old age.

But who would care for Matilda in *her* old age?

He would have rather enjoyed the evening if she had not been there. But every moment he was aware of her and hated the fact. He had been aware during dinner and had deliberately avoided looking her way and perhaps meeting her glance. He had relaxed briefly while the men were alone together after dinner. But then he had been aware of her again in the drawing room.

He had no real idea *why.* He had been involved in a brief, passionate romance with her when they were both very young, had been rejected by her father when he had asked to pay his addresses to her, had been rejected by *her* afterward to the extent that she had told him firmly to go away and refused ever to speak to him or so much as look his way ever again. And that had been the end of that. It had been surely the sort of disappointment that most men, and probably many women too, suffered during their volatile youth. He had not pined with unrequited love for long. Maybe a few days. Perhaps a few weeks. No longer than that.

He had promptly got on with his life.

And it had happened all of thirty-six years ago, for the love of God. Why was it, then, that he was so aware of her now and so irritated by her — and for her? Society was full of aging, fussy spinsters who were used by their relatives and lacked the spirit to fight back. But none of the others irritated him or aroused ire in him on their behalf.

She was standing over at one end of the room, talking with a couple of the other ladies. After they had moved away she remained there, straightening a pile of sheet music on top of the pianoforte. Then she looked across the room toward her mother. Perhaps, Charles thought, this needed to be settled — whatever *this* was. He strode toward the pianoforte before she could hurry away to see if her mother's shawl needed straightening again.

"How *do* you do, Matilda?" he asked, emphasizing the one word. She had not been given the chance to answer the question earlier.

"Oh." She looked into his eyes and kept her gaze there. "My mother thought you were addressing her."

"Even though I was looking at you?" he said. "Does she imagine you are invisible?"

She drew breath and closed her mouth.

Then she drew breath again when it must have become obvious to her that he was waiting for her answer. "I do not suppose so. I do not know what you expect me to say."

"I expect you to tell me how you are," he said. "It would be the courteous thing to do, to answer a question politely asked, would it not?"

She tipped her head slightly to one side, and he was instantly assailed by memory. It had been a characteristic gesture of hers when she was twenty, and apparently it still was.

"I am well," she said. "Thank you."

"Why did you not say so when I asked earlier?" And why was he pressing the point? He had no idea except that he was still feeling the irritation she seemed to arouse in him.

"My mother answered," she said.

"To inform me that *she* was well," he said. "Does she always answer questions that are addressed directly to you?" He frowned at her.

"It would perhaps have embarrassed her if she had realized it was me you were asking," she said. "Charles, what is this about?"

It was a good question. He did not have an answer. She looked her age, he thought.

But she was not actually a faded creature, as one might expect her to be under the circumstances. She was tall, still as straight backed as she had been as a young woman, her posture elegant, even proud. She was no longer slender. But she was well proportioned and elegantly dressed. Her face was virtually unlined, her hair still not noticeably graying. She was what might be called a handsome woman. She had been pretty as a girl, with a spark of animation to make her beautiful in his eyes. She might have married any of a dozen eligible men during that first Season of hers. She had not married him. She had not married anyone else either. Or during all the Seasons after that.

"Are you happy?" he asked her, his tone sounding abrupt even to his own ears.

She frowned but said nothing.

"I expected every time I opened the morning papers for a year or more afterward," he said without stopping to explain what he meant by *afterward,* "to see a notice of your betrothal to someone rich and eligible and respectable. It never happened, even after I stopped specifically looking. Are you happy?"

"I scarcely know what to say," she told him. "I make myself useful. My mother needs me, and it is a comfort to my sisters to know that she has constant companionship."

He gazed steadily at her. He had his back to everyone else in the room. But he did not suppose his conversation with her was being particularly remarked upon. Why should it be? He had conversed with most of the rest of the family by this stage of the evening. Why not with Lady Matilda Westcott too? No one in this room with the exception of her mother would remember their brief, intense courtship. And even if anyone did, it was a long time ago.

What would life have been like if they had married? It was impossible to know. So much would have been different. Everything would have been. Gil would not exist. Neither would Adrian nor Barbara nor Jane. Nor any of his grandchildren. But perhaps other children and grandchildren who had never been born would have had existence in their stead.

"Do you live to serve, then?" he asked her.

"There are worse ways to spend one's life," she told him.

"Are there?" It was not really a question he expected her to answer. "Why did you not marry?"

She recoiled slightly before recovering and looking beyond him to smile briefly at someone he could not see. "Perhaps," she said, "no one asked."

"That is nonsense," he said. "And untrue. *I* asked."

Her eyes focused fully upon him again. "Perhaps there was no one I wished to marry," she said.

"Not even me?"

He watched her draw a slow breath. "Your son — Gil — was born a mere year or so later," she said. "Whether I wished to marry you is not the point. The point is that I was wise not to do so."

That was inarguable. He had been known as wild even before he met her. But it had been the wildness of a very young man testing his wings and sowing a few wild oats, if that was not a hopeless mingling of metaphors. His real notoriety as an unsavory character and a rake came afterward. Would it have happened if he had married Matilda? He could not know the answer. He had not married her.

"It was wise, then," he said, "not to marry anyone else either?"

"Perhaps," she said.

"But perhaps not? Do you regret remaining unmarried?" He could not seem to leave the matter alone.

"Regrets are pointless," she said.

"Yes." She did regret it, then?

"The tea tray has been brought in," she said, looking beyond him again, "and Wren is pouring. I must go and add the correct amount of milk and sugar to my mother's cup and take it to her. She likes her tea just so."

And no one else was capable of doing it quite right? No one else knew the exact number of grains of sugar or drops of milk? He did not ask aloud. He stood aside and let her pass. As she did so he got a whiff of her perfume, so subtle that it could not be detected unless one was close to her. He was rocked by the memory of that same perfume and a shared kiss behind a potted aspidistra on the balcony outside a ballroom where they had danced a minuet together. A brief, passionate kiss. Lady Matilda Westcott had always — *almost* always — been carefully chaperoned by her mother.

Why would he remember that kiss when he had surely forgotten hundreds of others and the women with whom he had shared them? She had pressed her lips to his and brought her bosom against his chest, her spine arching inward beneath his hands. And he had smelled her perfume and been lost in sensual bliss — and an intense sexual desire that had never been fully satisfied.

Why was he remembering? Just because of that whiff of perfume?

# Three

Matilda took her mother a cup of tea, made just the way she liked it, as well as a piece of cake, and stayed close even though there was no need to. Both her sister Louise and cousin Althea, Alexander's mother, were seated close to her and engaging her in conversation. The younger women were agreeing that this evening's gathering had been a good idea of Alexander's and that it was encouraging that Viscount Dirkson had come and had even brought Mr. Sawyer, his son, with him.

"Well, I do *not* like it," Matilda's mother said. "All I can say is that I hope it is not a case of like father, like son. Viscount Dirkson was a crony of Humphrey's, which is *not* a great recommendation even though Humphrey was my son."

"Mama, do not upset yourself." But when Matilda would have handed her mother the smelling salts she always kept in her reticule, her hand was pushed aside.

Mr. Adrian Sawyer spoke up at that exact moment. He was addressing his father, but loudly enough to draw everyone's attention.

"Bertrand is getting up a party to go out to Kew Gardens tomorrow, Papa," he said. "He wants me to go with them. Will you mind terribly if I do not after all accompany you to Tattersalls, as I promised I would? May we make it next week instead?"

"And who is to be of this party, pray, Bertrand?" Louise asked, raising her voice.

"Well, my sister and Adrian for sure, Aunt," Bertrand replied. "And Boris."

"And me," added Jessica — Lady Jessica Archer, Louise's daughter. "I may go, may I not, Mama, instead of going visiting with you?"

"And my particular friend, Charlotte Rigg, to make numbers even," Estelle, Bertrand's twin sister, said. "I am sure her mama will let her come. I believe she has designs upon Bertrand." She laughed as he grimaced. "Her mama, that is, not Charlotte herself."

"Oh bother," Louise said. "That will mean I ought to accompany the party in order to reassure Mrs. Rigg that it is properly chaperoned. There are some ladies I particularly wished to call upon tomorrow."

"Oh, Mama," Jessica protested, "we will all be cousins and siblings. There will be absolutely no need of a chaperon. Besides, I am twenty-three years old."

"A veritable fossil," Avery, Duke of Netherby, said on a sigh, looking with lazy eyes at his half sister through his jeweled quizzing glass.

"But Miss Rigg is neither anyone's sister nor anyone's cousin," Louise pointed out. "Nor is she twenty-three. I doubt she is even nineteen. And her mother will not be able to accompany her. I heard just this afternoon that she has taken to her bed with a nasty chill."

"Well, bother," Jessica said.

"I daresay I could accompany the young people," Charles said, causing all eyes to turn his way — including Matilda's, though she had been trying to ignore him, having been considerably discomposed by that strange conversation of theirs. Heavens, did he seriously believe the Westcott family, not to mention Mrs. Rigg, would consider him a suitable chaperon for a group of six that included three young ladies, none of whom was related to him? But he was not finished.

"Provided there is a lady who is prepared to come as cochaperon, of course," he said.

"But if I go, as it seems I must," Louise

said, "you may save yourself the trouble, Lord Dirkson. I —"

"I suppose I could —" Viola began at the same time.

Charles cut them both off.

"Perhaps Lady Matilda Westcott?" he suggested, turning his eyes fully upon her. "If the dowager countess can spare her for a few hours, that is."

What? *What?*

*"Me?"* Matilda said foolishly, spreading a hand over her bosom while she felt all eyes turn her way. Though she was really aware only of his eyes and of the disturbing feeling that she might well swoon. Yet she gave no thought to the smelling salts in her reticule.

"Oh yes, do come, Aunt Matilda," Jessica cried, turning eagerly toward her. "It is really rather dreary to be on an outing with one's own mama as chaperon." She laughed and looked fondly at Louise. "No offense intended, Mama. I am sure you felt exactly the same way when you were my age."

"Oh yes, please do come, Aunt," added Bertrand, who had informed her a few weeks ago that she was a great gun after she had ridden in his sporting curricle all the way to Charles's house without clinging or squawking in alarm. It had actually been one of the most exhilarating experiences of her life. She only wished he could have sprung the horses. "You can keep a strict chaperonly eye upon Estelle." He grinned at his twin.

*"Chaperonly?"* His father, the Marquess of Dorchester, raised his eyebrows.

"Will you please come, Aunt Matilda?" Boris asked. "I have a hankering to see the pagoda at Kew. I have never been there."

"May I add my pleas, ma'am?" Mr. Sawyer added, smiling sweetly at Matilda. "And you will be comfortable with Papa, will you not, since you know him?"

It seemed to Matilda that the room grew suddenly silent and that all eyes turned accusingly upon her. Perhaps she was imagining it. But her cheeks felt as though they had caught fire.

"It is a very slight acquaintance," she hastened to explain. "I met your father, Mr. Sawyer, when my brother was still alive and I had just made my debut into society." She wondered if he would remember her calling his father Charles rather than Lord Dirkson when she had appeared at his house with Bertrand a few weeks ago. And heavens, she willed him not to mention that visit. Her mother and the rest of the family would be scandalized at the very least. "We danced together at a few balls that Season. It was many years ago, as you may imagine. I would be delighted to play chaperon for Jessica and Estelle and Miss Rigg tomorrow if I may be spared. It is ages since I was last at Kew. Mama?"

"Of course you can be spared, Matilda," her sister Mildred said. "I will spend the afternoon with Mama."

"I do not need anyone to cosset me," their mother protested.

"I will spend the afternoon with you anyway," Mildred said. "You may cosset me if you prefer. At least I will be able to relax, knowing for once where Boris is. He will be under the eagle eye of my sister."

*"Mama,"* Boris protested, clearly mortified.

"Then it is settled," Bertrand said, rubbing his hands together. "We merely have to make arrangements for Charlotte Rigg to come with us."

"Oh, there will be no problem over that," Estelle assured him. "Not when her mother is too sick to take her anywhere herself and Aunt Matilda will be accompanying the party. There is no one more respectable."

"Thank you, Estelle," Matilda said. "You make me sound very staid and very dull."

"You are not dull at all," that young lady

cried, startling her by rushing at her and catching her up in a hug. "Or staid."

"What I want to know about," Boris said, "is your flighty youth, Aunt Matilda, when you were in town with Uncle Humphrey and made your come-out and knew Lord Dirkson. Was everything very different back then?"

"Oh yes, indeed," Matilda said, slightly dizzy over the fact that everyone's attention was upon her. "We lived in caves, you know, and wore animal skins."

"And hunted down our food with stone mallets," Charles added to the great delight of the young people.

Matilda, catching his eye and noting the twinkle there — oh she *recognized* that twinkle — felt suddenly giddy with joy.

*Joy?*

When had she last felt joyful? When she had also felt youthful? A long, long time ago. Back when they lived in caves and rubbed sticks together to make fire. Even before the time of bows and arrows.

"And did you waltz at those balls, Aunt Matilda?" Boris asked.

Alas, no. The waltz had not been invented until long after she was young.

"We stamped about barefoot to the beating of drums," Charles answered for her, actually grinning for a moment.

Matilda laughed aloud and then felt horribly self-conscious. For though the young people and most of the adults were laughing too, Charles's eyes were fixed upon her, and suddenly he was not laughing at all. His eyes had even stopped twinkling.

Ah, but she wished, wished, *wished* the waltz had become popular thirty years or so before it had. It was surely the most romantic dance ever. She wished there was the memory of waltzing with him, even if only once.

"It was decent of you to offer to accompany our party," Adrian said the following morning as he rode his horse alongside his father's through the streets of London.

"I shall enjoy seeing Kew on my own account," Charles said. "I just hope you will not feel constrained by my presence."

"Not at all." Adrian grinned. "If I wish to become amorous, I am sure I will discover some bushes behind which to slink while you are looking the other way."

"You fancy one of the ladies, then, do you?" Charles asked.

"Lady Jessica Archer has a court of admirers large enough to fill our drawing room," Adrian told him. "I would be totally lost in the crowd. And I do not *fancy* Lady Estelle Lamarr, though she is exceedingly pretty and I like her. I do not believe I have met Miss Rigg, though I may recognize her when I see her. I have no intention of fixing my interest for many years yet."

The group was to gather at Archer House on Hanover Square, home of the Duke of Netherby, Lady Jessica's half brother. They were to take one carriage, provided by young Bertrand Lamarr's father. The ladies would ride in that. The men would accompany it on horseback. And they had perfect weather for the excursion. After a few cloudy, blustery days, the sun was shining and the wind had died down at last. It was going to be a warm day, though probably not oppressively hot.

Why the devil *had* he made the offer to accompany the young people? Obviously he could not be the sole chaperon of a group of unmarried young ladies. Yet without them there would have been no need of chaperonage at all. He could fulfill his role only if there were an older lady with him, yet he had no wife. Had he imagined the shocked silence with which his offer had been received? He knew why he had made it, of course, for he had already had a lady chaperon in mind.

Strangely, he had not really thought of the implications of his suggestion until later. It had been such a spur-of-the-moment thing. It had hardly occurred to him that he was dooming them both to spending the day in company together. He had thought only that *Matilda* was free to go with the young people, that she would probably be well accepted by them all since she was the mother of none of them. He had thought that she would probably enjoy a day out with young people, free of her own mother. He had thought that she would enjoy a day at Kew. She had enjoyed it thirty-six years ago. And yes, Adrian, there were bushes there behind which a couple could slink for a quick kiss.

He had wanted her to be *visible.* They were a decent lot, the Westcotts, but they had one collective shortcoming that had irritated him all evening. None of them saw Matilda. Oh, they did not ignore her. She was a part of their family and was included in all their activities and conversations. But none of them *saw* her. None of them, with the exception of her mother, had seen her, lovely and graceful, eyes bright, cheeks flushed with animation, dancing a minuet. None of them *knew* her. A presumptuous thought, no doubt, when he had had no dealings with her for well over thirty years and had known her even all that time ago for only a few brief months.

But she was a *person,* by God, even if she was past the age of fifty. Even if she was a spinster. She deserved *a life.*

But now he was stuck with being in company with her all day. It was not a happy thought, though he had found himself dressing with greater than usual care this morning — to his great annoyance when he had realized it.

"I think I want to meet him," Adrian said abruptly.

Charles turned his head to look at his son.

"Lieutenant Colonel Bennington," Adrian explained. *"Gil."*

"He lives in Gloucestershire," Charles told him. "I doubt he will want to meet you, Adrian. He has no desire to see me ever again."

"A man can travel," Adrian said. "A man can knock on a door. It can remain closed to him, of course, but he can do those things."

Charles frowned. "And will you?" he asked as they turned their horses into Hanover Square.

His son shrugged. "Maybe," he said. "Maybe not."

There was no further chance to consider

what Adrian had just said. Dorchester's traveling carriage as well as a cluster of horses was drawn up outside Netherby's house. A chattering group of young people was gathered on the steps and out on the pavement while the young Duchess of Netherby and the dowager duchess, Lady Jessica's mother, looked on from the top step, presumably preparing to wave them on their way. Lady Matilda Westcott was standing by the open door of the carriage.

He had once told her, Charles remembered suddenly, that pale blue was her color, that she should wear it as often as possible. Where the devil had that memory come from? She was wearing it now. It might have been thought to be too youthful a color for a woman of her age, but the dress and the spencer she wore over it were smart and elegant, neither youthful nor dowdy. She wore a small-brimmed navy blue bonnet, neat, with no added frills or flowers or feathers. She had spotted him and inclined her head, rather prim mouthed. He wondered if she regretted agreeing to his suggestion. But she had done it without hesitation. And then she had made that light, humorous answer about living in caves and wearing animal skins to the question one of the young people had asked about life when they were young. And then, when he had added his own silliness, she had laughed aloud with what had sounded like genuine glee.

And, ah . . .

She had been Matilda in that moment, as she had once been. As though all the years between had fallen away.

"Mr. Sawyer," Lady Estelle Lamarr cried gaily, addressing Adrian as they rode closer. "There you are. You are almost late. And you see? We have added two more members to the party. Mr. Ambrose Keithley and Dorothea, his sister, have agreed to join us." Miss Rigg and the Keithleys were identified and made their bow and curtsies.

"How do you do, Lord Dirkson?" Bertrand Lamarr called, grinning up at Charles. "Both Mrs. Rigg and Lady Keithley accepted you without question as a chaperon for their daughters."

"I believe, Bertrand," the dowager duchess said, "it was the fact that Matilda was to go along with the group that persuaded both of them. Good morning, Lord Dirkson, Mr. Sawyer."

Charles touched his hat to the ladies and smiled at Matilda. Her lips grew even primmer. Even her kid gloves, he noticed, were pale blue. Had she dressed with as much care as he had this morning? Had she remembered what he had told her about the color? Or had she discovered for herself over the years that it suited her?

"If the horses are not to stage a rebellion at being kept waiting so long," she said, *not* specifically addressing Charles, "we should perhaps think of being on our way."

"Oh yes, indeed," Lady Estelle cried. "You will sit on the seat facing the horses, Aunt Matilda. We are all agreed upon that. The rest of us drew spills, and Jessica won the seat next to you, the lucky thing. Charlotte, Dorothea, and I will squeeze onto the other seat, our backs to the horses."

"How fortunate the gentlemen are," Miss Keithley said, "being able to ride the whole way in the fresh air. We ought to have drawn also for the middle seat. Now we will have to squabble over it."

"Not in my hearing," Matilda said. "You may occupy it on the way there, Miss Keithley, and Estelle on the way back."

"Bravo, Aunt Matilda," young Boris Wayne said. "You keep them in line."

Miss Keithley laughed and climbed into the carriage. The other three young ladies lost no time in following her, all talking and laughing at once.

"Matilda," Charles heard the dowager

duchess say to her sister, "I hope you know what you have taken on. I doubt they will stop giggling all the rest of the day."

"I expect to survive the ordeal, Louise. I was once young myself," Matilda replied before looking, obviously startled, at Charles, who had dismounted in order to hand her into the carriage. "Thank you, Lord Dirkson."

She rested her hand lightly upon his outstretched one and he closed his fingers about it. It was a slim, long-fingered hand and warm through her glove. And then she was inside the carriage and turning to sit beside Lady Jessica, and the coachman was putting up the steps and closing the door before climbing to the perch and gathering the ribbons in his hands.

Charles mounted his horse again, and the whole cavalcade set off on its merry way to Kew. Adrian was already laughing with the other young men, perfectly at his ease.

Now *this,* Charles thought, was a new experience. The rake turned chaperon.

Bertrand had thought overnight of a friend of his who would be sure to want to join them. Perhaps more significant, Matilda had understood from the studied carelessness with which he had made the explanation, the friend had a sister who was very pretty and vivacious and had danced a set with Bertrand at her come-out ball a month or so ago in addition to several since then. So the carriage was more crowded than originally planned, and three of the young ladies were forced to sit squashed together on the seat opposite the one she shared with Jessica. Their spirits did not seem to be in any way dampened by discomfort, however.

It was a merry group indeed. Matilda had half forgotten how the very young behaved when they far outnumbered any older persons. She might have tried impressing a more sober decorum upon them and thus securing some peace for herself, but why should she? She was actually pleased to discover that her presence seemed not to have any inhibiting effect upon the spirits of her charges.

"Mama was not at all inclined to permit me to come," Miss Keithley said when the carriage was nicely under way, "even though Ambrose was to come too. I almost *died.* But then she was told that *you* were to chaperon us, Lady Matilda."

"Oh dear," Matilda said, twinkling back at the girl. "Does that mean I have a reputation as something of a dragon?"

It was a quite unwitty remark, but it

nevertheless set off a renewed gust of giggles from all four of her fellow travelers.

"Not at all," Miss Keithley assured her. "Mama said you were *eminently respectable* — her exact words."

"Ah, a dragon, then," Matilda said. "I shall try not to breathe fire over any of you, however. Provided, that is, you all display your most sedate conduct from this moment on."

For some reason that suggestion called for another burst of merry laughter, and Matilda felt happy for no reason she could explain. She had not felt at all happy all through a night of disturbed sleep. She had never been a chaperon. More to the point, she had never been a chaperon *with Charles Sawyer.* Whatever had possessed him to offer her name when Viola had been about to suggest going with the young people and Louise had been about to make a martyr of herself by agreeing to go herself? Mama had not been at all pleased. She had told Matilda on the way home last night that she ought to have put that man in his place with a very firm refusal. Since he was going too on this ramshackle excursion to Kew, who was going to chaperon Matilda?

*Mama,* Matilda had protested. *I am fifty-six years old.*

*And Viscount Dirkson is a rake,* her mother had retorted.

*Was a rake,* Matilda had said. *His own son is to be of the party, Mama.*

She had lain awake wondering why he had suggested her name and why she had agreed with such alacrity and what she would do if any of the young people misbehaved. Surely that would not happen, though. They were all properly brought up young persons. And she had wondered what she and Charles would talk about if they happened to be paired together, as was surely very likely since the young people would want to be with one another. She had wondered if he would offer his arm and if she would take it. The very thought had interfered with her breathing and she had wondered if she could develop a head cold or smallpox or something similarly dire overnight so that she could send her excuses and beg Viola to go in her stead. But there was her notoriously healthy constitution. No one would believe her.

But now she felt happy and carefree, almost as though she were one of these youngsters herself. Almost as though she had suddenly shed thirty-six years and might start giggling too at any moment. Goodness, they would all look at her as if she had sprouted another head.

"One thought bothered me last evening," she said. "The excursion was planned to include six young persons. But it was going to be impossible, I thought, for the six to be sorted out in such a way that *two* were not going to be paired with either a sibling or a cousin. What a dreadful waste of an outing and lovely weather *that* would have been."

Again the delighted, trilling laughter.

"But now that the number has increased to eight," Matilda continued, "you may each walk with a gentleman who is not related to you in any way at all."

The laughter this time was mingled with a few blushes.

"And that includes you, Lady Matilda," Miss Rigg said. "For there are ten of us in all, are there not?"

"Well, goodness me, yes, you are quite right," Matilda said, hoping she was not about to become one of the blushers. "Now let me see. I need to avoid Boris Wayne, as he is my nephew, and Bertrand Lamarr, since he is my former sister-in-law's stepson. Does that make him in any way my relative? Hmm. Maybe not, but he does call me Aunt Matilda. He is very handsome, is he not?"

"He is," Miss Keithley said with a scarcely disguised sigh.

"Bertrand and I both consider you our aunt," Estelle told Matilda. "And do not tell him he is handsome or his head will swell."

"But you will be paired with Lord Dirkson, Lady Matilda," Miss Rigg told her in all seriousness, as though there were any alternative.

"I suppose you are right," Matilda said, "since he is the only one close to me in age. Well, he is rather handsome too, is he not?"

"I think Mr. Sawyer is nice looking," Estelle said. "He has kind eyes and a sweet smile."

"Was Viscount Dirkson really a friend of Uncle Humphrey's?" Jessica asked. "And did you really meet him all those years ago, Aunt Matilda, and dance with him at balls? I think he must have been very handsome as a young man. He must have looked a bit like Gil but without the scar. Did you fancy him?"

*"Fancy?"* Matilda said, raising her eyebrows. "Is that the sort of language your mama encourages you to use, Jessica?"

But Jessica only laughed with glee, as did the other three. "Were you in love with him?"

"Oh, head over ears," Matilda told her. "So was every other girl on the market that year, and probably a few who were not. But there were many other very gorgeous young men to ogle too. I am convinced men were more handsome in those days."

"Oh, Aunt Matilda," Jessica said, still laughing, "is that the sort of language Grandmama encouraged you to use? *Ogle?*"

"Touché," Matilda said, and patted her niece on the knee.

The attention of the young ladies turned beyond the windows at that point. They would have claimed to be admiring the scenery, no doubt, if asked, while what they were really admiring was the gentlemen, who often rode within sight of the windows. They did it deliberately, Matilda believed, in order to see and be seen. Oh, she had forgotten so much about the mating rituals of the very young. But how easily the memory of it all came back — the preening and flirting, the fan waving and pretended indifference, even disdain.

Men always showed to advantage on horseback, provided they had reasonably trim figures and good posture and well-muscled thighs and rode as though they and the horse were a single entity.

All of which *Charles* had and did. The thought was in Matilda's mind before she could guard against it. He was fifty-six years old, for heaven's sake. But he was still gorgeously handsome and attractive. Though probably only in her eyes. She doubted any of her companions were sparing him a glance when there were Bertrand and Boris to gaze at, and Mr. Sawyer and Mr. Keithley.

She wondered if he had noticed she was wearing pale blue. She *hoped* not, or, if he had noticed, for after all he had eyes, she hoped he did not remember once telling her that she should always, always wear blue of the palest shade because it accomplished the seemingly impossible and made her even prettier and more desirable than she already was. He had actually used those words — *more desirable.* She had been shocked and thrilled to the core. But how foolish to think that he might remember. So many years had passed. She had not chosen her outfit deliberately for that reason. She had tried three different dresses first — the dark green, the tan, and the dark blue — before she had instructed her maid to pull this one from the back of her wardrobe. She had worn it only once before even though she had possessed it for two years. She had concluded after that one occasion that it was too youthful. But today she had tried it on and had felt immediately happy in it. She might be going as a chaperon, but she was not *ancient.* Not quite, anyway. And she wanted to look her best.

She had deliberately not asked herself why.

It felt very strange not to be with her mother. Not to be watching her every moment to make sure she was comfortable and warm and not in need of a shawl or a fan or a cup of tea. Not to be a shadow whom no one really saw except her mother, who was more often than not irritated with her for constantly fussing. Why did she do it, then? Because she needed to be needed by someone? It felt wonderful to be free of all that. The whole of today — well, the rest of the morning and the afternoon anyway — stretched ahead of her with nothing further to do except watch eight young people who really would not need any watching at all and enjoy the beauties of Kew Gardens, which she had not seen for ages. And on a perfect day, with scarcely a cloud in the sky or a breath of wind.

A whole afternoon to spend in Charles's company. And she was not going to feel self-conscious about it or fearful that he would find her dull, though he surely would. For *he* had asked *her.* She had not even thought of volunteering her services. She was going to enjoy herself, though she was feeling somewhat apprehensive about the end of the journey and the pairing up that would happen as soon as the men had dismounted and the ladies had stepped down from the carriage. She was perhaps the only one who knew exactly with whom she would be paired.

She was going to enjoy herself anyway. And if he thought he was going to throw her onto the defensive as he had done last evening, then he was going to have a rude awakening. She did not owe Charles Sawyer an explanation for *anything* she had done with her life. If anyone owed an explanation, it was he. Though that was not quite right. She, after all, was the one who had broken off both their romance and their acquaintance — because she would not have been able to carry on with the latter without the former. She had dismissed him and thus set him free to do and to be whatever he wished. He had done just that. But she would not even *think* of the past for the rest of today.

"This is going to be *such* fun," Miss Keithley said. "It is the first time I have been out without Mama since we came to London."

"But if you think your mama is a strict chaperon," Matilda said, "wait until you discover what I am. Dragons may appear mild in contrast. You may well beg your mother to accompany you everywhere you go for the rest of the Season."

A renewed burst of happy giggles greeted her dire warning and she smiled.

And then stopped smiling.

They had arrived.

# Four

Bertrand Lamarr and Boris Wayne wanted to go straight to the Chinese pagoda and climb to the top.

"Two hundred and fifty-three stairs," Boris said, "winding around the center."

"And spectacular views from each story," Bertrand added.

"Are there really golden dragons on the roofs?" Miss Rigg asked. But she wanted to go first to the orangery because it had been recommended by a cousin.

"But it is said to be too dark inside for the fruit to flourish," Miss Keithley told her.

"I want to see some of the temples," her brother said. "We missed them when we came last year because everyone else wanted to see the pagoda."

Lady Estelle Lamarr wanted to see Kew Palace, and Lady Jessica Archer would prefer the Queen's Cottage.

"All the royals used to have picnics in the

gardens there when they were children," she said. "Queen Charlotte used to arrange them."

"It is such a beautiful day," Adrian said, "and the gardens are so well laid out and so full of varied trees and plants and green expanses of grass that I would be content just to stroll about without any particular destination, seeing what is to be seen as we come to it."

Everyone had expressed a preference almost before Charles had handed Matilda down from the carriage and turned it over with all the horses to the care of the grooms and the coachman.

"I daresay we can spend at least a couple of hours here," he said, "before feeling the need to seek out a late luncheon or early tea, whichever seems appropriate when the time comes. There will be a chance to see everything and even just to relax and look about us and enjoy the sunshine. Lady Matilda, you are the only one who has not voiced an opinion. With what shall we start?"

"Me?" she said, spreading a hand over her bosom. Charles guessed that her preferences were not often consulted. "Well, I do not mind."

"The pagoda, Aunt Matilda," Boris said,

grinning at her.

"The Queen's Cottage."

"The temples."

"The orangery."

"Kew Palace."

They all clamored to be heard, and there was much laughter interspersed with the raised voices. Ambrose Keithley was elbowing Bertrand Lamarr in the ribs for some unknown reason and was being elbowed back. Miss Keithley had raised her parasol and set it spinning behind her head. Adrian was pretending the poke of it had caught him in the eye as he clapped both hands over it. Matilda held up a staying hand, and miraculously order was restored.

"You all have a great deal of pent-up energy," she said. "It needs to be used. Two hundred and fifty-three stairs, did you say, Boris? Perfect. We will begin with the pagoda. Besides, I want to see those dragons even if they *are* only gilded wood and not solid gold."

"But you have to climb to the top, Aunt Matilda," her nephew said, waggling his eyebrows at her.

"Was there any question of my *not* doing so?" she asked. "*Of course* I will be climbing to the top. Let us go. I did not agree to chaperon you all just in order to stand here procrastinating for the rest of the day."

And they all paired up and moved off along a wide grassy avenue in the direction of the pagoda, which was clearly visible from most parts of the park. Charles offered Matilda his arm. She looked smart and prim, her manner brisk. Yet there was about her a suggestion of exuberance that one did not see when she was playing the part of aging spinster daughter tending her mother's needs. He had been a bit afraid that the journey here in a carriage filled with flighty, giggling young ladies would sap her of all energy and patience. The opposite seemed to have happened.

She looked at his arm before slipping her hand through it, then glanced up at him. "I have not climbed to the top of the pagoda since —" She closed her eyes briefly before turning her head away. She did not complete the sentence.

Since they had done it together when they were twenty?

"Neither have I," he said.

He had been to Kew a number of times since then, of course. He had even been close to the pagoda. He had been urged a few times to climb it but had always declined. He had never really asked himself why. Was it fanciful to imagine now that it was because he had once climbed it with Lady Matilda Westcott?

"It was a day much like today," he said.

"Yes," she said softly. And then, a little more firmly, "Was it? I cannot remember."

They walked behind the young people, who were, as she had observed, full of high spirits. They were in pairs, but they were chattering as a group.

"*Have* you forgotten, Matilda?" he asked.

"Yes," she said.

"We were in a group like this," he said. "I believe there were six of us, not counting the parents of one of the young ladies — I cannot recall who. But they were not *your* parents. They were a little more indulgent. Your brother was one of our number."

"I have forgotten," she said.

"Whoever those parents were," he said, "they did not climb higher than the second story. They remained there while the rest of us wound our way to the top. The others did not remain there long. They went clattering back down the stairs almost immediately, leaving the two of us to enjoy the view."

"I will take your word for it," she said. "I have no interest in the distant past. I am here now. It is a beautiful day, and I want to enjoy everything as it is."

"Very well," he said, briefly covering her hand on his arm.

He had kissed her, surrounded by carved wood and vast sky and green expanses below. It had not been their first kiss, but it was the first one that could be prolonged. He had told her, his mouth against hers, that he loved her. And she had told him after he had kissed her that she loved him.

They were words he had not spoken to any other woman. He had grown up fast after Matilda and had abandoned such immature, sentimental drivel.

Her mouth now, he saw when he glanced at her face, was set in a prim line.

"We will enjoy everything as it is now, then," he said. "Were you driven to near insanity on the journey here?"

He was startled by her sudden smile and the twinkle in her eye as she looked back at him.

"Not at all," she said. "What a delight young people are, Charles."

"Giggling?" he said. "And chattering?"

"Well," she said, "I giggled and chattered right along with them." She looked self-conscious suddenly and turned her head away, hiding her face behind the brim of her bonnet. "Why not? It seemed the best form of self-defense."

Matilda! Ah, Matilda. What had her parents done to her? Or was that unfair? If Barbara or Jane had wanted to marry a young man as wild as he had been at the age of twenty, would he have given his consent? He knew he would not. But would he also have forbidden them all future contact with that young man? Would they have obeyed him without question if he had?

Ought he to have waited? If he had given up his wild ways and approached her the following year, would he have been able to persuade her to change her mind? And her father his? And her mother hers?

"*Why* did you not marry, Matilda?" he asked.

Her head turned sharply back toward him. "I never *wanted* to," she said.

"You wanted to marry me," he reminded her.

"I was young," she said. "And foolish."

Even now, ridiculously, it stung.

"You never loved anyone else?" he asked her.

"No." She frowned.

"Was it that you never wanted to marry?" he asked her. "Or was it that you never found a man to love?"

"Enough," she said. "Please, Charles, enough."

And he was a bit horrified to see that her eyes were rather bright, but not from the sunshine or the pleasure of the outing.

"I beg your pardon," he said. "Forgive me."

"And why should you care?" she asked him. "You fathered a *son* very soon after. And there were other women. Many of them. One could not help hearing about them. And you married a few years later and had children and grandchildren, all the while acquiring an ever worsening reputation as a rake among other things. Much you loved *me,* Charles. I will be forever thankful that my mother and father talked sense into me. My life as it has been is *far* better than it would have been if I had married you."

Every word felt like a blow. And every word was true. Except four of them, spoken with biting sarcasm — *much you loved me.* Literally they were true, but she had not meant them literally.

He *had* loved her, but he had proved it in the worst possible way, by going completely to pieces after she would have nothing more to do with him. He could not even blame immaturity. His unsavory reputation had been well deserved for years and years.

"I am sorry," he said. "I am so sorry."

"We have arrived at the pagoda," she said, and she smiled brightly at the young people, who had stopped walking and stood in a group to admire it from the outside.

"There are ten stories," Miss Keithley said. "I counted them."

"Impressive, Dorothea," her brother said. "You can count that high."

"I am not sure I will be able to step out onto any of those balconies," Miss Rigg said, "if that is what they are called. Not on the higher stories anyway. They must be terrifying."

Each story had a balcony outside it and a protruding roof above. But it was not necessary to step outside to appreciate the views. There were tall, round-topped windows all about each story.

"Take my arm," Boris said to her. "I promise not to let you fall."

"That is kind of you," she said. "But will we be able to climb the stairs two abreast?"

They all stepped inside to find out, exuberant and chattering. They had not yet worked off much of their overabundance of energy, it seemed.

"I love the dragons," Matilda said, looking up at the series of roofs. "They *look* as if they are made of gold."

"Do you really want to go to the top?"

Charles asked. "You are under no obligation."

"Oh, but I am," she said. "I was challenged by my nephew and accepted."

"Is he in the habit of issuing challenges to you and grinning and waggling his eyebrows at you?" he asked.

"Oh good heavens, no," she said. "He has always treated me with the utmost respect as his mother's elder — *considerably* elder — sister. I believe he is enjoying teasing me."

"And you are enjoying being teased," he said.

"Yes." She sighed. "Sometimes it is a little lonely being a staid maiden aunt." But she colored rosily as she said it and looked as though she would dearly like to recall the words. No one really liked to admit to loneliness. And perhaps no woman liked to admit to being a maiden aunt, as though those two words described everything there was to know about her.

"You are not my aunt, fortunately," he said. "You are Matilda."

"Oh." She looked at him a little uncertainly, her head tipped slightly to one side.

"Shall we go after the young people," he asked, "and make sure none of them try hanging from the balcony rails by their fingertips? I would hate to fail during my first stint as a chaperon."

"Oh goodness me, yes," she said. "What a horrid thought. And it is just the sort of thing young men do to impress young ladies. Not hanging *from* the balcony rails, perhaps, but certainly *over* them. The mere thought of it gives me heart palpitations."

They huffed and puffed their way up the stairs, winding about the interior middle of the pagoda, stopping only once, briefly, at the fifth level to look out through the windows while they caught their breath. Loud exclamations of wonder as well as the habitual laughter came from the floors above.

"Oh," Matilda said, "I had forgotten how much higher a tall building seems from the inside than it looks from the outside. And we are only halfway up."

"Are you sure you do not want to claim that you won half a challenge?" he asked her, almost hoping she would say yes. Sometimes one forgot that being fifty-six years old was a little different from being twenty.

For answer she turned and continued the climb. Coming up behind her, Charles admired beneath the pale blue of her dress the sway of her hips, still shapely though no longer youthful. And he admired the fact that she kept her spine straight and climbed steadily upward without slowing. By the time they came out on top, the young people were moving about the full circle of the room, looking out and exclaiming at the height and pointing out to one another all the landmarks they could see both within Kew Gardens and beyond.

"It is a bit like being up in a hot air balloon," Adrian said, "except that there is more than empty air beneath our feet."

"You have been up in a balloon?" Lady Estelle asked him.

"Yes," he told her. "Last year. It was exhilarating and frankly terrifying. But I lived to tell the tale."

"If I did not know differently," Lady Jessica said, "I would swear this pagoda is swaying. Would someone please assure me that it is not?"

"I think it is," Bertrand said, staggering and then grinning at her. "You had better hang on to me, Jessica, and stop me from falling."

She tutted and slapped his arm.

And everyone was ready to go down and set out on another adventure.

"After coming all this way up," Charles said, "I intend to stay awhile and admire the view at my leisure. My leisure is going to last at least ten minutes."

"It takes that long to recover your breath?" Mr. Sawyer asked, grinning rather cheekily.

"And that too," his father admitted.

"But you do not all have to wait for us at the foot of the pagoda," Matilda said. "We can do our duty quite adequately from up here. It makes a splendid watchtower. I daresay there is not a square inch of the Gardens that will be invisible to us."

Mr. Keithley groaned aloud and clutched his chest.

There were lots of trees, of course, and a person could not see into them or under them from up here. But young people must be allowed some time alone together. And what could they get up to in ten minutes? Though of course it would take about that long again to get down from here, and then one would no longer be able to see to all corners of Kew, let alone into all the crannies. But —

"I trust you all to behave yourselves as young ladies and gentlemen ought," she added in her severe Aunt Matilda voice. Not that she had ever been a severe aunt. She had never interfered with her brother and sisters or her in-laws concerning the ways they chose to deal with their children.

"That was very sly of you, Aunt Matilda," Boris told her. "Now you have forced us to be good."

"Not that we would ever dream of *not* being good," Dorothea Keithley said as she followed Mr. Sawyer down the winding staircase. "Don't look at me that way, Ambrose."

"Do you have eyes in the back of your head?" her brother protested, offering his hand to Jessica to help her onto the top stair.

Soon they were all gone, clattering downward noisily and cheerfully.

"We will all gather outside the orangery in half an hour's time," Charles called down after them.

And Matilda was aware of the sound of wind all about the outside of the pagoda, and of nothing else. She stepped up to one window and gazed down upon trees and lawns and the red-bricked front of Kew Palace. She moved to the next window and saw temple follies among the trees and land stretching to infinity beyond the Gardens. She moved again and simply gazed. She was aware of the warmth of Charles's right arm along her left, though they were not touching. She could smell his cologne.

"Oh, there they are," she said, pointing downward. "They have stayed all together."

"I can spot no budding romance between any of them," he said, "with the possible exception of Bertrand Lamarr and Miss Keithley. They are merely enjoying one another's company."

"Yes," she said.

"In a similar situation we were only too eager to snatch time for ourselves," he said. "And we were fortunate enough to have a pair of chaperons who were happy to remain well below the top story of the pagoda."

He had kissed her here, maybe on this very spot. He had told her he loved her and she had not for a moment doubted the truth of his words. She had told him she loved him and had meant the words with all the passion of her young heart. But not a month later she had sent him away, told him she would not speak with him or even see him again. She had told him when pressed, when it had seemed the only way to convince him, that she did not love him, that she never really had.

"*Did* you mean it?" he asked now, and she knew he had turned his face toward hers, was no longer looking at the view but at her. "I have often wondered."

"Did I mean what?" she asked, but she knew what he meant. It was as though he had read her thoughts.

"That you loved me," he said.

She frowned and watched a horse and cart inching along a ribbon of roadway on the distant landscape.

"I do not remember," she said. "Are you talking about the time we were here together all those years ago? How am I to recall what I said or what I meant?"

"You told me you loved me," he said, "after I had said I loved you. And then, not long after, you turned me away. But the cruelest cut of all came with the words you spoke as you did it. You did not love me, you said, and never had. But you did love me when we were here. You did mean it, did you not?"

From beneath contracted eyebrows she returned his gaze. Why was the answer important to him? "You have lived a lifetime of memory-bringing events since then," she said. "You fathered Gil. You married Lady Dirkson and had children and then grandchildren. You lived through years filled with . . . with riotous living. Why try to remember now what happened or did not happen here years and years ago when we were young and foolish and could not possibly have known our own minds? Why bother to remember? We have scarcely seen each other since. We have spoken only a few times, all of them very recently. What is the point of all this, Charles? If we ever had a . . . a chance, it is long gone. Those things happened to other people in another lifetime. We are not the same people now. Not even close."

"*Were* we foolish?" he asked her. He had turned to look downward again. Matilda could see the young people, still in a group together, making their way along a grassy avenue toward one of the domed temples. "But yes, of course I was. I was young and in love and then hurt as only the young can be. I was blinded by hurt. Instead of waiting for a year and then trying during the next Season to get you to change your mind and to get your father to see that I had changed, I immediately leaped into wild pleasure seeking in an attempt to forget you and soothe my bruised sense of self. I never did try to win you back. Yes, I was foolish. Were you?"

"Foolish?" she said. "No. I had always been obedient to my parents. I had always believed they knew what was best for me and loved me. I believed them when they told me you were no suitable husband for me, that your wild debaucheries would bring me nothing but misery."

"Debaucheries?" He turned to look at her

again. "At *that* stage of my life? Hardly. So you were *wise* to break off with me? To tell me you did not love me?"

"Yes," she said.

He was looking steadily at her, and almost inevitably she had to turn her own head and look back.

"Tell me," he said, "that that at least was not true. And please do not tell me you do not remember."

"Why should I remember?" she asked. "It was a lifetime ago. Oh, Charles, *of course* I loved you. We were young as these young people are young now." She gestured with one hand toward the window, though she did not look out. "You were handsome and you were paying court to me. You danced with me and talked endlessly with me and smiled and laughed for me alone, it seemed. Of course I loved you. It would have been strange if I had not."

"But you stopped?"

"Of course I stopped," she said, remembering her broken heart, her shattered dreams, her conviction that she would surely not be able to live on. "Did you imagine that I have been nursing a tendre for you all these years? Do you see me as a poor, frustrated spinster, sighing herself to sleep each night with memories of the one man with whom she shared a romance when she was no more than a girl? That is both absurd and insulting."

"Did I say I imagined any such thing?" he asked. "I am sorry. I have upset you."

"I am not upset," she said, swiping at her cheeks with the heels of both gloved hands and feeling the humiliating wetness of tears there — she, who never wept.

"Let us not talk or even think about all the years between," he said. "I loved you when we were last here together, Matilda, and you loved me. It is a bitter memory because of all that came so soon after. But there is a very definite sweetness about it too. We were a young couple in love. I have never been in love since."

"What nonsense," she said.

"Perhaps," he said. "But true nevertheless. I do not believe you have either, have you?"

"Me?" she said. "Of course I have — No, I have not. Is there anything shameful about that? I had chances. But I would not marry without love. I was a stubborn young woman."

"Yes," he said. "I know."

"Well," she said, "it *is* a sweet memory, Charles. It was also something that happened to two people who no longer exist."

"But we do," he said. "We are those very same two people thirty-six years later. There are gray hairs — more for me than for you — and lines carving themselves on our faces and somewhat thickening figures. But you still look very good. Perhaps I can say so because I look at you through fifty-six-year-old eyes. To me you look good, though I would like to see your mouth primmed less often and smiling instead — as it has smiled today whenever we are in company with the young people. I would like to kiss that mouth again."

She stared at him as though she were welded to the floor. She was too shocked to smack his face. At the same time she felt a renewed rush of awareness — of their aloneness up here, of the last kiss they had shared here, of *him,* of his solid presence, of his continued good looks, of his maleness. Of his *mouth.* But she was middle-aged. On the far side of middle age, in fact. Kissing was for the young. She no longer knew how to do it. The last time she had been kissed was . . . thirty-six years ago. It would be embarrassing. It would be bizarre. It would be . . .

She licked her lips, and his eyes dipped to follow the gesture. Her nipples were tingling. There was an ache between her thighs.

She had not experienced such things for many years. She was past the age . . . But even before then she had suppressed the nagging needs that brought her nothing but empty frustration and misery. She could not now . . .

She took a step closer to him, and when *he* stepped closer to *her,* she ignored the instinct to jump back in fright and she let herself rest against him instead, closing her eyes as she did so. Even through his coat and waistcoat and shirt she could feel that he was warm and firm muscled and male. She felt enclosed by the smell of him, his cologne, the starch that must have been used on his cravat and neckcloth, the essence that was Charles himself. It was ridiculous, perhaps, to feel that it was all somehow familiar, but it was nevertheless. With her thighs she could feel the powerful muscles of his own. With her lower legs she could feel the supple leather of his Hessian boots. It was all surely sufficient to make her swoon — if she knew how to do it.

She would remember this, she thought, just as she had always remembered the last time. She would remember for the rest of her life. With her dying breath she would remember that she loved him, that she had always loved him even if there had been days, weeks, even perhaps months through her life when she had not thought of him a single time. Oh no, never months. Or even weeks. Love never quite goes away. It was always there, dormant, waiting to be revived. Broken hearts were always aching to be mended.

His arms had come down along hers and he found her hands with his and twined his fingers with hers as their arms rested against their sides. He lowered his head and tipped it slightly to one side. She felt his breath against one cheek and opened her eyes. His own searched hers from a mere few inches away and somehow she did not feel like an embarrassed and dried-up old spinster for whom such things were merely a present embarrassment and a dream of what might have been a long time ago and could never be again. He did not look like an aging man who surely should be past such things.

"Allow me?" he murmured, his lips almost against hers.

For answer, she shut her eyes again and closed the distance. And —

Oh my.

*Oh my.*

Oh . . . *my goodness me.*

Her thoughts were no more coherent than that for however long the kiss lasted. It was probably a few seconds. No, surely longer than that. Minutes? Hours?

Had it been like this all those years ago? All the physical sensations? All the emotional yearnings? All the inability to *think*? But if it had been, how could she possibly have let him go?

Ah, how could she have let him go?

*Charles.*

"Charles?"

He had moved his mouth away from hers and was gazing at her with eyes that were impossible to read. They were still touching along their full length. Their fingers were still entwined at their sides. It had been really, she thought, by any objective standard, a rather chaste kiss. It had also been nothing short of earth-shattering. No, that was far too mild a term. It had been *universe*-shattering.

For her anyway.

He, of course, must have participated in a thousand such kisses with as many women.

*Don't exaggerate, Matilda.*

*Was* it an exaggeration?

"We are neglecting our duty," she said.

A wave of something so fleeting that it was impossible to name passed across his face. Amusement, perhaps? Regret? Longing? None of those? All of them?

"You are the one who told the young people you trusted them," he said. "I would have remained right behind them, treading upon the heels of the last in line."

"Oh, you would not," she said. "You were the one who told them you needed ten minutes up here before following them."

"Because I am an old man and needed to catch my breath and give my arthritic knees a rest," he said.

"Nonsense." She was very aware that they were still touching each other, front to front, and their fingers were still tangled up together.

He released her and took a step back. There was definite laughter in his eyes now. "I am sorry for discomposing you, Matilda," he said.

"You have done no such thing," she assured him.

"There is another reason why you are cross, then?" he asked.

"I am not cross," she protested, running a hand over the front of her dress and making sure her bonnet was still straight. "But we came as chaperons and . . ."

"And ended up needing some of our own," he said. "Come. We will go down. I will go first so that you do not have to peer into the abyss with every step."

Oh. *Oh.* He had surely said exactly the same thing the last time. But how ridiculous to believe that she could remember such a trivial act of gallantry thirty-six years later.

"Thank you," she said, and wanted to weep.

Yet again.

# Five

During the week following the excursion to Kew Gardens, Charles concentrated upon getting his life back to normal. The only trouble was that he was not sure it was going to be possible — not, at least, if *normal* meant the way it had been until a month or so ago.

For one thing, he had let go the mistress he had employed since not long after his wife's death. He had paid her off abruptly the very evening after Matilda had made her unexpected call at his house, though at the time he had not believed there was any connection between the two events. He had assumed that he would replace his mistress soon. But he had not done so in the ensuing weeks, though he was not at all sure celibacy suited him. Neither was he sure it did not. Actually, it was sex for sex's sake that no longer satisfied him, but he did not know what *would* satisfy him instead. Or if he did, he was not willing to give it serious thought.

For another thing, there was Gil. His son had been in his life for thirty-four years, in a purely peripheral way, but that had changed with all the business over the custody battle and then the breakfast to which his son's wife had invited him and his first-ever face-to-face meeting with his son. To say that meeting was uncomfortable would be to severely understate the case, but it had been difficult afterward to accept the possibility that he would never see Gil or hear from him again.

But hear from him he had a couple of days after Kew — or at least *about* him from Abigail, Gil's wife. She had written a letter filled with cheerful details about the Gloucestershire village in which they lived and their house and garden, which was dominated by both the sight and smell of roses. Interspersed with those details were seemingly random anecdotes about Katy, his granddaughter. And there had been one mention of Gil, who was being transformed from soldier to farmer, complete with muddy boots, for which Abigail had scolded him when he stepped inside the house with them one day without cleaning them off adequately on the boot scraper outside the door. Charles found reading the letter painful more than pleasurable, yet he read it at least a dozen times in the course of the rest of the day.

Then there was Adrian, who had renewed the friendship he had enjoyed with Bertrand Lamarr at university. He had also become friendly with Lamarr's sister and with Boris Wayne. The four of them had apparently called upon the Dowager Countess of Riverdale the day after Kew in order to thank Lady Matilda Westcott for accompanying them and making the day such fun for them — Adrian's word. She had apparently tried to persuade her mother to put her feet up on a stool while they were there, but the dowager had declared she was quite capable of keeping her feet on the floor and became quite cross with her daughter for fussing.

"And *I* ended up feeling quite cross too," Adrian reported. "There were none of the smiles and twinkly eyes from Lady Matilda that we saw yesterday, or the mock severe admonitions. I think the dowager countess stifles her, Papa. It is a shame, and it is not right. It is not easy to be a woman, is it? Especially a spinster. I wonder why she never married."

"Perhaps she chose not to," Charles suggested.

"But the *alternative . . .*" his son protested.

Charles ended up feeling irritated himself — but as much with Matilda as with her mother. Why did she behave like that? Why had she allowed herself to become the stereotypical fussy spinster daughter of an autocratic mother? He did not want to think about Matilda. He wished he could erase the memory of the day at Kew, especially of that half hour or so at the top of the pagoda. He did not know what to make of what had happened there. She had aroused in him memories that had been so deeply buried that he would have thought them completely obliterated if her reappearance in his life had not brought them flooding back. Not just memories of facts, however, but memories also of feelings and passions that should be laughable now but were not.

Matilda! There was no way on earth he wanted to become involved with her again. It would be ridiculous. And his guess was that she would agree with him.

Then there were his daughters. Barbara and her family returned from her in-laws' anniversary celebrations on the same day as Jane arrived in town with her family after recovering from her bouts of nausea. They came together the following day to call upon Charles, bringing their children with them.

He talked and played with all three of his grandchildren and admired various toys and treasures they had brought with them for his approval — including the proud treasure of a bruise the size of a bird's egg acquired from slipping off the back of a pony that had become suddenly frisky. The children were then taken up to the nursery by Barbara's nurse, and Charles was left alone with his daughters. Barbara had an invitation for him. Her birthday was coming up soon.

"I know," Charles said. "I never forget birthdays, do I?"

"I wish every man were like you in that regard, Papa," Jane said, shaking her head, and clucked her tongue. "Wallace, for example." Wallace, Lord Frater, was her husband.

"Instead of having a family dinner at home as usual," Barbara continued, "we are going to have a family celebration at Vauxhall Gardens. Edward has reserved a box and we will feast there and listen to the orchestra and dance and watch the fireworks. It must be three years or more since I was last there."

"We went last year," Jane said. "But I am always happy to have an excuse to go to

Vauxhall. It is sheer magic if the weather is good."

"Oh, the weather will be perfect for my birthday," Barbara assured her. "It would not dare be otherwise. Adrian will be coming. He has asked Lady Estelle Lamarr to accompany him. Do you know her, Papa? She is making her debut this year, though she is well past the usual age. I have seen her once or twice. She is a beauty — very dark coloring."

"I have an acquaintance with her," Charles said. "Her twin brother was at Oxford with Adrian."

"It would be lovely, in order to keep numbers even," Barbara said, "if you would invite someone too, Papa."

"Mrs. Summoner, perhaps?" Jane suggested.

Mrs. Summoner, who had been widowed about the same time as Charles had, had signaled on several occasions that she would not mind indulging in a discreet affair with him. She must be all of twenty years his junior. He held up a staying hand.

"If I must bring someone," he said, "I will choose for myself. I shall ask Lady Matilda Westcott."

He did not quite know what made him say it — and he certainly did not know if she would accept — except that he had been trying to pluck up the courage to talk to his daughters about something they needed to know, and this would make it somewhat imperative that he say it now.

"Lady Matilda Westcott?" Jane frowned. "Do you mean *Abigail* Westcott, Papa? But she is no longer *Lady* Abigail, is she? She lost the title several years ago. Besides, she is too young for you."

"And she has recently married, I have heard," Barbara added.

"I said Lady *Matilda* Westcott," Charles told them. "She is Abigail Westcott's aunt — Abigail Bennington now. She recently married Lieutenant Colonel Gil Bennington. My son."

They stared at him blankly.

"Did you say *'my son'*?" Jane asked, and laughed.

"I did," he said. "Gil Bennington is my natural son. He was born thirty-four years ago, before I even met your mother. His mother was the daughter of a village blacksmith. She raised him without my assistance, though assistance was offered. The only help I ever gave him came after her passing, when I purchased a commission for him in the foot regiment in which he was a sergeant. He refused any further help not long after that. I saw him for the first time a few weeks ago after he arrived in London with his new wife. They came to appear before a judge who was to decide who would have custody of his daughter. She was living with her maternal grandparents at the time. Now she is with Gil and his wife. I was at the hearing. I spoke up in Gil's defense. He has since taken his family to their home in Gloucestershire."

It all came out in a rush.

Jane's smile had disappeared. Both daughters were staring blankly at him.

"You have a *son*?" Jane asked. "Apart from Adrian?"

"Does Adrian *know*?" Barbara asked. "Dear God, it will kill him."

"He knows," Charles said. "He came with me last week to a dinner given by the Earl of Riverdale and his wife. A number of the other members of the Westcott family were there too. It occurred to me when I was invited that the truth was almost bound to leak out at last and that it would be better that you all hear it from me than from *ton* gossip."

His daughters were looking identically stunned, rather as Adrian had looked when Charles told him.

"And you are going to invite Abigail Bennington's *aunt,* one of the Westcotts, to Barbara's birthday party?" Jane said.

"Unless Barbara objects," Charles told her. "Obviously I have not asked her yet. She may say no even if I do."

"Lady Estelle Lamarr has some connection with the Westcott family too, does she not?" Barbara said, frowning in thought. "Her father married the former Countess of Riverdale a few years ago? Abigail Westcott's mother?"

"Yes," he said.

"And Adrian is bringing her to Vauxhall," Barbara said. "Yet he *knows.*"

"Yes," Charles said again.

"Oh goodness." Barbara sat back in her chair and placed her palms against her cheeks. "I feel as though I were in the middle of some bizarre dream. We have a *half* brother, Jane."

"If you happen to have a feather about your person," Jane said, "someone could easily knock me over with it. How is it possible we never knew of this? And how *could* you, Papa? Oh, of all the dreadful things. Whatever will Wallace say when I tell him? What is he like, Papa? Though I am not at all sure I want to know."

They were none too happy, Charles realized. It was unsurprising. He was not himself. He had kept the secret for so long that it felt disconcerting to have the truth out in the open to upset his children. His wife had never known.

"I believe he is a good man," he said.

He proceeded to tell them some facts about his son. And he wondered as he did so whether he ought to ask Matilda to go to Vauxhall with him and thus keep alive the connection between her family and his. Perhaps his children would resent it. Though Adrian did not seem to do so. Quite the contrary, in fact.

How would she answer if he did ask her? Would she accept? And what would it mean if she did? It was to be an intimate event *with his family.* Would anyone get the idea that he was *courting* her?

And would he be?

When Matilda received a written invitation to join Mrs. Barbara Dewhurst and her family for an evening at Vauxhall Gardens in celebration of her birthday, she thought at first that the lady must have mistaken her for someone else. But only for a second.

"You look as if someone had just died, Matilda," her mother said from across the breakfast table. "Whatever has happened?"

Matilda looked up blankly. She would

have loved to take the card upstairs to digest its contents in the privacy of her room, but it was too late for that. Apparently her face had betrayed her.

"Who is Mrs. Dewhurst?" her mother asked after Matilda had read the invitation aloud.

Matilda knew. She had known when Charles married and whom he married and where. She had known when each of his children were born — and married. She knew when his wife had died. For someone who had obliterated him entirely from her mind and memory over thirty years ago, she knew a lot about him. And she had suffered a great deal over each milestone in his life while denying every pang.

"She is Viscount Dirkson's elder daughter," she explained.

"But why would she be inviting you to join a family party?" her mother asked. But she did not wait for an answer. She set down her half-eaten slice of toast, dabbed at her mouth with her linen napkin, and sat back in her chair, regarding her daughter the whole while. "Do you have the viscount himself to thank for this?"

"I do not know any more than you do, Mama," Matilda said. Except that he had kissed her, and she had had a hard time both eating and sleeping in the week since, poor pathetic creature that she was.

"You fancied yourself in love with him once," her mother said.

"Oh goodness." Matilda laughed and stirred her coffee, even though the cup was already half-empty. "That was a long age ago, Mama." She looked up as she set the spoon in the saucer. "But I did not *fancy* myself in love with him. I loved him with my whole heart and soul."

Her mother continued to regard her steadily, and Matilda waited for the tirade of anger and ridicule that was bound to be coming. Instead her mother set down her napkin beside her plate and sighed.

"I know," she said.

Matilda lifted her cup, changed her mind, and set it back down on the saucer. She raised her eyes.

"I am not sure I knew about the 'heart and soul' part at the time," her mother said. "Though I understood it later, when you would have nothing to do with any of the many perfectly eligible gentlemen who would have courted you in the years after. I told myself it was infatuation. I told myself you were merely *in* love, something girls fall in and out of a dozen times before they settle into a sensible marriage."

"I fell only once," Matilda said. Oh goodness, she and Mama never talked like this.

"Yes, I know," her mother said again. "He ran wild with Humphrey, Matilda. Humphrey was my own son, but I was never blind to his many faults. Viscount Dirkson, or Charles Sawyer as he still was in those days, was a year older. I blamed him for leading Humphrey astray, or deluded myself into blaming him. My heart broke at the prospect of you marrying him and having to endure a wretched marriage for the rest of your life. I was not wrong about him. He grew worse than just wild as the years went on."

"I know, Mama," Matilda said.

"But," her mother said, "I have always lived with the guilt of denying you that misery — or that happiness. For it is impossible to know if his life would have proceeded differently if you had married him. Did he love you heart and soul too?"

"I believed so," Matilda said. "Indeed, I knew so."

"Being a parent is a hard job," her mother told her. "One so very much wants one's children to be happy. One wants to do all in one's power to prevent their being miserable. But where does wise guidance end and blind interference begin?"

Matilda frowned across the table at her mother. "You and Papa did the right thing," she said.

"Did we?" Her mother lifted her napkin again and proceeded to fold it neatly. "You were my firstborn, Matilda. I hesitate to say you were my favorite, for you were *all* my favorites at different times and in different circumstances. But you were special. You were my . . . my *firstborn.*"

Matilda found herself blinking back tears. Her mother *never* talked this way. And she had never been a demonstrative parent. She had never before said that she loved her eldest daughter, let alone that she had been the favorite.

"I must go and send an answer to Mrs. Dewhurst," Matilda said, getting to her feet. "I will decline, of course."

"Why?" her mother asked.

"I do not belong with that family," Matilda said. "I would feel embarrassed and awkwardly out of place."

"Why?" her mother asked again. "It is obvious that it was Mrs. Dewhurst's father who suggested your name. Why else would she have thought to ask you? I daresay she does not even know you."

Matilda could think of no answer. *Why* had he suggested her? He had said nothing during or after the journey home from Kew about seeing her again. There had been nothing from him since. She had assumed he was bitterly regretting some of the things he had said. Not to mention that kiss.

"Did you enjoy the day at Kew?" her mother asked.

"Yes, of course I did," Matilda said. "The young people were delightful. I was touched when Mr. Sawyer came the following day with Boris and Bertrand and Estelle to thank me. It was thoughtful of them."

"And was Viscount Dirkson delightful?" her mother asked.

Matilda sat back down. "He was pleasant company, Mama," she said. "I believe all the young people liked him."

"But did you, Matilda?" her mother asked.

"Yes, of course," she said. *He kissed me. Me, a fifty-six-year-old spinster.*

"Then you must go to Vauxhall with him and his family," her mother told her.

"Mama," Matilda began, but her mother held up a hand.

"Matilda," she said, "you have driven me to the brink of insanity several times in the years since your papa died."

"I know," Matilda said. "I want to care for you, Mama, but I know you resent my every move."

"You drive me insane with *guilt,*" her mother said. "Believe me when I tell you I did not understand just how much you loved him, Matilda. Perhaps the advice your father and I gave you was sound. It seemed so at the time. But I have looked upon you in all the years since as a millstone of regret and guilt about my neck. We ought to have advised you and then trusted you to make your own decision. We ought at least to have put a time limit on our refusal. We could have insisted that your young man wait a year before applying to your father again for permission to address you."

"Mama!" Matilda cried, hearing only that she had been a millstone about her mother's neck.

"Matilda," her mother said, getting to her feet while her daughter shot to hers in order to rush to her assistance — an impulse she reined in before she had taken more than two steps. "Matilda, *I love you.* When I snap at you, it is because my heart hurts for you and I know I am to blame for everything you have become. Now, I am going to my sitting room to read the morning papers. I can get up the stairs with the assistance of the banister rail and my own feet. You are to go to the morning room to write to Mrs. Dewhurst. You are to thank her for the kind invitation and inform her that you will be delighted to make one of the party. Or you may write to refuse. The choice is yours."

Matilda, dumbfounded, watched her mother leave the room. For the first time in what must be years she did not rush after her to offer assistance that was not solicited. It took a great deal of resolution.

She accepted the invitation. Having placed it on the silver tray in the hall and drawn the attention of the butler to it, she went up to her room and lay down on her bed, something she never did in the daytime, and stared up at the canopy.

*I love you.*

Not in the voice of a man from years and years ago, but in her mother's voice. For perhaps the first time ever. If her mother had said it before, Matilda had no memory of it. She had always chosen to believe it must be true anyway, though she had doubted of late. But oh, the craving to hear those words from one's own mother. And now they had been spoken.

*I love you.*

Matilda rolled over onto her side, hid her face against the pillow, and wept.

*I love you.*

*Why* did he want her to go to Vauxhall with his family?

*Did* he regret that kiss at the top of the pagoda in Kew Gardens?

*I love you.*

He too had spoken those words to her once upon a time long, long ago.

Life, her dreary, endless life, had suddenly become too full of emotion to be borne. She was not accustomed to strong emotion. She did not know what to do with it.

Except weep.

Something she never did.

She wept.

As soon as he had heard from Barbara that Matilda had accepted the invitation to Vauxhall, Charles wrote to inform her that he would bring his carriage to her mother's house and escort her there himself. He did not look forward to calling at the house, but it was the correct thing to do, and he was not really afraid of the dragon. Was he? But when he arrived on the appointed evening and was conducted to the drawing room, it was to find that the dowager countess was alone there.

His heart sank even as he girded his loins for battle.

"Ma'am," he said, making her a bow.

She looked him up and down from her chair beside the fireplace, her expression stern, even hostile.

"Lord Dirkson," she said. "Your daughter has a lovely evening for her party."

"She is fortunate," he said, "considering the fact that we have had nothing but drizzle and blustery winds for the last several days."

"Tell me," she said. "Did I make a mistake all those years ago?"

Her words took him completely by surprise. He did not know for a moment how to answer. "I understood," he said, "that the Earl of Riverdale, your husband, rejected my suit because my wild ways made me an ineligible suitor for his daughter. I was twenty years old. I behaved as a large number of young men behave at that age. Wildly, that is. I was prepared to reform my ways after I had made the acquaintance of Lady Matilda. Whether I would have done so or not cannot be known for sure. I daresay you believed at the time that you were acting in the best interests of your daughter. Subsequent events would seem to have justified you in that opinion."

"You loved her?" she asked.

"I did, ma'am," he said. "Very dearly. I do not expect you to believe me."

"Age does not necessarily strengthen a person or insulate her from pain," she said. "My daughter is as fragile now as she was then, Viscount Dirkson, even though she may appear to be set in her ways and incapable of deep feeling."

Matilda did not appear that way to him in either regard.

"Are you asking me my intentions, ma'am?" he asked.

She did not reply for a moment as she looked steadily at him. "I am," she said then.

He felt like a young man again, being hauled up before suspicious parents as he pursued their daughters. It was a little bizarre. But one thing was clear. The old dragon cared after all. He did not like her, but she cared. At least he assumed she did. Perhaps she was only anxious at the possible loss of her longtime slave.

"They are honorable, ma'am," he assured her. "I have no wish to hurt Lady Matilda. I will do all in my power not to do so. I never did hurt her, if you will remember. I am not the one who ended our connection."

What the devil was he saying? Was he committing himself to something? Events of the past couple of weeks or so had left him with the uneasy feeling that he was being drawn into some sort of trap. But . . . a trap of whose making? Not Matilda's, certainly. Not her mother's either, or any of her family's. Of his own, then? He was the one, after all, who had suggested first himself and then Matilda as chaperons for that youthful excursion to Kew. He was the one who had suggested her name to Barbara.

"Do you still love her?" the dowager asked him.

He raised his eyebrows. "I *care* for her, ma'am," he said.

She narrowed her eyes and then nodded curtly. "Matilda is an adult," she said. "She has been an adult for many years. It is time I learned not to interfere in her life. I am sure you would agree with that, Lord Dirkson."

"I am sure, ma'am," he said, "that your concern for her arises from love."

He was sure of no such thing. But before she could reply, the door behind him opened and he turned in some relief to watch Matilda hurry into the room, her evening gown an icy, shimmery silver gray, a blue cashmere shawl over one arm, her hair styled with simple elegance, her posture more erect even than usual, her cheeks slightly flushed, her lips in a prim line.

And dash it all. He fell in love. Again.

# Six

They crossed the river by boat instead of by the bridge, a convenience Matilda had always considered unromantic ever since it opened a few years previous. Charles took her shawl from over her arm just when she was starting to feel a bit chilly and wrapped it around her shoulders. For a moment he kept his arm about her, holding the shawl in place, but he soon removed it and sat more decorously beside her, making light conversation. It must be twenty-five or, more likely, thirty years since she had been anywhere escorted by a gentleman alone. She had been relieved that her mother had not suggested her maid accompany her. How humiliating it would have been if that had happened in his hearing.

He had arrived a bit early. She had not been quite ready. But she had hurried, alarmed that he was going to have to face her mother alone in the drawing room. And sure enough, Mama had been looking severe when she arrived there, and he had been looking stern. He had not told her — and she had not asked — what had transpired between them. Merely a stilted, banal conversation about the weather, she hoped.

"Oh," she said now. "Just look." They were foolish words, since they were facing the opposite bank of the Thames and he would have to be blind not to see the dozens of colored lanterns strung through the branches of the trees of Vauxhall Gardens, swaying in the breeze, their reflections shivering across the flowing water. "Is it not sheer magic, Charles?"

"It is indeed," he agreed, but when she turned her head to look at him it was to find that *he* was looking at *her,* his eyes shadowed by the near darkness and the brim of his tall hat.

She smiled and turned her face away. He had used to do that all the time. She had questioned him about it once. *Why are you always looking at me?* she had asked. He had had a ready answer. *Because there is nothing and no one in this world I would rather look at.* Foolish, flattering words that had warmed her to her toes. She did not ask the same question now. Who knew how he would answer?

"It was very kind of your daughter to invite me to join her birthday celebrations," she said. "Her card mentioned the fact that it is to be a *family* party."

"Immediate family, yes," he told her. "Barbara and Jane will be there with their husbands. Adrian has invited Lady Estelle Lamarr. And I have invited you. Social events are always better when there is an even number of men and women."

"Will Estelle indeed be here too?" she asked, pleased. "I had not heard. I like your son, Charles. He is a very pleasant young man."

"He likes you too," he told her. "He says you have a permanent twinkle in your eyes."

"Oh," she said, "I do not."

"No, I know," he said. "But you ought to, Matilda. You were born to arouse happiness in those around you. You used to do it. When I won your affections — for a short while at least — it was against brisk competition."

"That is so untrue," she protested.

"You were unaware of your own charms," he told her. "It was one of the endearing things about you. You were much admired, Matilda, largely because of the sparkle of happiness you exuded."

He must be wrong. Oh, surely he must.

She had had other suitors, of course, a tedious number of them after she had sent him away. But she was Lady Matilda Westcott, eldest daughter of the Earl of Riverdale. She came with a large dowry. She was extremely eligible. The attention she received had not been at all surprising. There had been nothing personal about it. He was quite wrong about that.

"This is a silly conversation," she said.

He laughed — and her insides turned over. "Then it is a good thing it is at an end for a while," he said as the boat drew in to the bank and all the magic and pleasures of Vauxhall awaited them, as well as the nervousness of meeting his daughters and their husbands as a member of their family party just as though . . . Well, just as though Charles were *courting* her.

She was *so* unaccustomed to being out alone, Matilda thought. For a moment she longed for the prop of her mother to fuss over. Then she set her hand in Charles's, got carefully to her feet against the sway of the boat, and stepped out onto the jetty. She rearranged her shawl about her shoulders as an excuse to release her hand from his, straightened her spine, and nodded briskly to indicate that she was ready to proceed. Colored lanterns swayed above their heads. The distant sound of music enticed them to come closer.

"Matilda." He offered his arm. "I chose you as my companion for this evening because I wanted you here. Everyone will be prepared to like you. You need not look as though you were about to march into battle."

"Do your daughters *know*?" she asked as she took his arm. "About Gil, I mean?"

"Yes," he said.

"And they know he is married to my niece?" she asked.

"Yes," he said. "And to Lady Estelle Lamarr's stepsister. They know. They are dealing with the knowledge."

As was she, Matilda thought. She was still dealing with it, with the knowledge that Charles must have fathered Gil a mere few months after declaring his undying love for and fidelity to her.

They strolled along a wide avenue in the direction of the rotunda, surrounded by other people, their senses assailed by the sounds of music and voices and by the sight of colored lamplight. She was here with a companion who was not her mother. She was here with a man who had deliberately chosen her. She was here with *Charles*. Whoever could have predicted any of this?

"Do you remember," he asked her, his voice low, "the last time we were here together, Matilda?"

How could she possibly *not* remember? The magic, the exhilaration, the pure joy of that evening. The heady feeling of being young and in love. The anticipation of a lifetime of love together. She had never doubted his eligibility, even though she knew he had been embroiled in some pretty wild escapades with Humphrey. He had been heir to a viscount's title, after all. And that evening had been one of the very few times they had been able to snatch more than just a few short moments alone together. They had wandered along one of the narrower, darker paths among the trees until they had stopped and he had kissed her.

"It was a long time ago," she said.

He did not answer. They had reached the rotunda with its tiers of open-fronted boxes arranged in a horseshoe shape about the dance floor. The orchestra was positioned in the center.

"It looks as if we are the last to arrive," he said. "But everyone else was coming via the bridge. My children, it would seem, have no sense of romance."

"And you do?" The words were out of her mouth before she could rein them in.

He turned his head to smile at her. "And I do," he said.

Then they were at the family box and Matilda was being presented to Mr. and Mrs. Dewhurst and Lord and Lady Frater, all of whom smiled amiably at her and shook her hand. Mr. Sawyer shook her warmly by the hand too, and Estelle beamed at her and kissed her cheek.

"It was only half an hour ago that I learned you were coming here too with Viscount Dirkson, Aunt Matilda," she said. "I was so delighted. Is this not the perfect evening for Vauxhall?"

"It is indeed," Matilda agreed. "And may I wish you a happy birthday, Mrs. Dewhurst?"

She was a pretty young lady and favored her mother in looks, as did her brother. Lady Frater more closely resembled her father.

"Thank you, Lady Matilda," Mrs. Dewhurst said. "But will you call me Barbara, please? And I am sure my sister would rather be called Jane than *Lady Frater.*"

"I would indeed," that young lady said. "Do come and sit down, Lady Matilda. The food will be arriving shortly. Vauxhall always has the *best* ham. And strawberries."

"Edward will pour you and Papa some

champagne," Barbara said as her husband got to his feet.

Oh, this, Matilda thought, gazing about her at Charles's family and beyond the box at the sights and hearing the sounds of Vauxhall, was wonderful. *Wonderful.* She was going to tuck every single detail away in her memory to hoard for the rest of her life.

Her eyes rested briefly upon Charles's face and she smiled.

The thing was, Charles thought, that Matilda looked every bit her age. She had attempted nothing to minimize it. And she behaved with a certain primness. At the same time there was something almost youthful about her — a certain innocence and wonder over her surroundings. There was no bright sparkle in her eyes, very little laughter, not a great deal of conversation, very few outright smiles. But . . . What was it about her? At every moment while they ate supper and listened to the music and watched the dancers and conversed, she looked . . . happy? Was that a strong enough word? She looked as if she really wanted to be here. She appeared fully present. She looked upon his children, his sons-in-law, her stepniece, as though she really liked them and was enjoying being with them. She looked very little at him, but when she did it was with almost a questioning expression, as though she did not quite know why she was here with him, but for this evening anyway was contented that it be so.

He suspected there had been very little joy in Matilda's adult life. And very few outings that did not include her mother or other members of the Westcott family.

He sensed that his daughters liked her, even knowing of her connection to Gil. He knew that Adrian did.

"I want to dance," Barbara announced after the remains of their supper had been cleared away. "And the next one is to be a waltz. Come, Edward."

"I believe almost every dance at Vauxhall is a waltz, Barbara," Wallace said. "Jane?" He held out a hand for his wife's.

"Have you been approved yet to dance the waltz, Lady Estelle?" Adrian asked. "I know this is your first Season."

"I have," she told him.

"I am not sure the rules apply so strictly here at Vauxhall anyway," Charles said as Lady Estelle got to her feet and set her hand in Adrian's. He turned his head. "Matilda?"

"Oh," she said, "I have never waltzed. The dance was not even performed in England until a few years ago." There was a certain wistfulness in her voice.

"But you know the steps?" he asked her.

"Yes, of course," she said. "I always think it must be the most romantic dance ever invented. Young people now are very fortunate."

"I do not believe," he said, "there is any prohibition upon the not-so-young waltzing too." He stood and extended a hand for hers.

"I would make a cake of myself," she protested. "And humiliate you."

"Matilda." He leaned a little toward her. "Do you not trust me to hold you and lead you and prevent you from tripping over your own or anyone else's feet? And do you not trust yourself to perform the steps you have seen and yearned to dance?"

"I have not yearned —"

"Liar," he said softly, smiling at her. "Your eyes give you away."

"Oh, they do not," she protested.

"Waltz with me," he said.

She raised her hand and placed it in his. She primmed her lips and squared her shoulders and he almost laughed. But it was not the moment for laughter. Only for tenderness. He knew that the bright, youthful star that had been the young Matilda was still locked within her, long repressed. All the warmth and vitality and love he remembered were still there too. He was not imagining it. It was not wishful thinking on his part. His Matilda still existed, but she had grown older, as he had, and he was not sorry for it. He was no longer interested in youthful beauty and allure. A fifty-six-year-old Matilda suited him perfectly. But the *real* Matilda, not the one shaped by her sense of duty to her mother and the perceptions of her family, who saw her merely as a spinster sister or aunt.

"You will be sorry," she warned him.

"Only if you are," he said. "I am wagering on my ability to make sure that you are not."

He led her onto the floor with a number of other people, including his son and his daughters, and waited for the music to begin. He looked up, beyond the colored lanterns, and saw the moon, almost but not quite full, and stars against a black sky.

"Look," he said, and she gazed upward with him.

He lowered his eyes to her face and the music began. He placed a hand behind her waist while hers came to rest on his shoulder. He took her other hand in his and held her firmly, close to but not quite touching his chest. And he led her into the steps of the waltz, tentatively at first, avoiding any fancy twirls. She kept her eyes on his, though she was not really seeing him, he knew. She was concentrating upon the steps she had seen performed but had never danced herself. And then she smiled fleetingly and then more brightly, and he knew she was seeing him and beginning to enjoy herself.

He led her into a simple twirl, and she laughed. With pure delight. He smiled back into her eyes. She was warm and vital in his arms, and he was where he wanted to be more than anywhere else on earth — not at Vauxhall specifically but within the loose circle of Matilda's arms. He was where he had surely always yearned to be, long after he had consciously and then unconsciously let go of the memory of her and his passion for her.

"Neither of us is going to be sorry," he murmured beneath the sounds of music and voices and laughter.

"No," she said. And then, with a touching sort of wonder in her voice, "I am *waltzing*, Charles."

He felt a curious tickle in his throat as though — alarming thought — he was about to weep.

"*We* are waltzing," he said.

And Vauxhall wove its magic around them.

All about them couples old and young, plump and thin, rich and not so rich, were waltzing. And Matilda waltzed with Charles among them.

She would not feel self-conscious because she was a staid spinster who always sat among the chaperons on the rare occasion when she attended a ball with her mother, or because she was past the age of fifty. She was not past the age of wanting to waltz or to indulge in a little romance. She was not too old to enjoy the feel of a man's hand at the back of her waist, his other hand in hers, the whole of the waltz to be danced face-to-face, almost body to body. She could feel his heat. She could smell his cologne as well as something equally enticing that seemed to be the very scent of him. She was not too old to feel the pull of his physicality. Or to dream.

Or to fall in love.

Though perhaps it was impossible to fall into anything one was already in. To fall in love again, then. Could one fall in love twice, with the same man, when one had not really stopped loving him the first time? Was it possible . . .

"What is amusing you?" he asked, and Matilda shivered at the low intimacy of his voice against her ear. He knew, as many people did not, that in order to make oneself heard amid music and a babble of voices, one needed to pitch one's voice beneath the general hubbub rather than try to shout over it.

"I am merely enjoying the waltz and the myriad sensations of being here at Vauxhall on a lovely evening," she told him.

"No," he said. "There was *amusement* in your face, Matilda. Something tickled you."

"Oh," she said, "I was wondering if it is possible to have the same feelings twice in a lifetime about the same subject, or whether that would mean that really there had been only one feeling spread over a long period of time, even if perhaps it was dormant for a while, and not two separate feelings at all."

And if he could interpret *that* it would be a wonder.

He led her into a series of twirls that had her marveling that this accomplished female dancer, who did not once trip over her own feet or anyone else's for that matter, was *she.* Matilda Westcott. Though she knew it was really the accomplished dancing of Charles that made her look good.

"I can see why you were so amused, then,"

he said. "Those were enormously amusing wonderings."

His eyes were laughing. Oh, he had used to do that all the time. And Matilda could not stop her own laughter from bubbling out of her. Then his mouth was smiling too and all sorts of lines showed themselves on his face, mostly at the outer corners of his eyes. Wrinkles in the making. Or, rather, laugh lines. Very attractive ones.

And she had never — oh, surely she had never before in her whole life, even when she was in love at the age of twenty — been happier than she was now, at this precise moment. Waltzing at Vauxhall. With Charles. She wanted to pinch herself. No, she did not. If this was a dream, she did not want to wake up. Ever.

But the waltz came to an end. Life always forged onward whether one wished it to do so or not. Matilda returned on Charles's arm to the box, only to have her hand solicited for another waltz by his son.

Oh my. She was about to refuse. No one ever danced with Matilda. She never expected it. But now *two* partners in one evening? She might never recover from the vanity of it all. Charles, she could see, was extending a hand for his elder daughter's and leading her out into the dancing area.

"Well, thank you," she said. "I have just danced my first waltz, you know. I hope I do not make a cake of myself and a spectacle of you during the second."

He laughed as they took their place on the dance floor. "I am my father's son in some ways," he said. "I will see to it that you come to no harm, Lady Matilda."

"Ah," she said, "but can you also see to it that *you* do not?"

He laughed again.

He was as good a dancer as his father, she decided after they had waltzed for a couple of minutes without talking — and without mishap — though he was *not* Charles, of course. He was not quite as tall and he was fairer of coloring and considerably younger. She doubted he had ever given his mother a moment's anxiety over wild oats he was sowing. Though he had been a mere boy, of course, when his mother died.

His eyes were upon hers. "You know my half brother, Lady Matilda," he said. "When you came to our house that day with Bertrand Lamarr, it was to tell my father about the custody hearing, was it not?"

"Yes," she said. "I thought he might be able to help. It was very much in the balance, you see, whether the judge would order that the little girl remain with her grandparents or be restored to her father."

"The little girl," he said. "My niece. My half niece."

"Katy, yes," she said.

She guessed that he was still grappling with the knowledge that there was another member of his father's family he and his sisters had known nothing of until very recently. Just as they, the Westcotts, had had to deal with the appearance of Anna, Humphrey's only legitimate daughter, in their midst six years ago. It had not been easy. It had been harder for some of them than for others.

"Lady Matilda," he said, "tell me about your niece."

She thought for a moment that he was moving on to another subject. "Estelle?" she said. "She is not really my — Oh, you are asking about Abigail, are you?"

"About Mrs. Bennington, yes," he said.

"She is the youngest of my brother's children," she told him. "She was always sweet and quiet, but a happy girl, I thought. She was on the brink of making her come-out into society when her father died and the discovery was made that he had never been legally married to her mother. She seemed to be the one who took the blow the best. She remained quiet and sweet. But her happiness was gone. And actually she became quieter than she had been — withdrawn and insistent upon being left to live her life her own way. We were all worried. My heart ached for her with that helpless feeling one gets when one wants desperately to help while knowing that all one's efforts to do so are not wanted and are therefore useless."

The story of her life.

"Ah, but she would have known herself loved," he said. "That is invaluable in itself, ma'am."

He was a kind young man, she thought. Some young lady was going to be very fortunate when he decided to settle down.

"And then this year she met Gil Bennington," she told him, "and married him without a word to her family — except her brother, who was the sole family member at her wedding. None of us were quite easy in our minds about it, for he is a taciturn, stern, dour man, very military in his bearing. But it became clear to us at the custody hearing and afterward that he loves his daughter to distraction and probably — *very* probably — Abigail too. And she glows with happiness, though she is as quiet and reserved as ever. There is a certain look about two people in love, Mr. Sawyer."

Matilda was surprised to realize that they were still waltzing, surrounded by other couples. She had forgotten her fear of tying her feet in knots.

"She is my half sister–in-law," he said. "If there is such a relationship."

"Your father loves you and your sisters no whit the less for the fact that he also loves his natural son," she told him. "Love is not a finite thing to be equally apportioned among a limited number of people. It is infinite and can be spread to encompass the whole world without losing one iota of its force. And goodness, just listen to me. If you wish for life advice, come to Aunt Matilda. Tell all your friends."

He laughed. "It is a jolt to the system, you know," he said, "to discover at the age of twenty-two that one has a thirty-four-year-old brother. And now I will not rest until I have met him. And Mrs. Bennington. And Katy."

Matilda smiled. How she liked this young man. Under other circumstances he might have been hers. But no. What a stupid, ridiculous thought. He was the son of Charles and his late wife.

"When you and my father knew each other as young people," he said, "were you in love, Lady Matilda? And what an impertinent question that is. Do please ignore it."

She continued to smile at him as Charles and Barbara danced by, laughing over something one of them had said.

"We were both very young," she told him. "Just twenty. Whatever was between us, Mr. Sawyer, was over long before your father met your mother. I saw very little of him during the years of their marriage, and even that little was from afar. We never spoke. There was never anything between us."

"Except when you were very young," he said. "As though young love is foolish and not to be taken at all seriously. I am twenty-two, Lady Matilda. Only two years older than my father was then. I know I am young. I know it will be years before I acquire any serious sort of wisdom. But the feelings of the young ought not to be dismissed or made light of. They are very real. I am sorry that something happened — and I am *not* going to ask you what it was — to separate you and my father. I like you."

Matilda smiled and blinked her eyes rapidly. Was it because of something to do with life after the age of fifty-five that she was becoming a watering pot these days?

"Thank you," she said. "It was not your father's fault, you know. It was mine. But it is also ancient history. *Very* ancient."

They lapsed into a not-uncomfortable silence for what remained of the waltz. How lovely it felt to be *liked,* Matilda thought in some surprise. One tended to imagine sometimes that only being *loved* was of any significance. But there was something enormously touching, something genuine, about being told that one was liked. By a young man who had no reason to feel anything at all for one.

Charles's son.

After the dance was over and while the orchestra took a break they all indulged themselves with the strawberries with clotted cream for which Vauxhall Gardens was famous. And then Jane suggested a walk, something they all agreed they needed after feasting upon such rich foods. Besides, during the darkness of evening there was about Vauxhall a beauty that beckoned one beyond just the area around the boxes.

They all set off together, Mr. Sawyer and Estelle leading the way along the broad, tree-lined avenue, well illumined by the light from the colored lanterns, Charles and Matilda bringing up the rear "like a couple of conscientious chaperons," Charles remarked.

"However," he added a minute or two later, "I believe it is to Barbara that the

Marquess of Dorchester entrusted Lady Estelle's care this evening. That leaves us free of all responsibility, Matilda."

For some reason his words left her feeling breathless.

The avenue was crowded with revelers. It was difficult for a group of eight to remain together. But she and Charles did not need to try. Both his daughters were with their husbands. Estelle was under the care of one of them and being escorted by surely a very respectable young man.

How lovely, Matilda thought, to be without responsibility and walking alone with a man in the crowd.

As she had been with the same man in the same venue thirty-six years ago.

# SEVEN

Thirty-six years ago they had walked this avenue with a group of other young people. Oddly — or perhaps not so strangely considering how long ago it had been — Charles could not recall who any of the others had been, though he thought Humphrey had been there. The parents of one of the young ladies had chaperoned them, but they had been a cheerfully careless pair and had enjoyed the pleasures of Vauxhall on their own account without keeping too close an eye upon their charges, a fact that had delighted those charges.

Charles and Matilda had turned off onto a side path, narrower than the main avenue, more thickly enclosed by trees, more sparsely lit by lanterns, and close to being deserted. They had been able to walk side by side, but only because each had an arm wrapped about the other's waist. Her head had come to rest upon his shoulder after a while until, in a small clearing to one side of the path, they had come to a halt and he had kissed her.

He had stopped short of making full love to her, and she had indicated just as he was pulling back that she would not have allowed it anyway. But they had shared a long and passionate embrace before that moment. Afterward, while they were recovering their breath, his forehead against hers, her hands spread over his chest, he had told her again that he loved her, that he wanted to marry her. She had said yes, oh yes, oh yes, she wanted to marry him too. She would love him with all her heart forever and ever.

Soon after, they had returned to the main avenue to rejoin their party and begin living happily ever after. Less than a week later he had called upon her father . . .

"Matilda," he said now as they walked along the main avenue, "how long did it take you to stop loving me?" For she *had* loved him. He had doubted it for a long time, when the pain was raw, but no longer.

"About as long as it took you to stop," she said. "Gil was born the following year."

"I dealt with my unwanted love in a thoroughly unbridled and immature way," he said. "I suppose I remained immature long after the age at which most men settle down. Until ten years or so ago, in fact. I did not love Gil's mother, though I do not want to speak disrespectfully of her. She was not a woman of loose morals. I believe she genuinely thought I loved her and would marry her. She punished me very effectively when she understood that I did not and could not."

"By keeping you away from your son?" she said.

"Yes."

"Are you telling me, then," she asked him, "that all the behavior for which you became notorious was because of me? Did I hurt you so very badly?"

"I was hurt," he admitted. "But my behavior was mine to own. You were not responsible for any of that, Matilda."

"Humphrey always assured me whenever I asked," she said, "that you were not hurt at all, that you had been lying to me when you told me you loved me, that you were incapable of love just as he was. You were a capital fellow in his estimation. He told me to grow up to the real world and not expect love outside the pages of a book."

"And you listened and believed?" he said. *She had asked her brother about him?*

"I did not look for love from any man," she said.

"Because of me?" he asked.

"No, of course —" She stopped. "Yes. Because of you."

He drew a slow breath and let it out on an almost audible sigh.

"Your mother treats you poorly, Matilda," he said. It might seem to be a non sequitur, but it was not. "You gave up love and marriage in order to be treated with impatience and irritability even before strangers? Do you not regret —"

"Regrets are pointless," she said sharply. "My mother is sometimes impatient with me because I *coddle* her. I have fully realized it only lately. I have always been so determined to show my love and devotion, to make my life seem meaningful, that I have treated her, at least in recent years, like an old woman rather than as a person of dignity still able to be in charge of her own life. I have been a severe trial to her — as she has been to me. Don't judge from the outside, Charles. She has her own demons to deal with. She feels guilty for blighting my life. My presence forever at her side and my . . . fussy behavior are a constant reproach to her. I could have behaved differently all those years ago. I could have fought for myself instead of giving in so meekly to my parents' fears and commands. I could have married someone else of whom they *did* approve. Oh, but regrets are pointless, Charles. Must we spoil this most wonderful of wonderful evenings by talking of the past?"

The avenue was crowded. They dodged other revelers and probably annoyed a number of them with their slow pace. The orchestra had resumed its playing, but the music was almost drowned out by the sounds of raised voices and laughter.

Perhaps her mother was not such an ogre, then, Charles thought. Apparently she had a conscience. Perhaps she loved her eldest daughter after all. Probably she did, in fact. And Matilda loved her in return, even though her mother had blighted her life — an interesting choice of words. No, he must not judge. Close human relationships were often a great deal more complex than they seemed to outsiders. His own relationship with his wife, for example, had been far from simple, far from one-faceted. On the whole it had been a decent marriage, even though he had been a wayward husband much of the time and she had told him even before they wed that she had no real interest in men but recognized the necessity of conforming to society's expectations by marrying him. Yet they had produced three children who had grown into affectionate, sensible adults of whom they had both been proud.

"We will not spoil the evening," he said. "It *is* wonderful, is it not?"

He could not be sure in the dim, swaying light of the lanterns, but it looked to him as though her eyes had filled with tears. And how much she had revealed about her feelings!

*. . . this most wonderful of wonderful evenings.*

Ah, Matilda.

"Come," he said, turning her onto a side path just as he had more than thirty years ago. "Let us seek a little more privacy."

He could not be sure it was the *same* path. But it did not matter. It was narrow as the other one had been, a little too narrow for two people to walk comfortably side by side. He drew his arm away from hers and encircled her waist with it. Far from showing any outrage or resistance, she set her own arm about him and very briefly rested the side of her head against his shoulder.

*Just* like last time.

"This is better," he said. "The noise seems more muted here."

"Yes," she said. "Charles —"

"Mmm?" He waited for her to continue.

"Surely this is impossible," she said.

*"This?"*

"It surely is," she said. "Impossible. More than three decades have gone by. I am *old.*"

"I take exception to that word," he told her. "For if you are old, then I am older. Three months older, I seem to recall. We are not old, and even if we are, we are not *dead.* Only in that circumstance would I be forced to agree with you that this is impossible. Though perhaps I would be unable then either to agree or to disagree. I would be dead. We are *alive,* Matilda."

"But this sort of thing is for young people," she protested.

"Slinking into the trees to set our arms about each other's waist?" he said. "Embracing?"

"Oh, not that," she said hastily. "It would be most unseemly."

And she sounded so like a prim, middle-aged spinster that he smiled into the darkness. He loved her primness. But only because there was also her passion. And passion very definitely lurked within her. It had shown itself briefly during their kiss on top of the pagoda. And in some of her looks and words since — *this most wonderful of wonderful evenings,* for example.

"Most," he agreed.

"You are laughing at me," she said.

"Yes."

She turned her face toward his, though he doubted she could see his laughing eyes. "That is unkind."

"Is it, my love?" he asked her.

*"Charles!"* Her voice seemed half agony, half outrage.

"Do you not want me to call you that?" he asked. "My love?"

"Ch-a-a-arles."

He stopped walking. There was a little open-fronted rain shelter in a small clearing to the right of the path, a bench inside it, a lantern suspended from the branch of a tree before it to illumine the interior. He led her toward it, though he did not sit down with her. He faced her instead and laced his fingers with hers at their sides, as he had done at the pagoda. He could see her face dimly, as she would be able to see his. She was gazing wide-eyed at him.

"That was no answer," he said. "Do you not understand that is what you are to me — my love?"

"Oh," she said, "you cannot possibly love me, Charles."

"I do not see why not," he said. "And apparently it is possible. I have tested the idea and can find no flaw in it. Do you love me, Matilda?"

He watched her lick her lips, lower her gaze, first to his mouth, then to his neck-cloth. "Of course I do," she said, sounding almost cross.

"You cannot possibly," he told her, and her eyes shot up to look accusingly into his again.

"I never stopped," she said. "Do you think I did — or could? I followed all the events of your life from afar and lived for the few glimpses I had of you down the years. I bled a little inside every time I heard something about you that reaffirmed my conviction that I had done the right thing by refusing to have anything more to do with you. The pain dimmed as time passed until there was almost no pain at all. The memories dimmed until they became almost unconscious, lost somewhere in the recesses of my mind. But always, always, I have known that I love you, ridiculous as it seemed to be, ridiculous as it would have seemed to anyone who had ever suspected."

He had turned very still inside. His love for her must have lain dormant in him for more than half his life, but he had given it almost no thought since a year or so after she had rejected him. He had given *her* no thought, or almost none. Yet his love must not have completely died — or why had it been revived so easily now in all its intensity? Why was it that after such a brief time he was surer than he had been of anything else in his life that he loved this woman who was his age and looked it and dressed without glamour or obvious allure? Yet to him she seemed the most beautiful woman on earth. Why was it he had fallen in love only twice in his life, and with the same woman? It shook him to the core that even though she was the one who had rejected him all those years ago, she had remained true to him ever since. For he knew she must have had numerous chances of marriage to other men, at least during the ten years or so after him.

"Matilda." He sighed and drew her to him, one arm about her waist, the other about her shoulders. "You put me to shame with your steadfast fidelity."

"But I am the one who sent you away," she said.

"For reasons that seemed sound to you at the time and possibly were," he said. "How can either of us be sure I would not have turned out just as I did even if we had married? I do not *believe* I would have, but I cannot be certain. Perhaps we needed to wait until we were older. We might have had a very unhappy marriage if we had wed when we were young."

"And we might not have," she said, infinite sadness in her voice.

"You said earlier that regrets are pointless," he said, resting his forehead against hers. "You were right."

"Yes," she agreed.

And he kissed her.

She kissed like someone who had never kissed before, with slightly pursed lips and stiffened limbs — even though they had kissed at Kew. But there he had not had his arms about her. Perhaps she felt more threatened this time. He raised his head.

"Put your arms around me," he said. She had her hands clutched about his upper arms. She tipped her head slightly to one side in a familiar gesture before releasing her hold and sliding one arm beneath his about his waist and wrapping the other about his neck.

"Charles," she said. "I am no good at this. I will only make a cake of myself."

"I do not believe there is a manual," he said. "Or any rules at all, in fact. Just kiss me, my love, and I will kiss you."

"You ought not to call me that," she said.

*"My love?"* he said. "Why not?"

She pursed her lips, looked as though she was about to say something, and changed her mind. "I keep waiting to wake up," she said at last.

"So do I," he told her. "But while we are both asleep, shall we share the dream?"

She tightened her arms about him. "Very well," she said so primly that he almost laughed.

He smiled instead and kissed her again, drawing her against him, moving his hand lower down her back to draw her closer yet. He probed the seam of her lips with his tongue, and when they trembled apart he explored the inside of her mouth, stroking and circling her tongue. She moaned low in her throat, and he could feel one of her hands tangling in his hair.

And though she was different from the way she had been at the age of twenty, there was something about her that was unmistakably Matilda, and he knew he had never really stopped loving her. It was why he had never fallen in love with anyone else. For always, somewhere in the recesses of his being, there had been Matilda. And now — yes, it was like a dream — he held her in his arms again.

They were gazing into each other's eyes then in the dim, pink glow of the lantern, her head tipped back.

"I never did ask you to marry me," he said. "Your father said no, and then you sent me away, and the question remained unasked."

"Yes," she said. "I am so sorry, Charles. I know now that you suffered just as I did."

"Can we put the omission right at last?" he asked her. "Will you marry me, Matilda?"

Her eyes widened and she took a step back, dropping her arms to her sides. "Oh," she said. "But it is impossible."

"Why?" he asked.

"There is your family," she said. "And mine. There is . . . our age."

He turned his head to eye the bench inside the wooden shelter and led her to sit there. He took one of her hands in his and held it on his thigh. "Shall we dispense with the last objection first?" he said. "Is there an age limit upon love and marriage? If we wish to spend the rest of our lives together, does it matter whether we are twenty or fifty-six — or eighty?"

"People would laugh," she said.

"Would they?" He stroked his thumb over her palm. "How strange of them. *Which* people, exactly?"

"They would laugh at *me,*" she said.

"I cannot think of anyone who might," he

said. "But in the unlikely event that someone did, would you care?"

She frowned in thought, her eyes upon his. "I think I might," she said. "If I became the subject of a sneering on-dit with the *ton* I believe I might mind."

And the thing was that such a thing was possible. Lady Matilda Westcott was known to the *ton* as a staid, fussy, aging spinster who hovered constantly over her mother. *Would* she be seen as a figure of fun if she suddenly announced her betrothal and went about looking as she looked now? Like a woman in love? All April and May?

"Then I suppose you will have to decide which course of action you would prefer," he said. "Would you rather keep your familiar image and thus be largely invisible to the *ton*? Or would you prefer to announce your engagement to me and become the sensation of the hour and very much *not* invisible?"

"Oh," she said, still frowning. "Oh dear."

"Thirty-six years ago," he said, "you were given no choice at all. You were told what to do and you did it. You have lived with the consequences ever since. Now, after all these years, you do have a choice. You can continue as you are. Or you can marry me. *You* have the choice, Matilda."

"But it is still impossible," she said. "For we are not the only ones concerned. There is your family. And mine."

"My children like you," he told her. "I know Adrian does. He has told me so. And I sense that Barbara and Jane do too. They do not often like the women I escort. For they always look upon them as potential wives, and they all come up wanting in one way or another."

"Surely I would quite as much as anyone else," she said. "They cannot help but compare other women to their mother. They surely cannot *want* you to marry again."

"I believe you are wrong in that," he said. "Much as I do not deserve such good fortune, I have children who love me and wish to see me happy. They loved their mother, but they accept the fact that she is gone while I am still here. And what of the Westcotts, Matilda? They seem a decent lot on the whole. Why would you expect them to object to your finding happiness at last?"

"Oh," she said, "it is not that they do not wish for my happiness. But to them I am just Matilda. Or Aunt Matilda. I am the sister who stayed home to look after my mother while the other two married. They would all . . ."

"Laugh?" he suggested when she did not

immediately complete the thought.

"No." She was frowning again. "Not that. They would not be so unkind. But they would be . . . incredulous."

"And perhaps a little bit happy for you?" he suggested.

"I am not sure," she said. "They certainly might doubt my judgment. When they first learned that you were Gil's father they immediately recalled your unsavory reputation."

"It was a well-deserved notoriety," he said, "and has been hard to shake, even impossible in some circles. I can understand the concern they will feel for you. However, if you decide to marry me, they will learn that I have changed. Perhaps some of them already know it. They all treated me with warm courtesy when I attended Riverdale's dinner."

"But you were not my betrothed then," she said.

"And I am now?" He smiled at her. "Then I will have some work ahead of me. I will have to persuade them that I love you, that you are all the world to me and always will be. And you, if you decide to marry me, will have to show them that you are not *just* sister Matilda or Aunt Matilda but *Matilda* without any qualifiers, a person in your own right, free to make your own choices. A person deserving of happiness. *If,* that is, you love me more than you fear change or the incredulity of your family and society."

"Oh, Charles." She sighed.

He released his hold on her hand, set his arm about her shoulders, and drew her head down onto his shoulder.

"Two simple questions," he said. "First, do you love me?"

"You know I do," she said. "I always have."

"Second," he said, "do you *want* to marry me?"

There was a long silence before she answered. "Yes," she said at last.

"One somewhat more complex question, then," he said. "*Will* you marry me, Matilda?"

"Oh," she said.

He waited.

"Yes," she said then, her voice barely audible. "Oh yes, Charles, I will."

He released the breath he had not realized he was holding. "Then let us rest upon that for tonight," he said. "We love each other. We are to marry and spend the rest of our lives together. Sometimes life really is that simple."

"But —" she began.

He set one finger across her lips. "No buts.

Not tonight."

"And tomorrow we awaken from the dream?" she asked against his finger.

"There is a funny thing about tomorrow," he said. "It never comes. Have you noticed? For when the day that ought to be tomorrow arrives, it is actually today. And today we are in love and planning to marry."

She gazed at him and then laughed — with that delightful merry sound that could always make his heart turn over. "How absolutely absurd," she said. "You have set my head in a spin."

He grinned at her and kissed her again before sitting quietly with her, gazing out into the pink-hued darkness and listening to birdsong and the distant sounds of music and voices and laughter.

"We are going to be *married*?" she asked him after a while. *"At last?"*

"At long last," he said softly, his cheek against the top of her head. "And it will be good, Matilda. I promise."

"Yes." She smiled, and in the glow of the lamp he watched one tear trickle down her cheek and disappear beneath her chin.

He did not show that he had noticed. He closed his eyes instead and rested a little longer upon his happiness.

# EIGHT

Charles had been very wrong about tomorrow. It *did* come. It also became today in the process, as Charles had said it would, but it was very different from yesterday's today.

Oh goodness, she was beginning to think like him, in a head-spinning way. Suffice it to say that today — *now,* this morning — was very different from yesterday, last evening. Then she had been caught up in the magic of Vauxhall Gardens and all things had seemed possible. It had been the most wonderful evening of her life. It had culminated in fireworks and in a journey home in a darkened vehicle, their hands clasped upon his thigh. It had ended with a warm kiss as the carriage drew to a halt outside her door. And the unspoken promise of happily-ever-after.

This morning she was Matilda Westcott again, a little pale and droopy eyed because she was not accustomed to late nights or to dancing and kissing handsome gentlemen and agreeing to marry them. She was not used to laughing and even giggling a time or two. Oh dear, had she really behaved in such an unseemly manner, as though she were a *girl*? Whatever must everyone have thought? Today the idea of marrying Charles seemed utterly absurd. He could *not* have been serious, or, if he had been, today he would be feeling a certain horror at what he had said on the impulse of the moment.

This morning she was feeling elderly and frumpish and mortally depressed and irritable and not at all herself. She wanted to be herself again. Instead she felt like weeping.

"Your evening out," her mother said, setting down the letter she had been reading and regarding her daughter across the breakfast table, "must not have been a great success."

"I would have been happier if I had stayed at home," Matilda said. "I worried about you being alone." With a rush of guilt she realized she had spared her mother scarcely a thought all evening. And now she had lied and made herself feel worse.

"I was alone with a houseful of servants and a library full of books," her mother said.

"Matilda, I do not *need* you."

Well, there. She had been justly punished for her lie.

"I only love you," her mother added.

Her mother *never* talked like this. Matilda frowned and looked down at her plate. She was rather surprised to see half a slice of toast spread with marmalade there. She could not remember eating the other half, or anything else for that matter.

"It was a pleasant enough evening," she said. "Vauxhall is always worth a visit. Mrs. Dewhurst appeared to enjoy her birthday. Everyone was very amiable and kind."

*I waltzed. I laughed. He kissed me — and I kissed him back. I accepted his marriage proposal.*

"And Viscount Dirkson?" her mother asked.

"He was amiable and kind too," Matilda said, getting to her feet. "Mama, let me get you a fresh cup of coffee. That one has grown cold while you have been reading your letter."

"I do not need a fresh cup," her mother said with a flash of her old irritability. "Don't fuss, Matilda. I am sorry if the evening was not everything you hoped it might be. I am . . . sorry."

"I had no expectations," Matilda said.

"And it really was very pleasant."

But her mother was on her feet and making her way toward the door. It was time for one of her meetings with the housekeeper to discuss the meals for the coming days and other household matters. She had never allowed Matilda to take over those responsibilities from her. Neither had she ever offered to share them.

Matilda went to the morning room to write letters to her nieces, Camille in Bath and Abigail somewhere in Gloucestershire in her country cottage, which she shared with Gil and Katy. Charles's son and granddaughter. There was no getting away from him, was there?

But did she want to? Had she not accepted a marriage offer from him last evening? Had he not held her hand all the way home in the carriage and kissed her before his coachman opened the door and set down the steps? He had not said anything about seeing her again, though. But surely he meant to. It would be most peculiar if he did not, even if he had changed his mind.

*As he surely must.*

Oh, he had been wrong about tomorrow. Tomorrow definitely came, and it was not the same as yesterday. But what happened to *today* while one made the contrast between *yesterday* and *tomorrow*? Strange thoughts.

He could not *possibly* love her.

There was no way on earth he could really want to marry her.

Just *look* at her.

The first visitors arrived early in the afternoon. It was not unusual for Matilda's sisters to call, as they were attentive to their mother and knew she enjoyed hearing the latest on-dits that had not yet found their way into the morning papers. It was unusual for them to come together, however, as they did today, and for Louise to bring her daughter, Jessica, and Anna, Duchess of Netherby, her stepdaughter-in-law, with her. And no sooner had the four of them arrived and exchanged greetings and weather reports and seated themselves than Viola, Marchioness of Dorchester, Matilda's former sister-in-law, was ushered into the room too.

"It seems we all had the same idea this afternoon," she said, and kissed cheeks, asked after the dowager's health, and commented upon the fact that it would be a lovely day if the wind were not so cutting. "I knew you at least were here, Louise. Your carriage is outside the door."

"Thomas came home from White's Club this morning," Mildred said, "with word that you were seen at Vauxhall last evening, Matilda, in company with Viscount Dirkson. You were strolling along the main avenue with him, apparently without even your maid for company. I thought whoever told Thomas that must have been mistaken, but when I called upon Louise, she informed me that Jessica danced with young Bertrand Lamarr last evening, and he told her when she asked about Estelle that she had gone with Mr. Sawyer and one of his sisters for a birthday party at Vauxhall Gardens. And Mr. Sawyer told Bertrand while they were waiting for Estelle to finish getting ready that his father had invited *you* to accompany him, Matilda."

"I was charmed, Aunt Matilda," Jessica said.

"Yes, I was there," Matilda said. "It was a pleasant evening."

"Only pleasant?" Viola smiled warmly at her. "Estelle was bubbling over this morning about all her experiences there. And she was very happy that you were there too. She told us about how you appeared very different from how she had always thought of you. About how, both at Kew Gardens last week and at Vauxhall last evening, you were full of sparkle and laughter and *fun* — her words, I do assure you. *Did* you enjoy yourself?"

"Well, I did." Matilda felt horribly uncomfortable. She was not accustomed to being the focus of anyone's attention, even her family's. "It was a birthday party, and they are a close family and were greatly enjoying the occasion and one another's company. How could I not show pleasure too? It would have been uncivil to look bored or even just solemn."

"Aunt Matilda." There was sheer mischief in Anna's smile. "Do you have a *beau*? I do hope so."

"Anna," Louise said reproachfully.

"Oh, do say it is true, Aunt Matilda," Jessica said, a spark of mischief in her eyes. "I thought when we were at Kew that Viscount Dirkson was particular in his attentions toward you."

"And we heard, Matilda," Viola said, "that you *waltzed* last evening. More than once. With Viscount Dirkson more than with anyone else."

"I believe you are in love," Jessica said, laughing and clapping her hands.

*"Jessica."* Her mother's outraged voice put an instant end to her merriment. "Your aunt

Matilda is *not* a figure of fun. She is a lady of mature years and must be treated with the respect that is her due. The very idea of her being in love, as though she were a giddy girl. And with Viscount Dirkson of all people."

"I must agree with Louise," Mildred said. "I cannot stand by and listen to my sister being teased upon such a matter. She is far too mature to be in love or to *have a beau.* And she is far too sensible to lose her head over a man like Viscount Dirkson. He may have reformed his ways in recent years, but he once had a very unsavory reputation indeed and even now ought not to be welcomed into society with wide-open arms. It was probably unwise of Alexander and Wren to invite him to dine with us. Just consider what followed. He had the effrontery to suggest that Matilda share the duties of chaperon with him for the young people's excursion to Kew. And when I heard this morning that he had taken her to his daughter's birthday celebration, I was very angry. You ought not to be subjected to such disrespect, Matilda, and I am sorry it has happened. I shall ask Thomas to have a word with Viscount Dirkson. It would not hurt, Louise and Anna, if you persuaded Avery to do likewise."

Matilda sat quietly in her chair, fighting the urge to jump to her feet to fuss over her mother for some imaginary need.

"Thank you," she said. "Thank you for coming and showing your concern. You speak *of* me as a mature woman, Louise. And you too, Mildred. Yet you speak *to* me as though I were a child, someone lacking in the knowledge and experience needed to command her own life and make her own decisions. You speak of me as though I were someone who needs a *man,* a family member, to protect me from all the wicked harm that awaits me beyond my doors."

"Well, you must admit, Matilda," Louise said, "that your experience of life is severely limited. You have lived all your days with Mama, and Papa while he was alive, sheltered within the safety of home. We *care.* We do not want to see you the subject of gossip."

"We could not bear to see you humiliated," Mildred added. "Or hurt. We love you, Matilda. You are our *sister.*"

Matilda drew breath to answer, but her mother spoke first.

"And Matilda is my daughter," she said. "My firstborn. The eldest of you all. Quite old enough to decide for herself what she wants to do with her life, even if it is only to go to Kew Gardens with a party of young people and the father of one of them, a man whose reputation once set him beyond the pale of polite society. Or even if it is to go to Vauxhall under the escort of the same man and in company with his son and daughters and their spouses. She is old enough to decide for herself whether she will sparkle and laugh and have fun, as Estelle put it. Such careless language, Viola! And Matilda is old enough to decide whether she will waltz under the stars. *She is old enough.* Perhaps it is disrespectful, Louise and Mildred, to question the judgment of your elder sister."

There were a few moments of incredulous silence while everyone — Matilda included — gawked at the dowager countess. *Gawked* was the only appropriate word.

"I really meant no offense, Matilda," Louise said at last. "You must know that. I am merely concerned for you. Of course you may . . . But do you have an *attachment* to Viscount Dirkson?"

"Is it true," Jessica asked, "that you were once in love with him, Aunt Matilda?"

"And that you are again?" Anna asked. "But we are embarrassing you. Do forgive us. We really *do* care, you know. If we did not, we would not tease you. We care about your happiness. And about you. Do let us shift the subject a little. Were there fireworks last evening? Were they as amazing as they usually are?"

But before Matilda could answer, the butler appeared in the doorway — no one had heard his discreet knock — and they all turned to hear what he had to say.

"Viscount Dirkson, my lady," he announced, and Charles came striding into the room.

Charles had seen the two carriages outside the door. He had even recognized one of them as belonging to the Duke of Netherby. For a moment he considered driving his curricle right on by and returning later, but there was always a chance that he had already been spotted from the drawing room window. Besides, he had no reason to hide from the Westcott family. Indeed, he had every reason not to.

He was a bit disconcerted a few minutes later, however, when he stepped into the drawing room on the heels of the butler and found the room seemingly full of ladies. All of them were members of the family. Matilda, he was happy to see, was not hovering behind her mother's chair today but was seated very straight backed on the edge of another chair, two spots of color in her cheeks.

"Ma'am." He bowed to the dowager countess and looked around at the others. "Ladies. Matilda." He smiled at her.

She looked back at him with what he could describe only as acute embarrassment as everyone else rushed into greetings, which varied from subdued to effusive. He guessed they had been talking about him before his arrival. He wondered if Matilda had *told* them, as he had told his children — Adrian last night, Barbara and Jane this morning.

"Estelle was bubbling over at breakfast about last night's visit to Vauxhall," the Marchioness of Dorchester said. "What an inspired idea it was, Lord Dirkson, to choose that venue at which to celebrate your daughter's birthday."

"It was entirely her idea, ma'am," he told her. "But it was indeed a lovely evening. Was it not, Matilda?"

"It was," she said, and surely it was not his imagination that all attention was suddenly riveted upon her. Her hands were clasped tightly in her lap. Her lips were in a prim line. "It was lovely."

Ah, she had not told them.

"I came to assure myself that you had

taken no chill or other harm," he said.

"It was kind of you," Louise, Dowager Duchess of Netherby, told him, "to invite Matilda."

"Kindness had nothing to do with it, ma'am," he said. "Or if it did, it was on Lady Matilda's part. She was kind enough to accept my daughter's invitation to be one of the party."

"Oh," Lady Molenor, Matilda's youngest sister, said. "The invitation came from your daughter, did it?"

"It did," he said. "At my suggestion."

"Estelle's invitation came from Mrs. Dewhurst too," the marchioness said. "At the suggestion of Mr. Adrian Sawyer, I believe. She had a splendid time."

"Do have a seat, Lord Dirkson," the dowager said, indicating an empty chair.

"I do not intend to stay, ma'am," he said. "I came to pay my respects and to ask Lady Matilda if she will drive with me in my curricle in the park later."

"Oh," the Dowager Duchess of Netherby said, "my sister has never ridden in a curricle. She would be terrified."

"I have, Louise," Matilda said. "I rode up with Bertrand one afternoon several weeks ago, and far from being terrified, I found it to be one of the most exhilarating experiences of my life."

"Matilda?" Lady Molenor said. "Impossible."

"With Bertrand?" the marchioness said. "Well, the rogue. He said nothing to us."

"Bravo, Aunt Matilda." The young Duchess of Netherby laughed. "How splendid of you."

"Indeed," Lady Jessica Archer agreed. "How did he persuade you to do something so daring, Aunt Matilda?"

"Exactly when was this?" the dowager countess asked eagerly.

Matilda was stretching her fingers in her lap and then curling them into her palms again. "Thank you," she said, looking at Charles and ignoring the questions her family had for her. "That would be delightful."

"Matilda —"

"Oh good, Aunt Matilda."

"Are you sure, Matilda —"

She continued to ignore them all. She licked her lips, her eyes still upon Charles, though it was clear she was addressing everyone when she spoke. "Last evening Viscount Dirkson asked me to marry him and I said yes."

Well, that silenced them — for a few moments anyway.

Charles smiled slowly at Matilda, and she

frowned back at him.

Part of his attention was caught by the sound of the dowager countess, her mother, drawing breath. He waited for the tirade that was sure to come.

"Well, thank God for that," was what she actually said.

Matilda thought her fingernails might well be drawing blood from her palms, but she could not seem to relax her hands. She thought her heart might beat a path through her chest cavity and ribs. She held her mouth in a firm line so that she would not . . . what? Laugh? Why would she feel an irresistible urge to laugh when she was so tense that her jaw felt locked in place?

She gazed upon Charles and could hardly believe he was the same man as the one with whom she had danced and laughed last evening. And kissed. The one with whom she had stood beyond the rotunda to watch the fireworks while exclaiming all the while in childish superlatives at the splendor of it all. The one who had stood behind her at last and encircled her waist with his arms so that she could rest the back of her head against his shoulder and not grow dizzy as she gazed upward — despite the fact that they might have been observed by half the *ton,* or even three-quarters.

Today he was an immaculately clad gentleman, handsome, solid of build, somehow remote from her. Except that . . . He had named her alone when he had entered the room and greeted everyone. He had *smiled* at her. He had come to make sure she had taken no harm last evening, though from what she might have taken harm she did not know. He had neatly turned the idea that *he* had been kind to invite *her* to Vauxhall into one in which *she* had been kind to *him* by accepting Barbara's invitation. And he had come — he had said it in front of her mother and sisters and sister-in-law and nieces — to invite her to drive in his curricle with him in Hyde Park. It must be thirty years or more since any gentleman had invited her to do that.

She was fairly bursting with her love for him. All last night's and this morning's anxieties had fallen away. *He had come.* And he had smiled and called her by name. He wanted her to go out with him. He still loved her.

Tomorrow had not come after all. It was still today. Eternally today in which to be with Charles, to enjoy his love, to return it in full measure, to . . .

"*Thank God,* Mama?" Mildred said.

"I thought my punishment was to be eternal," her mother said. "It is the millstone I have carried about my neck for well nigh forty years. I thought I would carry it to my grave."

"Whatever are you talking about, Mama?" Louise asked. "Are you well? Matilda, is Mama ailing?"

"Stop fussing," their mother said. "Start talking about a wedding instead. It must be a grand one. I will not stand for anything less. Matilda must have her grand wedding at last. And if you have anything to say to the contrary, Lord Dirkson, I would suggest that you keep your tongue between your teeth and allow the women to do what women do best."

He actually grinned as he clasped his hands behind his back. "Plan weddings?" he said.

"Precisely." She nodded briskly.

"Mama —" Matilda began.

"Ma'am." Charles spoke again. "I am quite prepared to allow the world to turn upon its axis as it always has done. However, I feel compelled to speak out on two points before I lose my voice altogether, and I fear that time is imminent. First, Matilda and I did not get as far as discussing our wedding last evening. I have no idea what sort of ceremony she wants or where or when she wants it to happen. She must make that choice — with me. I will not allow her to be bullied into giving in to what her family and mine may think appropriate. And second, when the women sweep in to organize us, as they no doubt will unless Matilda chooses to elope with me, it must be remembered that there are women in both the Westcott and Sawyer families. My daughters, despite my dire warnings this morning, very probably have my wedding half-planned already."

"I am still in shock," Anna said, getting to her feet. "But a very pleasant shock. Aunt Matilda! I cannot tell you how pleased I am for you. And you too, Lord Dirkson. Avery and I slipped off quietly to marry one afternoon, you know, while Grandmama and the aunts and cousins were busy planning a grand wedding for us. I was never happier in my life." She leaned over Matilda's chair and hugged her warmly. "And Abigail married Gil in the village church at home just a few weeks ago with no one present except Harry and the vicar's wife. I believe she will always treasure the memory. Perhaps you —"

"Thank you, Anna," Matilda said. "But I want a *wedding.*"

She had not thought of it until now, when

she had been almost afraid to believe in the truth of what had happened last evening. But it was true. All her life she had dreamed of a grand wedding, but for most of that time that was all it had been — an ever-fading dream. And, for the last twenty years or so, entirely faded.

"Then a wedding is what you will have, my love," Charles said.

*My love?* Oh. In front of half her family.

"St. George's it will be, then." Louise clapped her hands as though to draw the attention of thousands. "We must have the banns called next Sunday. It is already rather late in the Season and we do not want to wait until it is over and most of the *ton* has returned to the country. If Matilda is to be married at St. George's, the pews must be full to overflowing. Oh goodness, we must let Wren know and Elizabeth and Althea. They will want to be involved in the planning."

"We must arrange a meeting with Mrs. Dewhurst and Lady Frater," Viola said. "They will have ideas of their own. They already do, according to Viscount Dirkson."

"Alexander will want to host the wedding breakfast," Anna said. "But I know Avery will insist that the ballroom at Archer House has more room."

A *ton* wedding at St. George's on Hanover Square? A wedding breakfast in the ballroom at the town house of the Duke of Netherby? Matilda started to feel anxious again. Surely, oh surely, she would be the laughingstock. She had not meant anything quite so grand. Just a definite wedding with . . .

"Matilda," Charles said. "My curricle is outside your door. Why wait until later to go for our drive? I have the distinct impression that our presence here is de trop. Will you come now?"

"Yes." She got to her feet. "Oh yes. Thank you."

How many times had she participated in family conferences and family planning committees? She had usually been at the forefront of them all, busy planning how to extricate some family member from disaster or how to help them celebrate an event in their lives. Was she now to be the object of such family activity?

Oh. It did feel good.

"Matilda," Charles said when she joined him downstairs after going to fetch her bonnet and gloves and reticule, "I will not allow you to be bullied, you know. Even by me. Especially by me. You are looking worried, even a little stricken. There is no need. You must tell me as we drive what you want. And you shall have it. You are the bride. You are to make the decisions."

*You are the bride.*

She felt that growingly familiar urge to weep. She smiled instead as he handed her up to the passenger seat of the curricle and she remembered that heady feeling of being much farther off the ground than she had expected. The feeling of danger and exhilaration. She laughed aloud.

"But everyone would be so disappointed," she said, "if we were to run off with a special license to marry in secret. Besides which, *I* would be disappointed. And they would be upset if they planned and planned and I disapproved of everything. My family would be upset. So would Barbara and Jane. I think a marriage is for two people, Charles. But a wedding is for their families and friends. Shall we just let them plan?"

"It would save us a lot of anguish," he said, grinning at her as he took his place beside her. "When I walked into that room awhile ago and saw you, I feared you had changed your mind. You looked brittle and severe."

"But only because I was convinced *you* must have changed *your* mind," she said.

"Absurd," he told her.

"Absurd," she agreed, and they both laughed as though someone had just made an extremely witty remark.

"Charles," she said, laying a hand on his arm as he leaned down, took the ribbons from his young groom, and gathered them in his hands, "I wish we were in the country. I wish I could ask you to spring the horses."

He turned his head to look into her face, his own still filled with laughter. "*Do* you, my love?" he asked her.

"I know you are a notable whip," she told him. "It was always a part of your reputation."

"One day soon," he said, "when we are in the country, I will spring the horses and risk both our lives as they dash along at a neck-or-nothing pace."

"Oh, *will* you?" she said. "Thank you, Charles. I am not a staid old lady quite yet, you know."

"I have noticed," he said, and he risked horrible scandal by leaning toward her and kissing her briefly on the lips while windows in numerous houses all around them looked accusingly on and his young groom pretended to be looking intently elsewhere.

As the curricle moved off in the direction of Hyde Park, Matilda, in marvelous lady-like fashion, threw back her head and laughed.

# Nine

Several times over the following month, Charles sat alone in his library, wishing that he had not suddenly found himself at the center of a whirlpool or a tornado — both seemed appropriate metaphors. For of course the notice of his betrothal appeared in every London paper and perhaps a few provincial ones too. And wherever he went, he faced congratulations or — at his clubs — endless witticisms over which he was forced to laugh. His son and one of his sons-in-law dragged him off to his tailor and his boot maker and his hatmaker and Lord knew where else so that on his wedding day he would be able to astonish the *ton* with new and fashionable everything.

His daughters and every female on earth who had a connection with the Westcott family, no matter how slim, held meeting after meeting to discuss every aspect of the wedding that women invariably found to discuss and wrangle over. Though to be fair, he heard no reports of arguments or raised voices or heated discussions or rivalries between the two families. Early predictions proved quite accurate. The wedding breakfast was to be served at Westcott House, the home of Alexander, Earl of Riverdale, on South Audley Street. Invitations were sent. If any member of the *ton* then staying in or within a twenty-mile radius of London had been omitted, Charles would be enormously surprised. Relatives from farther afield had been summoned, including a few cousins he scarcely knew but whose presence on his wedding day was deemed by his daughters to be essential to his happiness.

Charles would just as happily have done what the Netherbys had once done and sneaked off to marry Matilda in an obscure church somewhere, special license in hand, while their families were in a flurry of plotting and planning for a grand wedding to outdo all others this year. But despite ever-changing misgivings and second and third and sixth thoughts through which Matilda suffered during the course of the month, he understood that a big public wedding was what she really wanted. And what Matilda wanted she would have. She had waited long enough for her wedding — thirty-six years.

What she had feared most was being laughed at. Charles felt no doubt that there were certain elements of society that ridiculed her behind her back. There always were. The world would never be rid of unkind people who compensated for their own insecurities by dragging down other happier, more successful people to their own level through their gossip. They were to be heartily ignored. She was well received wherever she went. Barbara held a soiree in her honor, and Jane had her as a special guest in Wallace's private box at the theater the very evening after the announcement appeared in the papers. The Duke and Duchess of Netherby hosted a betrothal party at their home, and the Marquess and Marchioness of Dorchester organized an afternoon tea. Charles took her driving in the park several times and escorted her to a private concert and a literary evening.

She received well-wishers with quiet dignity wherever she went. No longer was she the fussy spinster forever in her mother's shadow, though perhaps that had something to do with the fact that her mother flatly refused to have her there any longer. And Matilda need not fear for her care, her mother informed Charles when he broached the subject of her coming to live with them after their marriage.

"You need not fear either, Lord Dirkson," she had added. "I am quite capable of looking after myself. And has Matilda not told you? My sister is coming to live with me when I return to the country after the Season is over. She will be bringing her longtime companion with her, an estimable lady who will offer companionship without trying to worry me into my grave."

Charles had understood immediately that life had been about to change very much for the worse for Matilda, who would no doubt have found herself constantly being compared unfavorably with her aunt's ideal companion.

"I really do not know how I would have borne it," Matilda had admitted to him when he mentioned what her mother had told him. "I would have gone mad. Adelaide Boniface is the gloomiest creature of my acquaintance. And she *sniffs.*"

"Now I know," he had said, "why you accepted my marriage proposal."

"Oh, absolutely!" she had assured him, and laughed gleefully.

He loved her laughter. He loved her happiness. Oh, she behaved in public with quiet dignity, though even then he was aware of an inner glow in her that warmed him too. In private she smiled a great deal, and the glow was brighter. Her eyes when she looked at him had a sparkle that made them appear to smile even if the rest of her face was in repose.

He felt awed and humbled by her happiness.

And by the fact that he shared it.

He had never given much thought to being happy. It was not a word much in his vocabulary — though he *had* been happy when each of his children was born and whenever he had spent time with them during their growing years. He had been happy when his daughters married and when his grandchildren were born. He had just not used that particular word to describe his feelings. He had not known the conscious exuberance of happiness since Matilda had disappeared from his life when he was still no more than a puppy.

Now he knew himself happy again. Even if he *did* spend great swaths of time shut up in his library during the month before his nuptials wishing he did not have the ghastly ordeal of a grand *ton* wedding to face before he could bear Matilda off home and live out his life with her there. He was even dreaming of happily-ever-after, though fortunately it was contained inside him. Sometimes he could still think and feel like that young puppy he had been. It was downright embarrassing.

He was going to be very glad when the wedding was over.

In the meanwhile, he was equally glad that Matilda, despite all her frequent misgivings, was at last going to have the wedding she ought to have had more than thirty years ago.

Charles was quite right in his perceptions. There had been no wrangling, no unpleasantness between his daughters on the one hand and the ladies of the Westcott family on the other as they planned the wedding. All of them, once the Westcotts had recovered from the shock they had felt upon learning that Matilda, that most confirmed of spinsters, was going to marry at last, had thrown themselves with enthusiasm into the planning of the wedding of the Season. And if Louise and Mildred, Matilda's younger sisters, still felt wary of the bridegroom's notorious past, they soon set their fears aside in favor of rejoicing that their precious Matilda, that rock of sisterly support upon which they had leaned since they were girls, was to find happiness of her own at last. The bridegroom's daughters were genuinely pleased for their father, having concluded that Lady Matilda Westcott was vastly different from any of the other ladies he had escorted about London since their mother's passing. And vastly preferable too.

There was no wrangling, then. There was, however, an awkward moment. It came when they were making lists of potential guests and everyone was throwing out suggestions, most of which were accepted without question. Viola, Marchioness of Dorchester, had suggested Harry — Major Harry Westcott, her son — who was not far away at Hinsford Manor in Hampshire, and Camille, her elder daughter, who was in Bath with her husband and family. She was interrupted before she could say more.

"I certainly hope Camille and Joel will come," Wren, Countess of Riverdale, said. "But will they, Viola? With all seven children?"

All but one of those children were under ten years of age. Four of them were adopted, three Camille and Joel's own.

"They came to Hinsford a few months ago to see Harry when he came home from war at last," Viola said. "Whether they will now come all the way to London for Matilda's wedding is another matter, of course."

"They must be invited anyway," Elizabeth, Wren's sister-in-law, said. "It will be up to them whether they come or not."

"That sounds sensible," Mildred said.

"And what about Abby?" Jessica asked. "She and Gil must be invited too."

That was when the suggestion of an awkward moment happened. Jessica and Abigail had always been the closest of friends. Jessica had been as hurt as her cousin when Abigail's illegitimacy had been revealed just as she was about to make her come-out into society.

"They have only recently gone home to Gloucestershire," Louise said quickly. "It is too much to expect them to return so soon. I am sure you will write to them with the news, of course, Viola, if you have not already done so."

"But —" Jessica said.

"Who else?" her mother said more loudly than seemed necessary, directing a pointed look her daughter's way.

There was an awkward pause before Mildred rushed in with a new suggestion. "How about —"

But Barbara Dewhurst interrupted her. "No, really," she said. "We are quite well aware of who Gil Bennington is, are we not,

Jane? He is married to the former Abigail Westcott, your daughter, ma'am." She nodded in Viola's direction. "And he is our father's natural son."

"There is really no need —" Louise began.

"No, there really is no need to hush up all mention of his existence, ma'am," Jane, Lady Frater, said, interrupting her. "We know of him. Our father has told us. We also know that he will have nothing to do with Papa. That hurts him, though he has not openly admitted it. Our brother, Adrian, however, is determined to meet him sometime. It has been a shock to discover this late in our lives that we have a half brother. But we do feel as curious about him as Adrian does."

"We do," Barbara agreed. "And now there is this extraordinary circumstance of our father being about to marry Abigail Bennington's aunt."

"He has a young daughter," Jane said, sounding almost wistful. "Our niece. I do long to see her."

"Are you suggesting, then," Anna, Duchess of Netherby, asked, "that they be invited to the wedding?"

"Well," Barbara said, frowning, "our father would doubtless be horrified. And it seems almost certain Gil himself would refuse to come. But —"

"Perhaps Abigail will come alone," Wren suggested. "Though it would be a shame."

"*Shall* we invite them?" Anna asked.

"I really do not see why not," Jessica said. "Abby is as much a part of our family as any of us."

"And we *are* inviting Camille," Elizabeth said, "even though it seems equally doubtful that she will come. Perhaps we ought to send an invitation and let Abigail and Gil decide for themselves."

"What do you think?" Viola asked Charles's daughters. "Please be honest. And will you inform your father if we do invite them?"

Barbara smiled. "He has told us," she said, "that we may do anything we wish for this wedding provided we do nothing of which Lady Matilda would disapprove, and provided we do not expect him to have his ears assailed with details."

"Ah," Mildred said, smiling back. "Then we need to consult Matilda, do we? And let *her* decide."

"We know what her answer will be," Elizabeth said.

"Do we?" Mildred asked.

"Of course," Elizabeth said, laughing. "Matilda is a romantic. She always has been. She will certainly want them to be invited to her wedding."

"Oh, I hope so," Jessica said. "I *do* hope they come."

Matilda had asserted herself, something she had rarely done all her life, at least on her own account. Oh, she had allowed the women of her family and Charles's to organize her wedding according to their wishes, it was true. She had made the decision to have a grand society wedding, despite the fact that privately she changed her mind at least once every waking hour. Having done so, she was content to leave the details to the grand committee — of which she would have been a leading member if it had been anyone else's wedding.

But she had asserted herself in other ways. She had selected an outfit for the occasion, a simple, elegant walking dress of pale blue when her sisters had wanted her to wear a finer, more elaborate gown, one more suited to the occasion. And they had wanted her to choose a more vivid color, since pastel shades were associated with youth and she surely would not wish to be accused of trying to minimize her age.

She was now — on her wedding day — wearing the pale blue walking dress. She was also wearing a straw hat — *not* a bonnet — which was held on her head with pins and was tipped slightly forward over her eyes. It was trimmed with silk cornflowers, which were a slightly darker shade than her dress. Louise had described it as frivolous, and Mildred had suggested that she change the trim to a simple ribbon instead of the flowers. Matilda was wearing it this morning — complete with flowers.

She was also wearing silver gloves and silver slippers and silver earrings, something she rarely wore because after an hour or two she invariably found that the earrings pinching her earlobes caused excruciating pain if she did not pull them off. But that always left the lobes red and painful-looking, often with the imprints of the earrings upon them. This morning she had donned the earrings the last of all her accessories in the hope that she could get through her wedding and maybe even the breakfast afterward without screaming in agony. They were in the form of bells and tinkled slightly when she moved her head. Another frivolity.

And she had asserted herself over Abigail and Gil. *Of course* they must be invited, she had assured the delegation that had come to put the question to her — Viola and Anna and Louise and Mildred. It was very probable, she agreed, that Gil would refuse to come and that Abigail would not come without him. And it was altogether possible that if they *did* come, Charles would be horribly embarrassed and perhaps Adrian and Barbara and Jane too despite what the latter two had said to the contrary. But *of course* they must be invited. Rational adults ought to be allowed to make up their own minds about what they wished to do with their lives. It ought not to be up to their families to try to live their lives for them.

"Matilda," Mildred asked, looking thoughtful, "is that what happened to you? Was it Mama and Papa who tore you away from Viscount Dirkson when the two of you were young?"

"What happened more than thirty years ago no longer matters," Matilda told her firmly. "It is *now* that matters. We are together *now,* Charles and I, and we are to be married, and I want a wedding day that is perfect. Will it be more perfect if Gil and Abigail are the only family members *not* present or if they *are*? It is impossible to know the answer. But the decision ought not to be ours to make. It must be Gil's and Abigail's."

"Not Viscount Dirkson's?" Viola asked.

"He will say no," Matilda told her, "while his heart will yearn to say yes."

"We must do all in our power, then," Anna said, smiling, "to make sure he gets his heart's desire. And you too, Aunt Matilda."

"Well, I *do* want them to come," Matilda admitted, "though I would ask that the invitation not be sent until tomorrow. I ought, I suppose, to call upon Barbara and Jane first."

But those two young ladies, as well as Adrian, who happened to be with his sisters when Matilda called first upon Barbara, were genuinely curious to meet the half brother of whose existence they had not even known until recently.

"And if they come and Papa does not want them here," Adrian said, "I would really be very surprised. I believe he longs to be reconciled."

"But that would not make you unhappy?" Matilda asked.

"No." He frowned in thought for a moment. "Papa said something the day he told me about Gil Bennington. He told me how he had fallen in love with me the moment he saw me after I was born. And I daresay he fell in love in just the same way with my sisters. All my childhood memories confirm me in the belief that he was telling the truth.

He spent more time with us than most fathers of my acquaintance spend with their children, and he always gave the impression that he was as happy with our company as we were with his. I do not believe love has limits. Do you, Lady Matilda? I mean, the fact that there was always Gil and that our father obviously cared for him does not mean he cared the less for us. If Gil comes back into Papa's life now, it will not mean that we are diminished. Will it?"

"Not by one iota," Matilda assured him, remembering how, when Anna arrived unexpectedly in their family at the age of twenty-five, it had seemed at first that Humphrey's newly illegitimate offspring — Camille and Harry and Abigail — would be displaced. It had not been so. Just the opposite had happened, in fact. The whole family had bonded more firmly than ever before under the threat of attack. They had routed the threat with love.

Matilda did what never came quite naturally to her. She got to her feet and hugged first Adrian and then his sisters. And because Mr. Dewhurst, Barbara's husband, was also in the room, she hugged him too.

*"Diminished,"* she said. "What a foolish notion. Your family love is about to *expand,* not contract. Your father is about to marry

me, is he not?"

At which they all laughed, Matilda included.

And she asserted herself over which man of the family would give her away at her wedding. Thomas, Mildred's husband, had offered. So had Alexander, as head of the family. Harry — Major Harry Westcott, the eldest of her nephews — had written from Hinsford to offer his services. Avery, Duke of Netherby, had informed her one afternoon that she doubtless had dozens of family members fighting duels over the honor of leading her along the nave of St. George's, but if not — or if she did not much fancy any of the contestants — he would be happy to make himself available. Colin, Lord Hodges, Elizabeth's husband, had offered, as had Marcel, Marquess of Dorchester, Viola's husband. Even young Bertrand Lamarr had offered, grinning at her cheekily as he did so.

"After all, Aunt Matilda," he had said, "I believe I started the renewal of your romance when I agreed to escort you to Viscount Dirkson's house when you wished him to attend the custody hearing for Gil's daughter."

And since he had spoken publicly, the whole secret story came out and the family discovered that not long ago Matilda had taken the truly scandalous step of calling upon a gentleman in his own home with no one to chaperon her except a very young man who was not even related to her by blood.

Trust the young to keep a secret!

Matilda made her choice and announced it during the family dinner that preceded the betrothal party Avery and Anna gave for her at Archer House.

"Thank you to all of you," she said, looking at each man in turn — though Harry had not yet come up from the country. "I am touched that each of you is willing to stand in place of my father. However, I am fifty-six years old. The notion that someone — someone male — needs to give me away is a strange one. Give me away from *what*? I have been of age for thirty-five years. Although I have always lived with Mama, I have independent means. I can and will give myself away to the man of my choice. So I shall walk alone along the nave of the church."

"Matilda," her mother said, reproach in her voice. "It just is not *done.*"

"It will be done by me," Matilda said. "And that is my final word."

"Oh, bravo, Aunt Matilda," Jessica said.

"Jessica!" her mother said.

"I say," Boris said. "You are a jolly fine fellow, Aunt Matilda."

"A *fellow,* Boris?" Mildred asked. "A *jolly fine* one? Wherever do you get such language?"

But her son merely grinned at her and waggled his eyebrows.

"It cannot be allowed, Matilda," Louise said firmly. "You will be the —"

"I believe," Avery said in his usual languid voice, his jeweled quizzing glass in his hand, though he was not actually looking through it, "there is a little-known statute on the books to the effect that after the age of — ah — fifty-five, a woman must be considered entirely her own person and may do whatever she wishes without running the risk of being exiled for life for doing what no one has done before her."

"Oh, Avery," Estelle said, giggling. "You made that up on the spot."

"Well, of course he did, idiot," said her fond twin.

"Then that settles the matter," Matilda said. "Thank you, Avery. Though I would have done it anyway, you know, even if there had been no such statute."

"Quite so," he said.

And so here she was now, dressed in pale

blue and silver, wearing a frivolous hat at a jaunty angle on her head, knowing — though Charles did not — that Gil and Abigail and Katy had arrived late yesterday afternoon at Viola and Marcel's London home, and knowing too that no man awaited her downstairs to offer her a steady male arm to help her totter her way along the nave of St. George's to meet her bridegroom.

Her bridegroom! Her heart leaped within her bosom and performed a couple of headstands and a number of tumble tosses before leaving her simply breathless. Surely he would have changed his mind at the last moment and would not be there awaiting her when she arrived.

What utter nonsense and drivel!

Her bridegroom! Charles. Ah. At last. At long, long last.

And if she stood here, one glove on and one off, still in the hand of her maid, and entertained more of such idiotic thoughts, it was *she* who would not be turning up on time. Not that brides were expected to be on time. But she was not just any bride. She was Matilda Westcott. And Matilda had gone through life being punctual, on the theory that it was bad mannered to be late and waste other people's time when they might be using it to better effect elsewhere.

She was not going to start being late with her own wedding. She was not going to be early either. That would be embarrassing. She would be on time. To the minute.

And it was time to leave.

"Thank you," she said, taking her glove from her maid and pulling it on as she drew a few deep breaths.

Her wedding day!

Perhaps she would perform a few twirls on her way along the nave. Now *that* would make for a memorable wedding.

How dreadfully the mind babbled when one was nervous.

And she was very, very nervous.

Oh, Charles!

She straightened her shoulders, stepped out of her dressing room, and made her way downstairs and outdoors to the awaiting carriage.

# Ten

Charles was resigned to his fate as he awaited the arrival of his bride at St. George's. Behind him the pews had filled with family and the very crème de la crème of aristocratic society. At least, he assumed they had filled. He did not turn his head to look. But he could hear the rustling of silks and satins, the muted conversations, the cleared throats.

Given the choice, he would still opt for a quiet wedding. He was also still glad Matilda was to have her grand wedding at last. He sat in the front pew, wondering how her life would have proceeded if her father had not refused his suit quite so adamantly or if she had not refused to discuss the matter with him afterward. Or if he had had the gumption to fight for what he wanted instead of turning peevishly away to nurse his bruised heart by becoming one of England's most notorious rakes and hellions. Would they have married? Would his children be hers too — but different children, of course? But children of her own — and his. Would she have been happy? Would he? Her life would certainly have been different. Would his?

They were pointless thoughts, of course. Ifs were always pointless when applied to the past. If the past had been different, then so would the present be. He would not now be sitting here on full display before the *ton*, awaiting the arrival of his bride. She would not be living through her wedding day now, today.

He was glad it was now. He felt suddenly happy even as a twinge of anxiety nudged at him lest she be going through one of her many doubting moments and would simply not come.

Impossible! Of course she would come.

"Nervous?" Adrian murmured from beside him. His son was his best man.

"Of course," Charles murmured back. "Today is the start of a wholly new life."

But before anxiety could take hold of him, he heard a stirring from the back of the church and guessed that it heralded the arrival of Matilda, who was apparently coming alone. Her mother had arrived earlier with Mrs. Monteith, her sister, and Miss Boniface, her paragon of a companion who also, according to Matilda, sniffed. They had come earlier than originally planned in order to take up residence with the dowager countess and console her for the loss of her eldest daughter to marriage.

The clergyman, fully robed, appeared from somewhere and Charles rose with the rest of the congregation and the great pipe organ began to play. Charles turned to look along the nave. And sure enough, she came alone, a straight-backed woman of middle years, proceeding with slow — but not too slow — dignity along the aisle, her eyes fixed forward until they found and held upon him. She was dressed decently, elegantly, almost severely in pale blue — as he might have expected had he given the matter thought — with an absurdly pretty straw hat tipped forward over her forehead and with her silver-gloved hands clasped before her. Her face was pale, her mouth in a prim line until she was a few steps away from him. Then, unseen by all except the closest of the congregation, she smiled at him with all the sunshine of a summer's day behind her eyes.

He saw in that smile the vivid girl she had been. And he saw in the quiet poise of her demeanor the woman she had become.

He saw Matilda. His love. Always and ever

his love.

She set her hand in his, giving herself to him because, as she had explained, she did not need any man to do it for her, no matter how closely related to her that man was or how well meaning. She let her fingers curl about his own in a firm grip.

"Here I am," she murmured for his ears only.

"And at last," he said just as quietly, "so am I."

They turned together to face the clergyman.

"Dearly beloved," he began.

And just like that, within a very few minutes, they were married.

Charles was after all glad they had done it this way, with all the pomp of a high church service, with all their family and friends and acquaintances in attendance. He was glad for himself, for he wanted the world to know that he married this woman from choice and from love. He was glad for Matilda, for she glowed from the moment she first smiled at him until the moment when the clergyman pronounced them man and wife. And even then she glowed as he led her to the vestry for the signing of the register. When Alexander, Earl of Riverdale, witnessed her signature and then hugged her, and Adrian witnessed his signature and hugged her too, she glowed at them. She glowed as they left the vestry and proceeded, her arm drawn through Charles's, back along the nave, smiling from one side to the other as they passed the pews. It was impossible to see everyone who was there. But they would do that at the wedding breakfast in a short while.

She smiled still as they passed through the church doors and emerged into sunshine at the top of the long flight of steps down to their awaiting carriage — an open barouche decorated almost beyond recognition with flowers. She smiled at the crowd of onlookers that had gathered down there to applaud and even cheer. And she laughed when she saw her young nephews and his sons-in-law waiting farther down the steps to pelt them with flower petals before they could reach the dubious safety of the open carriage. And then, halfway down, when the petals were already raining about them in a brightly colored shower, she looked back up to where the congregation was beginning to spill outdoors after them and she lost her smile.

"Ah," she said, and Charles had the curious impression that she saw something she had been looking for. He looked backward even as he laughed at another shower of petals that was fluttering from the brim of his hat.

Quite a few people had come outside, his daughters and grandchildren, Matilda's mother and aunt and sisters among them. And one group a little separate from the others, three steps down from the top. A man and a woman, and a child between them, holding a hand of each.

When he thought about it afterward, Charles did not suppose that silence had really descended upon the congregation above, the gathering of the curious below, and the young people on the steps with their handfuls of petals. But it seemed to him at the time that they were suddenly cocooned in silence, Matilda and he, her arm through his, her face turned to look into his — with anxiety?

God. Oh good God.

Neither group moved for what was perhaps a second or two but seemed far longer at the time. Then the woman took a step down, impelling the child and the man to descend too. And Matilda took one step back up, forcing him to do likewise. Who descended or ascended the other steps between them Charles did not afterward know, or who first extended a hand. But suddenly he felt the warm, firm clasp of his son's hand even as he gripped it in return.

His elder son, that was.

Gil.

"Congratulations, sir," he said stiffly.

"You came," Charles said foolishly.

"We came."

And then Matilda was hugging first his son's wife and then his son and was then bending down to smile at the child — Katy — and say something to her. And Abigail was hugging Charles and lifting Katy to say *how do you do* to her grandpapa, and somehow — oh, somehow his son was hugging him too. Briefly, awkwardly, improbably, surely unintentionally, unforgettably.

"Congratulations, sir," he said again.

"You came," Charles said, just to be original.

After every wedding Charles had ever attended, the bride and groom left the church and ran the gamut of mischievous relatives who went out ahead of them in order to decorate their carriage with noisy hardware and throw flowers. The carriage was always on its way by the time large numbers of the congregation left the church behind them. All the greetings and congratulations, all the hugs and kisses, and slapping of backs, and laughter, came later as the guests arrived at the venue for the wedding breakfast.

This wedding was the exception to that tradition. It was too late to escape. Within moments they were surrounded by wedding guests. Matilda was being hugged and kissed and wept over by her mother and her sisters and sister-in-law and cousins and nieces and aunt. She had children about her — most of them, he believed, the offspring of her niece Camille from Bath — all trying to tell her things in piping yells while brushing at the flower petals with which she was strewn. His own daughters and grandchildren were soon gathered about her too. She was bright eyed and rosy cheeked and laughing and lovely. Her brother-in-law and nephews and cousins meanwhile were pumping him by the hand and slapping him on the back, as were his sons-in-law, having abandoned their petal throwing for the moment — or perhaps they had no more to throw. Adrian and Charles's daughters and grandchildren were hugging him. Other people were calling greetings.

Matilda, some little distance away from Charles, turned to find him and smiled at him in a way that would put sunshine to shame.

She was, he realized, elbowing her way closer to him until she could take his hand in hers, utterly happy.

As was he.

"We had better leave while we still may," he said, laughing.

"Oh, must we?" But she slid her arm through his and allowed him to lead her down through the path that opened for them and hand her into the barouche.

"I have just one wish remaining," she said as he sat beside her and took her hand in his, lacing their fingers. "I hope the young people tied a whole arsenal of pots and pans and old boots beneath the carriage. I want to make an unholy din on the way to Westcott House. I have always envied —"

But what or whom she had always envied was drowned out as the coachman gave the horses the signal to start and the barouche rocked into motion. So was Charles's laughter. And so were the church bells pealing out the good news of a new marriage.

Matilda's one remaining wish had come true.

She turned her face toward him, and he saw that she was laughing — until the laughter faded and her eyes became luminous beneath the brim of her hat.

Matilda.

What part had she played in bringing his elder son to him today of all days? What part had his younger son and his daughters played in it? Surely they had been consulted. What on earth had persuaded Gil to come for the wedding of the father he had not wanted to know? What did it mean exactly that he had come? Would he also come to the wedding breakfast?

It was impossible to ask any of these questions. The noise coming from beneath the carriage was deafening.

And the answers would wait.

He smiled at his bride, and her eyes filled with tears even as she smiled back at him.

"I love you," he said, and her eyes lowered to read his lips.

"I love you," her lips said in return.

And he dipped his head and kissed her. Propriety be damned. If he must suffer this din, which proclaimed to the world that a newly wedded couple was on its way through the streets of London, then at least he was going to let the world know that he was happy about it.

He lifted his head and grinned at her. Her eyes brimmed with tears and laughter.

He kissed her again. Or she kissed him.

They kissed each other.

# ABOUT THE AUTHOR

**Mary Balogh** has written more than one hundred historical novels and novellas, more than thirty of which have been *New York Times* bestsellers. They include the Bedwyn saga, the Simply quartet, the Huxtable quintet, the seven-part Survivors' Club series, and the Westcott series.

The employees of Thorndike Press hope you have enjoyed this Large Print book. All our Thorndike, Wheeler, and Kennebec Large Print titles are designed for easy reading, and all our books are made to last. Other Thorndike Press Large Print books are available at your library, through selected bookstores, or directly from us.

For information about titles, please call:
(800) 223-1244

or visit our website at:
gale.com/thorndike

To share your comments, please write:

Publisher
Thorndike Press
10 Water St., Suite 310
Waterville, ME 04901

# POE AND OUR TIMES

# POE AND OUR TIMES: INFLUENCES AND AFFINITIES

*EDITED BY*

*BENJAMIN FRANKLIN FISHER IV*

BALTIMORE: THE EDGAR ALLAN POE SOCIETY

ISBN 0-9616449-0-7

*To*
*Four Supporters of Poe in Our Times:*
*Richard and Lynn Hart*
*and*
*Al and Mary Rose*

## KEY TO RECURRING REFERENCES

Several works to which repeated citations are made, or from which quotations are frequently drawn, will be indicated in these abbreviations throughout this book.

*H* = *The Complete Works of Edgar Allan Poe,* ed. James A. Harrison, 17 vols. (New York, 1902; rpr. New York, 1965, 1979).

*M* = *Collected Works of Edgar Allan Poe,* ed. Thomas Ollive Mabbott, 3 vols. (Cambridge, MA, 1969-1978).

*O* = *The Letters of Edgar Allan Poe,* ed. John Ward Ostrom, rev. ed., 2 vols. (New York, 1966).

## *ACKNOWLEDGEMENTS*

First, and foremost, I thank Al Rose for his encouragement as regards putting together this book and his support of the project. A like debt is owed to Louis J. Budd and Erma P. Whittington, of the Jay B. Hubbell Center for American Literary Historiography, Duke University, for permission to publish the sketches of Killis Campbell and Thomas Ollive Mabbott. Maureen Cobb Mabbott, who saw to completion her husband's edition of Poe's *Tales and Sketches*—and who, despite any disclaimers on her part, is a Poe scholar in her own right, as well as an authority on Leonardo da Vinci, and a poet—has continued generous in assisting the work of younger scholars. I am also conscious of the examples set, long ago, by these former teachers: Sadie V. Shoener, Edna M. Rarick, Ethel M. Kimmel, Calvin D. Yost, Jr., and Arlin Turner. Finally, the contributors to *Poe and Our Times* have evinced memorable cooperation in this venture, and I thank them one and all.

*B.F.F. IV*
*OXFORD, MISSISSIPPI*
*19 JANUARY 1986*

## CONTENTS

## *INTRODUCTION*

### *The Shadow of Poe*

The essays gathered here support a single major theme, the considerable influence of Edgar Allan Poe upon literary culture from his day to our own. Considering that Poe might have lived into this century, and that Killis Campbell and Edith Wharton, to be mentioned subsequently in connection with him, were born in the 1860s, "our times" is a defining phrase of fair magnitude. Furthermore, and in despite of relentless attempts to discredit him and his work, when so popular a medium as the poster recently prepared to advertise Stroh's beer bodies forth a Poe, most likely bibulous, with sufficient exaggeration in the accompanying imagery from his writings to make the whole funny, we can not deny that he "has arrived." We also can not seem to lay to rest, however, an all-too-easily assumed mode of thought, or lack of thought, regarding our author's much-bedevilled reputation. That he was a habitual drunkard, not to mention a drug addict and debaucher of ingenuous women, many will unquestioningly affirm. Many in this camp will as adamantly argue that Poe and his narrators are interchangeable. Such affirmations reveal how strongly a body of ill-informed notions will persist, and in the face of solid demonstrations to the contrary. Nevertheless, a Poe who comes before us amidst comic and alcoholic trappings is altogether understandable. After better than a century of neglect, and, somewhat later, a deploring of his humor (that nevertheless elicited ready responses from his contemporaries), a major revaluation of Poe's workings in comedy has occurred during our times.[1] That increased breadth in viewpoints in no way negates perceptions of a decidedly serious, many-layered texture within his literary productions. Instead, many have come to understand how the tales in particular may yield simultaneously a multeity of surfaces, "edges," suggestions, call them what you will, each plausible and capable of coalescing with others in no jarring manner, for readers who come to these writings with varied attitudes.

A many-sided Poe is strongly attested in the following pages. His image, his mirth, his metaphysics, his crime and detective ventures, and much more, receive careful attention. Since the French response to Poe has for so long been open-minded and favorable, the collection opens appropriately with two studies covering Poe's French devotees through recent times. A similar survey of critical import underlies the thinking of John E. Reilly and Bruce I. Weiner, respectively on Poe's image among American playwrights and his place in mystery-detective writing. Just and exceptionally personable reminiscences pay tribute to Killis Campbell and Thomas Ollive Mabbott, without doubt a pair who labored mightily in contributing to a "Poe in our times," in

contrast to the figure conjured up by Griswold and his witting or unwitting followers. Modern writers have also tapped the wellsprings of the Gothic, of fantasy literature, and of folk myth, as they devolve from Poe, traits evident in the essays by Dwight, Menides, Ljungquist, Bennett, Peirce, McDaniel, Werner, and Fisher.

These studies present no isolated cases of influence and affinities. Poe's links with Robert Penn Warren, Richard Wright, Robert Frost, Vladimir Nabokov — to skim the readiest cream from vast quantities of such interconnections — have been astutely assessed, as have others.[2] Many more like studies will follow. Consequently we must realize that Poe's shadow, as it hovers above much artistic inspiration, extends to great length. We observe the continuing interest about Poe in editions of his works now in progress, in a spate of recent biographies, and in quantities of critiques coming out each year. Two organizations provide supportive functions to Poe's causes, as does a professional journal devoted entirely to him and his work. Films, tee-shirts, key-chains, comic books as well herald him.

Two writers, years ago, furnish what may be unintentional but significant perspectives on Poe's case today. H. L. Mencken touches sensitive chords in opining: "Americans, obsessed by the problem of conduct, usually judge their authors, not as artists, but as citizens...Edgar Allan Poe, I daresay, will never live down the fact that he was a periodic drunkard, and that he died in an alcoholic ward."[3] Vintage Mencken we encounter here, to be sure; and just as sure, like much else thought and published about Poe, it lands somewhat off the mark. Second, in the centennial year of Poe's birth, another voice spoke words that still ring true: "But POE is hard to stop talking about. Everything said about him seems to provoke a reply, and every reply a rejoinder. He is eminently debatable. That may be one source of his fame."[4] The essays in *Poe and Our Times* witness the pertinence of these opinions, even after many years, as does the greater panorama of Poe scholarship. They are true measures of Poe's magnetism.

Benjamin Franklin Fisher IV

## NOTES

[1] Merely one example, and many more could be marshalled, appears in the Charleston, SC, *Courier* for 2 January 1836: There Poe is characterized as "equally ripe in graphic humor and various Lore" (p. 138). I thank David K. Jackson for this item. See also Mary E. Phillips, *Edgar Allan Poe, The Man* (Chicago, Philadelphia, Toronto, 1926), 1. 427. She notes that plays based on Poe's writings, to be performed in New York

during 1919-1920, would bring forth his "very distinct and well-developed sense of humor, not always fathomed by Dr. Griswold and some others." Other, more recent and extended, commentary about the comic in Poe may be found in Benjamin Franklin Fisher IV, *The Very Spirit of Cordiality: The Literary Uses of Alcohol and Alcoholism in the Tales of Edgar Allan Poe* (Baltimore, 1978); Donald Barlow Stauffer, *The Merry Mood: Poe's Uses of Humor* (Baltimore, 1982); and [what stands as a sourcebook for the subject] *The Naiad Voice: Essays on Poe's Satiric Hoaxing*, ed. Dennis W. Eddings (Port Washington, 1983), which collects fifteen important essays and an excellent bibliography relevant to the topic. I acknowledge much assistance from Professor William J. Zimmer, in my work.

[2] John Cook Wyllie also sheds interesting light on the similarities of Madison Jones's novel, *The Innocent* (1957), to "Metzengerstein": "Guilt-ridden Dixie," *Saturday Review*, 23 February 1957, p.18.

[3] *Prejudices*, First Series (New York, 1919), p. 52.

[4] S., "Personal," *Harper's Weekly*, 30 January 1909, p. 6.

# PAUL VALÉRY AND THE POE LEGACY IN FRANCE

*LOIS VINES*

> "Rien de plus original, rien de plus *soi* que de se nourrir des autres. Mais il faut les digérer. Le lion est fait de mouton assimilé."
>
> Valéry, *Choses tues.*

Paul Valéry's death in 1945 marks the end of the century-long Poe cult in France, initiated by Baudelaire in 1846 when he discovered Poe's stories and decided to devote himself to the task of translating them into French. Baudelaire's vow to make Poe known in France was carried out with missionary-like fervor by his successors Mallarmé and Valéry. No major French author since Valéry has taken up the banner for Poe, to whom three generations of French writers were devoutly attached.

Although Baudelaire and Mallarmé have both been the object of extensive research relating their thought and work to Poe's, the influence of Poe on Valéry has not been examined in a comprehensive manner. Studies on the influence of Poe in France make only brief mention of Valéry.[1] The best essay on the subject is T. S. Eliot's article "From Poe to Valéry," written over thirty years ago.[2] Eliot's appraisal of Poe's effect on Valéry makes two essential points: first, Valéry's concept of pure poetry derives from Poe's idea that "a poem should have nothing in view but itself"; and, second, Valéry's interest in observing himself writing a poem comes from his reading of "The Philosophy of Composition." After Eliot's article appeared, twenty-nine volumes of Valéry's hand-written notebooks were reproduced (each containing some 900 pages) and three volumes of correspondence were published. This material brings to light additional aspects of Poe's effect on Valéry, which will be examined in the present discussion.

Baudelaire and Mallarmé both played a part in the influence of Poe on Valéry because of the intricate chain of relationships that existed among them. Although Poe's effect on Valéry was unique, the Frenchman did nevertheless share a certain image of the American poet handed down to him by his compatriots. This continuity of admiration is interesting in itself. Poe died a year after Baudelaire's first translation of one of his tales appeared in France. That Baudelaire had never met or corresponded with Poe did not diminish his devotion to translating Poe's stories, his cosmological poem *Eureka,* and some of his essays. Mallarmé admired both Poe and Baudelaire and supposedly came to Paris to meet the author of *Les Fleurs du Mal* but did

not have the courage to approach him at a bookstall. Mallarmé learned English, he said, in order to understand Poe better, whose poems he rendered into French, thus completing a difficult task Baudelaire had not attempted. With a sense of mission accomplished, Mallarmé dedicated the volume of poems to the memory of Baudelaire.

Valéry admired Poe, Baudelaire, and Mallarmé, with whom he had a personal association for seven years before Mallarmé died in 1898. Valéry's first contact with Poe's work was through Baudelaire's translations and the introductions that accompanied them. Baudelaire mentioned in his 1852 essay that he could not give an account of *Eureka* because it required a special article. Valéry wrote that special article, "Au sujet d'*Eureka*,"[3] as a preface to the 1923 edition of Baudelaire's translation of the cosmological poem. In an essay on Baudelaire, Valéry expressed most eloquently his own admiration for Poe.[4] Valéry also made a contribution to the French version of Poe by translating fragments from the "Marginalia."[5] The text is particularly interesting because Valéry added his own marginal notes alongside those he was translating.

Poe played a significant role in the relationship between Valéry and Mallarmé. The younger poet's first letter to Mallarmé, written from Montpellier when he was only nineteen, mentions Poe in a rather name-dropping fashion. Knowing Mallarmé's fondness for Poe, Valéry introduced himself as a person who is "*profondément pénétrée des doctrines savantes du grand Edgar Allan Poe—peut-être le plus subtil artiste de ce siècle.*"[6] When Mallarmé and Valéry met a year later in Paris, Valéry recalled that it was the subject of Poe that brought the two of them together in a close relationship. But they got an essentially different message from their common mentor. Impressed by Poe's devotion to the technique of writing verse, Mallarmé dreamed of perfecting the art of writing and of giving it a universal value to be realized in a book. Poe's effect on Valéry was, in one sense, just the opposite. Although he too was intrigued by poetic technique, it was not for him a means to the same end. Valéry's ultimate goal was not to create a supreme work, but rather to understand the mind, his own mind, during the act of artistic creation. This particular effect of extreme intellectual self-consciousness distinguishes Poe's influence on Valéry from that of his predecessors.

Early in his literary career Valéry was obsessed with reading Poe. Traces of this immersion are evident in three of his prose pieces composed between 1889 and 1895. His first literary essay, entitled "*Sur la technique littéraire,*"[7] is a naive paraphrasing of "The Philosophy of Composition." Valéry begins

by declaring that the most important consideration of the poet must be to create the maximum effect on the reader. As the essay continues, certain phrases bear a striking resemblance to Baudelaire's translation of Poe's essay. Valéry: *"le poème n'a d'autre but que de préparer son dénouement;"* Poe: *"le poème doit préparer son dénouement;"* Valéry: *"cent vers entreront dans les plus longues pièces;"* Poe: "[*le poème aura*] *une longueur de cent vers eviron."*[8] Valéry goes on to mention Poe by name, but there is no indication that the ideas he expresses in the first part of the essay come directly from Poe. The essay would have been published by the *Courrier libre* in Paris had the literary journal not gone out of business. The manuscript was found after Valéry's death and finally published more than half-a-century after it was written. Although the essay clearly lacks originality, it is interesting to our study because it shows that Valéry was indeed "penetrated," as he said, by the ideas of Poe.

Valéry's next attempt at writing an essay was very successful. His *"Introduction à la méthode de Léonard de Vinci,"* written at age twenty-three, is still considered to be one of his best prose pieces. The original approach to the subject was inspired by his reading of Poe. Having been invited to prepare an article on Leonardo, Valéry decided that instead of bringing together biographical details and descriptions of the artist's work, he would recreate the mind that engendered the work. Poe's description of how he wrote "The Raven" suggested to Valéry the possibility of a new critical method. He was convinced that the only valid means of evaluating an artist's (or a writer's) work was to examine the relationship between what the mind was attempting to do and how well it succeeded.

Since Valéry's approach to the study of Leonardo was different from anything that had previously been done, he begins the essay by explaining his new method to the reader. Here again, part of his explanation seems to come directly from "The Philosophy of Composition." In a paragraph beginning with the statement *"mainte erreur, gâtant les jugements qui se portent sur les oeuvres humaines, est due à un oubli singulier de leur génération,"*[9] Valéry puts forth the idea that our judgment of creative works is distorted because we are not aware of their genesis. He goes on to explain that most authors do not have the courage to take a look at how a particular work was created; other writers, says Valéry, could not even understand the process. Like Poe, Valéry attributes this failure to the vanity of the author, who would prefer to give the impression that his work sprang forth on its own. As both authors point out, inspiration plays a role in the creative process, but conscious effort, chance, and decisions made at the last minute are also

involved. Valéry was fascinated by the drama that takes place in the creative mind and believed that Poe was the first to describe it.

It was this *"comédie de l'intellect,"* as Valéry called it, that intrigued him for a lifetime. His essay on Leonardo sets forth his approach to literary criticism, which he was to use later to evaluate the work of other writers. Valéry never questioned whether Poe's description of how he composed "The Raven" was a hoax. It was of no importance. He believed that Poe placed the study of literature on an analytical basis, and that was the goal to which he himself aspired. He expresses this idea very clearly in one of his notebooks: *"Poe le premier a songé à donner un fondement théorique pur aux ouvrages. Mallarmé et moi-même. Je pense avoir été le premier à essayer de me ne pas recourir du tout aux notions anciennes mais à tout reprendre sur des bases purement analytiques."*[10] In the same way that Valéry recreated the mind of Leonardo, he also formed an image of Poe which we can piece together from remarks in his notebooks and correspondence. He pictured Poe as a literary innovator who could apply intellectual rigor to creative work.

At about the same time that Valéry was preparing his study of Leonardo da Vinci (1894-95), he began working on another prose piece that would eventually be titled *La Soirée avec Monsieur Teste.* His notebooks and letters show that during the same period he was reading Poe's tales, a fact that some critics have overlooked.[11] In a notebook dated 1894, he makes reference to an idea for a literary project, calling it for the moment *"La vie et les aventures de Ch. August Dupin."*[12] An unpublished manuscript of an early draft of *La Soirée avec Monsieur Teste* bears the title *"Mémoires du Chevalier Dupin."*[13] A careful examination of *La Soirée avec Monsieur Teste* and "Murders in the Rue Morgue" provides convincing evidence that Poe's story served as a model for Valéry when he created his own fictional character Edmond Teste.[14]

Valéry saw in Dupin a mind capable of observing its own analytical faculties. Not only was Dupin able to think logically, he also took pleasure in retracing the mental processes by which he discovered a coherent pattern in supposedly unrelated events. Teste is portrayed as an intellectual superman who understands how his own mind functions. He never engages in spectacular feats of logic that characterize Dupin. The only mystery he attempts to unravel is that of his own mind. He aspires to no practical application of his mental power and is absorbed by only one question, *"Que peut un homme?"*—what is a man capable of intellectually? Teste is in this sense a purified Dupin; he seeks intellectual self-comprehension for its own sake and makes no attempt to exhibit his superior mind in public.

The descriptions of Leonardo's creative mind and Edmond Teste's analytical brain reveal Valéry's obsession with intellectual rigor and self-comprehension. After publishing the prose pieces on Leonardo and Teste and several poems, Valéry went through a twenty-year period during which he devoted himself to observing his own mind. His main goal was no longer to try to publish, but rather learn more about how his own brain came to grips with mathematics, the sciences, and the creative process of writing a poem. His notebooks during those years contain many examples of mathematical equations interspersed with comments on literary problems. Looking back on this period in a letter to Albert Thibaudet, dated 1911, Valéry describes the role that Pole played in this shift of focus in his life:

> ...Celui qui m'a fait le plus sentir sa puissance fut Poe. J'y ai lu ce qu'il me fallait, pris de ce *délire de la lucidité qu'il communique.* Par conséquence, j'ai cessé de faire des vers. Cet art devenu impossible à *moi de 1892, je le tenais déjà pour un exercise, ou application de recherches plus importantes. Pourquoi ne pas développer en soi, cela seul qui dans la genèse du poème m'intéresse?*[15]

These lines express one of the most important aspects of Poe's influence on Valéry. This "demon of lucidity," as Valéry sometimes called Poe, pointed him in the direction of solving the mystery of his own mind. Valéry never claimed to have succeeded, but he never lost sight of his goal. The last line he scribbled in a notebook before his death was *"après tout, j'ai fait ce que j'ai pu...."*[16]

During the long period referred to above, Valéry did not actually stop writing. He continued to compose poems and to develop topics that interested him, but little of his writing appeared in print. Finally, André Gide convinced him to publish a collection of poems. The slender volume entitled *Charmes* came out in 1917, and Valéry was immediately recognized as an outstanding poet. A constant theme represented symbolically in many of the poems is the drama of artistic creation.[17] Valéry went one step farther than Poe. Not only did he observe himself while writing a poem; the creative process itself became the subject of his poetry.

Valéry's interest in Poe was not simply a youthful enthusiasm. Comments in his notebooks show that he continued to read Poe and think about him for the rest of his life. A series of references in his notebooks dated 1919-20 indicate that he was thinking about giving a lecture on Poe. He refers to Poe as *"la conscience consciente"* and as *"l'ingénieur de l'esprit."*[18] He mentions that he would have difficulty talking about Poe because he had read him so much. There are also several references to *Eureka,* which was to become the

subject of Valéry's only published essay on Poe, written when he was fifty years old.

Valéry saw in *Eureka,* once again, a drama of the intellect. He believed that any cosmogony is a myth, but at the same time he admired the heroic effort of the human brain as it tries to grasp the very notion of a universe and a beginning. This history of thought, says Valéry, might be summarized in these words: *"Il est absurde par ce qu'il cherche, il est grand par ce qu'il trouve."*[19] He admired Poe for his leap of the imagination backed up by scientific explanations. Valéry did not like several features of *Eureka;* he was unimpressed by the pretensions of the author, did not care for the solemn tone of the preamble, and was disappointed that all the consequences were not deduced with precision. And, as a final criticism, Valéry says, *"il y a un Dieu."* Nonetheless, he was fascinated by the ideas developed in *Eureka.* Poe awakened in him an interest in science, which had been numbed by the dismal instructors of his school days. In Poe's discussion of the symmetrical and reciprocal relationship of matter, time, space, gravity, and light, Valéry recognized a similarity with the formal symmetry of Einstein's universe. In spite of his admiration for Poe's scientific affirmations, Valéry concludes that the universe escapes intuition and logic. He says however: *"c'est la gloire de l'homme que de pouvoir se dépenser dans le vide."*[20] He was convinced that imagination plays an important role in science and that scientific analysis is involved in creative achievements. Valéry believed that Poe was the first writer to see these relationships.

The admiration for Poe's poetic theory that Valéry expressed in his first literary essay did not diminish over the years. From 1937 until just a few months before his death, Valéry taught a course in poetics at the renowned *Collège de France,* where a chair had been established in his honor. Poe was often the subject of his lectures.[21] He explained "The Philosophy of Composition" and "The Poetic Principle" to his students while giving examples from his own experience, gathered from many years of observing himself write. Like Poe, he believed that writing poetry is a conscious act calculated to arouse emotion in the reader. Valéry liked creating verse within the strict rules of classical French prosody. A sudden inspiration or a stroke of luck might play a role in the creation of a poem, but for the most part, poetic composition requires a conscious, analytical approach to language. Valéry believed that Poe was the first to recommend eliminating from poetry all subjects that can best be treated in prose—history, politics, morality, etc. This was an important point for Valéry, and much has been made of his concept of *"la poésie pure,"*[22] which was reaffirmed by his reading of Poe.

Looking back on his literary career, Valéry remarked in 1933 that Leo-

nardo, Poe, and Mallarmé had a deep influence on him.[23] He explained the particular way in which this influence operated in his case. Certain aspects of the works of these men caught his attention, and he would then imagine the mind that had created the work. This mental image, formed in his own mind, had the greatest effect on him. Valéry wrote several essays about Leonardo and Mallarmé. Since he published relatively little on Poe, it has been necessary to sift through his letters and notebooks in order to recreate his mental image of Poe. There emerges from this material a striking portrait. Valéry's Poe was a literary genius, a logical thinker who attempted to place creative work on an analytical basis, and the first writer to explore the psychological aspects of literature. Several of the references to Poe in Valéry's final notebooks repeat Baudelaire's phrase describing Poe as *"ce merveilleux cerveau toujours en éveil."*[24] "That marvelous brain always on alert" appropriately fixes the image of Poe that became a legacy in France.

## NOTES

[1] Patrick F. Quinn states in the introduction to *The French Face of Edgar Poe* (Carbondale, IL, 1957) that he does not attempt to examine Poe's effect on Valéry. Célestin Pierre Cambiaire's *The Influence of Edgar Allan Poe in France* (New York, 1927; rpt. New York, 1970) mentions Valéry in two paragraphs, pp. 159-160.

[2] *HudR*, 2 (1949), 327-342.

[3] *Oeuvres de Paul Valéry*, ed. Jean Hytier, 2 vols. (Paris, 1957, 1969), 1:854-867.

[4] Ibid., "Situation de Baudelaire," pp. 598-613.

[5] "Quelques fragments des *Marginalia*," traduits et annotés par Paul Valéry, *Commerce*, 14(1927), 11-41. *Commerce* was a literary review published in Paris between 1924 and 1932. Valéry was one of the three editors.

[6] *Lettres à quelques-uns* (Paris, 1952), pp. 28-29.

[7] Valéry, *Oeuvres*, 1:1809-11. Henri Mondor obtained the manuscript in 1946 from Charles Boès, former editor of the *Courrier libre*, and published it under the title "Le premier article de Paul Valéry" in the collection *Dossiers*, 1 (Paris, 1946).

[8] Valéry, *Oeuvres* 1:1810. Poe, *Oeuvres en prose*, transl. Charles Baudelaire, ed. Y. -G. Le Dantec (Paris, 1951), pp. 984-985.

[9] Valéry, *Oeuvres*, 1:1156-57.

[10] Valéry, *Cahiers* (Paris, 1957-61), 12:703.

[11] For example, one of the most respected Valéry critics, Emilie Noulet, believed that he had not bothered to read Poe's tales. See Noulet, *Paul Valéry* (Brussels, 1951), p. 85. T. S. Eliot discusses Poe's tales in the article mentioned above, but makes no connection with Valéry's work.

[12] Valéry, *Cahiers*, 1:50.

[13] Valéry, *Oeuvres*, 2:1381. Jean Hytier describes the manuscript, which was exhibited in 1956.

[14] For a detailed account, see my article "Dupin-Teste: Poe's Direct Influence on Valéry," *FrF*, 2 (1977), 147-159. One of the most interesting similarities is the role of the narrator in both stories.

[15] *Lettres à quelques-uns*, pp. 97-98. The italics are Valéry's.

[16] Quoted in Valéry, *Oeuvres*, 1:70, by Valéry's daughter, who wrote the "Introduction Biographique."

[17] For a detailed discussion of this subject see Noulet, *Paul Valéry*.

[18] Valéry, *Cahiers*, 6:767-768.

[19] Valéry, *Oeuvres*, 1:862.

[20] Ibid.

[21] Valéry's lectures at the Collège de France were never published, but one of his students, Lucienne Julien-Cain, recounted what he said about Poe in her book *Trois essais sur Paul Valéry* (Paris, 1958); pp. 129-150.

[22] T. S. Eliot gives a good explanation in "From Poe to Valéry."

[23] Valéry made this remark and the explanation on influence in his introduction to René Fernandat's book *Autour de Paul Valéry* (Grenoble, 1933).

[24] Valéry, *Cahiers*, 22:489, 702; 23:74; 25:625; 27:234. These notebooks date from 1939-43.

## EDGAR POE AND FRANCE: TOWARD THE END OF A MYTH?

*ROGER FORCLAZ,* TRANSLATED BY *JAMES KELLY MORRIS*

The spiritual bond between Edgar Poe and Baudelaire is a unique phenomenon in the annals of literature. It is tempting to imagine them meeting; Barry Perowne has done so in a novel locating Poe in Paris in 1844[1] (in fact, certain biographies of Poe present a hiatus of several months for this period). There he meets Baudelaire, with whom he plots to dishonor the latter's father-in-law, General Aupick; but the ingenious plan elaborated by Poe is reduced to naught by unforeseen circumstances. Here we find again the Poe of legend, romantic hero *par excellence,* living in the world of his dreams and experiencing in life what he imagined in his tales; a person marked for misfortune, he wears "the haggard mask of tragedy" and states with bitterness after his defeat that nothing had ever been his "except the burden of his mistakes weighing on his back and growing always heavier."[2] Poe appears as a Byronic hero, trampled by destiny and victimized by implacable fatality, which he is as incapable of resisting as his heroes, like the unhappy one "whom unmerciful Disaster / Followed fast" in "The Raven."[3]

Perowne's novel attests the fascination Poe exerts, especially the force of myth attached to him, particularly in France. Baudelaire is chiefly responsible for this state of affairs; if he deserves the credit for having "discovered" the American story-teller, for having translated his works into French[4] and for having assured his glory, then Poe had to pay the price of this posthumous celebrity. Indeed, the author of *Fleurs du Mal* proceeded to select, somewhat arbitrarily, from the works of his senior, laying aside certain interesting and important stories; furthermore, he recreated Poe according to his subjective image of an inspired poet for whom intoxication was a method of work. The result was a double obstacle to the comprehension of the author of *Histoires Extraordinaires* (Baudelaire's edition of Poe's fiction): first because readers of French knew only a part of his work—significantly, the volume dedicated to Poe in the library of the Pléiade and regularly re-edited for more than forty years contains only Baudelaire's translations—and then because the image of Poe presented to them was distorted. It is all the more regrettable, a half-century later, that that point of view was given credence by so-called scientific criticism, especially by Emile Lauvrière and Marie Bonaparte. It is not to show Poe in his true light, though, merely to make of him an accursed poet, seeking inspiration in alcohol and opium, merely to see in him a being resembling his creations, a bohemian living on the edge of society and finding himself isolated from the America of his time. The true Poe is much different, as one may well perceive if he replaces the man's work in its literary and intellectual context and applies himself to studying the theories applicable to the work.[5]

We cannot understand Poe if we are limited to what Baudelaire translated; it is imperative to study his corpus, as Floyd Stovall has said: "We shall understand Poe best by a direct and earnest analysis of his total work."[6] Unfortunately, only a small part of this writing is accessible to French readers. True, the novels have been wholly translated; some of the stories not translated by Baudelaire were done by journalists and critics contemporaneous with the author of *Fleurs du Mal,* and, nearer our time, Léon Lemonnier newly translated all the tales laid aside by Baudelaire, including the almost intranslatable "Why the Little Frenchman Wears His Hand in a Sling."[7] There are also poems translated by Mallarmé, Gabriel Mourey and Victor Orban, then by Léon Lemonnier and Henri Parisot. It is rather the rest of Poe's works that remain unpublished in French, with the exception of isolated works such as the "Marginalia," the unfinished *Politian,* several critical articles, and certain letters.[8] Nothing exists in French comparable with the recent German edition, whose four volumes—more than 4000 pages—include, besides the complete fiction and poetry, *Eureka,* the "Marginalia" and most of the essays, as well as a selection of notes and letters; thus German readers may perceive the diversity of Poe's works.[9]

Fortunately, this gap is now partially filled thanks to Claude Richard, who published in the *Cahiers de l'Herne* a book on Poe.[10] This volume of nearly 500 pages is presented as a record of Poe's theoretical ideas, with, on one hand, the three manifestoes ("The Philosophy of Composition," "The Rationale of Verse" and "The Poetic Principle") that formulate his theory of literature, and, on the other hand, selections from the critical work where this theory finds its application. At the outset Richard states: "the corpus of texts translated by Charles Baudelaire has traced, once and for all, the frontiers of Poe's work," and he announces without ambiguity his intention to "render to Edgar Poe the entirety of his territory." Justly, he registers as inaccurate the image given by the author of *Fleurs du Mal:* "With Baudelaire, Poe, the man of procedure, complies with the frantic creation." He is original in his postulation of Poe's theoretical thought as a point of departure for understanding the writer and for affirming that "Poe's text is itself sufficiently meaningful." Richard's concern is first of all to allow the writer to speak rather than determining his words and actions for him, as, in the wake of Baudelaire, the French, with rare exceptions, have done. He emphasizes that "the interpreters who created the image of a poet of disorder could work out their theory only by disregarding numerous unedited texts"—unedited in France, that is. Furthermore, the texts selected by Richard, which occupy a third of his book, show us a Poe "forever careful about planning, elaborating

and ending" and make him appear as a poet of order and not of disorder, as the "literary engineer" that Valéry (almost the only one in France really to understand him) presented. We rejoin therefore Régis Messac, who, long ago, named Poe "one of the most extraordinarily lucid spirits that exist in all of literature."[11] Poe's audience in France deserves this quality of his genius—which appears equally in the detective stories, the genre he invented—the affinity between his and the French spirits, characterized by the preference for logic and clarity.

After the three manifestoes in which the writer enunciates his theory of literature, some twenty passages illustrate the development of Poe's critical thought; they are divided into three parts, with reflections on the theater, on the novel and short story, and on poetry. These texts, remarkable for their lucidity, reveal a Poe analyzing and dissecting the works of his contemporaries, but also stating principles and a coherent aesthetic doctrine. No one attached a greater importance to the conscious progression of the writer; no one placed greater emphasis on the will in literary creation. Thus it is that Poe praises Daniel Defoe's "faculty of identification" manifest in *Robinson Crusoe,* which he defines as "that dominion exercised by volition over imagination which enables the mind to lose its own, in a fictitious, individuality." Likewise, concerning Bulwer-Lytton: "Whatever may be the true merits of his intelligence, the merit of luminous and precise thought is evidently not one of the number." Poe goes as far as to reconstitute the course of the novelist, reproaching him for oversights in the construction of his plot; the writer, he says, forgets his basic plan in the course of composition, omitting certain details previously introduced into the plot and destined for importance in the *dénouement.* In reviewing two novels of Dickens, Poe likewise deplores the disadvantages of the serial formula, which hinders the writer from abiding by a predetermined plan. When Dickens entitled his novel *The Old Curiosity Shop,* Poe says, his plan was quite different from what it appeared to be in its final realization, and obviously he now should have given another title to his story, in which the shop plays a secondary role. The article on *Barnaby Rudge,* written, like the preceding article, in April 1841, furnished an even more striking illustration of Poe's analytical faculties. Did he not venture to predict the resolution of Dickens's novel, also serialized, when just eleven chapters were published, only to see his predictions prove essentially correct?[12]

A critic of penetrating mind, a remarkably lucid writer who formulated in his critical articles a coherent theory of literary creation, of poetry and of the short story: so Poe appeared in his texts, which reveal the importance he accorded to verisimilitude, particularly to rendering plausible the fantastic,

as well as the preponderance in his aesthetics of the combined effect on the reader. An important text that is yet little known in France is the review of Hawthorne's *Twice-Told Tales,* in which Poe formulates his theory of short fiction: "The tale proper, in our opinion, affords unquestionably the fairest field for the exercise of the loftiest talent, which can be afforded by the wide domains of mere prose." This article constitutes a counterpart to "The Philosophy of Composition"—translated by Baudelaire under the title "La Génèse d'un poème"; here Poe affirms the necessity for a writer to determine the *dénouement* even before beginning to write, as well as to put everything in harmony with the pre-established design: "no poet can afford to dispense with *any thing* that may advance his design."

Richard's work also contains a particularly interesting article, even if its attribution to Poe remains uncertain—a review of *Tales* (1845).[13] This article, in an ephemeral New York review whose editor-in-chief was Thomas Dunn English, later arch-enemy of our author, reflects Poe's opinion of some of his most famous stories and also expresses ideas dear to him, such as the importance of originality—"The creative power of the mind is boundless"—or the primordial role that he attributes to what he calls the "power of simulation": "A writer must have the fullest belief in his statements, or must simulate that belief perfectly, to produce an absorbing interest in the mind of his reader. That power of simulation can only be possessed by a man of high genius." It is not at all proven, however, that Poe is the author of the article in question, and one can reproach Richard for going a bit too far when he says that it is a "manifestation of the hand of Poe" and that it was published under the signature of the writer. Probably the article is the collaboration of Poe with English, written by the latter from what the author had furnished him.[14]

After the texts giving an outline of Poe's literary doctrine, Richard presents criticisms raised by the writer and his work, in three nearly equal parts. The first includes the testimonies of Poe's contemporaries, friends and enemies, beginning with his first biographer, the sinister Griswold, who worked at tarnishing his subject's memory in slanderous articles and in the posthumous edition of his works. Richard makes evident the errors perpetrated by Griswold, who did not hesitate to modify certain of Poe's letters to cast him in a bad light, nor to retouch the article by Lowell (who had written several years previously a study on Poe, reproduced by Griswold in his edition and figuring in Richard's work), which he deemed too favorable. This article aside, these texts make no pretension to criticism; instead they illustrate the controversy that raged after the writer's death between his partisans and his adversaries, and the tendency of most American critics during the nineteenth century to explain the work in terms of the man and to

condemn both in the name of bourgeois morality. The distorted image popularized by Baudelaire and continuing in France began in America. The articles of Griswold, Daniel and Thompson—the latter two were journalists from Richmond with whom Poe was associated—constitute in fact sources for the different articles that Baudelaire wrote in the preface to his translations. The French poet sometimes was content to translate entire passages from the essays of the American journalists; in his first article, published in the *Revue de Paris* in 1852, Baudelaire resorted to his informants for presenting to his compatriots works which he had not yet read, such as *Eureka* and *The Narrative of Arthur Gordon Pym* (which, according to Daniel, he named a "purely human book"). The French myth has truly "pitiable origins," emphasizes Richard, who justly entitles his introduction to this section "Birth of a Myth."

This chapter, which furnishes the pieces of the record for Poe's literary fortune in France, prefigures the next chapter, which shows the myth in full bloom, especially with Baudelaire and Mallarmé. The author of *Fleurs du Mal,* who had as much determination in defending Poe as Griswold had in disparaging him, added even more to the myth, affirming that America, that "great barbarity lighted by gas," had been merely a "vast prison" for the writer and that he had nothing in common with his country, to such an extent that his countrymen did not consider him American.[15] Therein, however, is one of the most tenacious legends received in France, emphasizes Richard, who likewise clears up another legend, that of the alleged superiority of Baudelaire's translations to the original texts. That said, it would be unjust not to recognize the merits of Baudelaire, both as a translator of Poe and as an artist worthy of his literary glory in France, as it would be unjust not to recognize that, thanks to his inspired intuition, the French poet discovered in Poe qualities that had escaped the ordinary reader, for example when he speaks of Poe's "driving aspiration toward unity." From this point of view, it is certainly exaggerated to allege, as Richard does, that the essence of two famous reviews by Baudelaire ("Edgar Poe, His Life, His Works" and "New Notes on Poe") is contained in the articles of Griswold, Daniel and Thompson and that therefore they need not be reproduced in his own book.

Two other texts presented by Richard also add to the record of the "myth": they consist of a very curious article by "Sâr" Péladan and an essay by Jules Verne—who produced almost simultaneously a notebook in the same series, containing a significant article on cryptography and on Poe's influence on his work in that field.[16] That essay, entitled "Edgar Poë [sic] and His Works" and published in 1864 in the *Musée des Familles,* probes the reason for the influence the American exerted on the author of *Extraordinary*

*Voyages* (is not the general title of his work derived from that which Baudelaire gave to Poe's stories when he translated them into French?). Its critical value is virtually nil, though, and it could have been replaced advantageously, for example, by the article that Barbey d'Aurevilly dedicated to Poe in *Littérature étrangère*. In return, other critiques have an undeniable value by reason of their authors' detachment with respect to the "myth." These include articles by Valéry—the two essays "Concerning *Eureka*" and "Position of Baudelaire" as well as a less known text, "On Literary Technique"—and the first critical study on Poe in French, published in 1846 in the *Revue des Deux Mondes* under the pen of Paul-Emile D. Forgues—who was also the first translator of Poe into French; he brings to light the essential characteristic of the writer's genius when he says of Poe's stories: "The logic is plain; it dominates everything; it is queen and mistress."

Finally, the third part of Richard's work—Edgar Allan Poe before his peers—presents varying judgments passed on the author by English and American writers, from Margaret Fuller to Richard Wilbur, by way of Henry James, Walt Whitman, R. L. Stevenson, G. B. Shaw, T. S. Eliot and others. Claude Richard's selection is representative of the range of attitudes toward Poe, from the enthusiasm of Shaw or of William Carlos Williams—who considered him "a genius intimately shaped by his locality and time"—to the unqualified condemnation of Henry James: "Enthusiasm for Poe is the mark of a decidedly primitive state of reflection." The reader will perhaps regret the absence of D. H. Lawrence's study,[17] but that is available in French; whereas Richard endeavored to present as many as possible unedited texts in our language, for which one can only praise him. This absence is elsewhere more than compensated for in a very little known article by John Cowper Powys and especially in two texts by T. S. Eliot, a "Note on Mallarmé and Poe" emphasizing the fundamental clarity of the writer,[18] and the lecture "Edgar Poe and France," which serves as a link with the preceding section. The author of *Murder in the Cathedral,* whom one cannot place among Poe's admirers since he questions the "enigma" of Poe's importance, attempts in fact to explain the divergence between French and Anglo-American criticism concerning the author of "The Gold-Bug." One cannot agree with the explanation he proposes—according to Eliot, this divergence occurs because English and American critics are more inclined to render isolated judgments on the different parts of a work, whereas French critics tend to consider the work as a whole—but one must concur when Eliot affirms the necessity of grasping Poe's work in its entirety.

Paradoxically, French readers will have to consult the work of Claude Richard to be able to put this recommendation into practice. This work—

which we reproach only for its abundance of printing errors, particularly annoying when one finds "reputation" instead of "refutation," as well as several errors in French within a text otherwise excellently translated[19]—will surely contribute to making Edgar Poe better known in French-speaking countries, presenting him in his true light, as a writer plainly in control of his resources and not as the inspired poet of the Baudelairean tradition. One must praise Richard for undertaking demythification. This enterprise, however, is not without danger. When he speaks of the "moving, but fallacious, mythical image of the *poète maudit* created by Baudelaire to enhance Poe's reputation" and when he emphasizes the "laborious banality of Poe's life," Richard falls into the defect of certain biographers who make of Poe someone rather ordinary, almost insignificant, and who see in him only a writer for hire and a needy journalist, thus losing sight of what was exceptional about him. Yet there was something that attracted Baudelaire to Poe; if he went too far in recreating Poe as he imagined him, the French poet was not mistaken in making of the author of "The Raven" the archetype of the accursed poet and in considering him his spiritual brother.

Almost inevitably, in attempting to react against the "myth," Richard goes to the opposite extreme; the fact remains that, thanks to him, Poe appears in an entirely new light, as a lucid writer and as a theoretician of literature. Certainly, many features still are lacking, thus preventing French readers from forming a complete picture of the American writer. We lack, for example, the letters—of which, happily, Richard announces an edition in preparation; we lack especially a selection of the journalist's articles showing that Poe was very much interested in the problems of his country and of his age. The merit of Claude Richard is, at the least, having done a pioneer work; thanks to him, let us hope, the "Aidgarpo" of the myth[20] will give place to the true Poe.

## NOTES

[1] *A Singular Conspiracy* (Indianapolis and New York, 1974). I am indebted to Dr. Forclaz and the Editors of *RLV* for permission to translate freely, but without altering its meaning, this essay. It first appeared in *RLV*, 43(1977), 348-356. Dr. Forclaz wrote to Prof. Benjamin Franklin Fisher IV, 6 August 1982, that he had discovered a French translation of *The Journal of Julius Rodman* (published in 1912), and that a sentence stating that no French version existed—p. 349 of *RLV*—should consequently be deleted from this translation.

[2] "He turned to Baudelaire the face of one marked for misfortune—the haggard mask of tragedy...Had anything, in all the uncaring world, ever been his—except the burden of guilt, growing always heavier, which rode upon his back?"—ibid., pp. 199, 202.

[3] Transl. Baudelaire.

[4] Note, however, that Baudelaire had been preceded by Isabelle Meunier and other contemporary journalists. For the history of the first translations of Poe in France, see the work of Léon Lemonnier, *Les Traducteurs d'Edgar Poe en France de 1845 à 1875: Charles Baudelaire* (Paris, 1928).

[5] See on this subject my work *Le Monde d'Edgar Poe* (Berne and Frankfurt, 1974). On the subject of the theories of Lauvrière and of Marie Bonaparte, cf. ibid., pp. 14-17, 66-69, and my "Edgar Poe et la Psychoanalyse," *RLV*, 36(1970), 272-288, 375-389.

[6] *Eight American Writers—An Anthology of American Literature*, ed. Norman Foerster and Robert P. Falk (New York, 1963), p. 14.

[7] Cf. *Histoires Grotesques et Serieuses, Suivies des Derniers Contes*, transl. Charles Baudelaire and Léon Lemonnier (Paris, 1950). This work is unfortunately out of print, but a new complete edition is in preparation in the library of the Pléiade through the efforts of Claude Richard. It is necessary to note that the uncompleted tale "The Lighthouse," the only tale not translated by Lemonnier, has since been done by Jacques Finné with the conclusion imagined by Robert Bloch in his anthology *L'Amérique Fantastique* (Verviers, 1973).

[8] One will find an almost complete list of French translations of Poe's work in the bibliography of the work mentioned in 10 (pp. 465-466). Cf. Jean Rousselot, *Edgar Poe* (Paris, 1962), pp. 214-218.

[9] *Werke, herausgegeben von Kuno Schuhmann und Hans Dieter Müller* (Brussells, 1966-73).

[10] *Edgar Allan Poe. Cahiers de l'Herne*, No. 26 (Paris, 1974).

[11] *Influences Francaises dans l'Oeuvre d'Edgar Poe* (Paris, 1929), p. 76.

[12] The article in question was published in the *Saturday Evening Post*, 1 April 1841, p. 4; it does not figure in the complete works of Poe, but a passage from it is cited in the review of the novel that the writer published in *Graham's Magazine* in February of the following year (cf. *H.* 11:58).

[13] "Poe's *Tales*," *Aristidean*, 1(1845), 316-319.

[14] That is especially the opinion of T. O. Mabbott: "The review of Poe's *Tales* must have been written after talking with Poe—it contains things only their author could have known. But the writer of the review was clearly T. D. English" (letter—T. O. Mabbott to Roger Forclaz, 19 January 1966).

[15] The two citations are taken from "Sa vie, ses oeuvres," Baudelaire's preface to his first volume of translations, the *Histoires Extraordinaires*.

[16] Jules Verne, *Cahiers de l'Herne*, No. 25, ed. Pierre-André Touttain (Paris, 1974). Cf. pp. 324-329 for the article "Jules et la cryptographie."

[17] Published in *Studies in Classic American Literature* (New York, 1923), pp. 93-120. Cf. *Etudes sur la Litterature Classique Americaine* (Paris, 1948) for the French translation of this work.

[18] "Il y a fort peu de l'halluciné chez Poe"—"Note sur Mallarmé et Poe," *Nouvelle Revue Francaise*, 27(1926), 525; cf. p. 407 of Richard's work.

[19] For example, the use of *emprise* as a masculine noun and the translation of *annual* for *annuel*, whereas the English *keepsake* is used in French in this particular case; the use of *bien que* with the indicative shows a certain laxness.

[20] Cf. Malcolm Cowley, "Aidgarpo," *New Republic*, 11 May 1945, pp. 607-610.

## POE IN AMERICAN DRAMA: VERSIONS OF THE MAN

*JOHN E. REILLY*

Tragedy, comedy, melodrama, mystery, fantasy, even opera and ballet: there have been more dramatizations of the life and character of Edgar Allan Poe than of any other figure in America's past with the exceptions of George Washington, Abe Lincoln, and possibly Pocahontas.[1] Most of these dramas about Poe exist only as unproduced and unproducible scripts resting undisturbed in the files of the Copyright Office or scattered here and there in theatre collections and among miscellaneous Poeana. Of the handful which have managed to reach the stage or screen, almost all have failed dismally and none has achieved anything more than modest success. Even when unstageworthy, all of these dramas, but especially those which have been produced professionally, are of interest at least to the extent that they represent versions of Poe and thereby record the impact of Poe, rather the impact of the image of Poe, upon the American mind.

The distinction of being the first drama about Poe to be staged in the legitimate theatre belongs to a play by George Cochrane Hazelton entitled *The Raven*.[2] It opened at Albaugh's Lyceum Theatre in Baltimore on 11 October 1895 with Creston Clarke, who was a grandson of Junius Brutus Booth and nephew of Edwin Booth, in the role of Poe. Although a review in the *Baltimore Sun* the following day commended Hazelton for following "closely the life of Poe as given by his biographers," his play in fact makes no serious effort to do so.[3] It is, instead, a conventional melodrama exploiting the prevailing romantic image of Poe.

The play opens on the lawn of the Allan home in Richmond. Poe is in love with Virginia Clemm, who is literally and conveniently the girl-next-door. Both his status in the Allan household and his love for Virginia are threatened, however, by Roscoe Pelham, A. M., an entirely fictitious character who is John Allan's secretary as well as the ubiquitous villain of the piece. When this scoundrel deliberately exposes our hero's gambling debts, John Allan disinherits and banishes his foster son. Act I closes with a proud Poe departing Richmond accompanied by Virginia and his faithful slave Erebus, determined to make his own way in the world. Ignoring almost the whole of Poe's literary career, Hazelton carries the action from Richmond presumably in the late 1820s or early 1830s to Fordham Cottage in January of 1847. Here we discover that Poe has been unable to make a living by his pen and that Virginia is in fragile and failing health. While she is alone in the cottage, Roscoe Pelham enters and is about to force his attentions upon her when Poe returns. Fearful that her impetuous husband will quarrel with the villain, Virginia feigns gaiety, bursts into song, ruptures a blood vessel, and dies

forthwith. In the very midst of mourning his child bride, Poe meets and falls in love with Helen Whitman, a wealthy poetess who resides in Fordham and to whom he is drawn by her uncanny resemblance to Virginia, a resemblance so close as to be little short of Morella-like reincarnation. Poe's plan to marry Helen is foiled, however, when who else but Roscoe Pelham, who just happens to be Helen's legal counselor, informs her that Poe has broken his temperance pledge. She dismisses Poe reluctantly, but, before exiting her life, he recites the whole of "The Raven," helpfully identifying it as "the heart-rending confession of my famished soul." The play closes with Poe deranged and dying in Baltimore, where one of Roscoe Pelham's henchmen has drugged him in order to use him as a repeater in an election then in progress, an election in which of course Roscoe Pelham is a candidate.

Hazelton's characterizations are no less fanciful than his plot. John Allan is more the stereotype of the plantation colonel than a Scottish merchant of Richmond. In the first act, Virginia is a coquettish Southern belle (presumably Hazelton's version of Sarah Elmira Royster). Thereafter she becomes the conventional heroine of melodrama, defending her virtue against the lascivious advances of the villain and sacrificing her life in the interest of her husband's well-being. Hazelton's Poe is equally unhistorical. In Act I he comes across as a bad imitation of something between Prince Hal and Romeo. Thereafter he degenerates into a ridiculous figure utterly lacking in either nobility or pathos. In Act III, Scene 2, for example, he is discovered kneeling at Virginia's grave holding a pistol to his temple while bidding a bitter farewell to a cruel world when he suddenly catches sight of Helen Whitman, drops the pistol, rises, and follows her off stage, "spell-bound." And in his final speech delivered in his last lucid moment, Poe refuses a glass of medicinal brandy offered to him by his friend Tony Preston:

> Nevermore! Thou demon of my life, at last I conquer thee! Oh, Tony, Tony, my heart is breaking! "I am a thing, a nameless thing, o'er which the Raven flaps his funereal wing!"

Presumably Hazelton intended this curtain speech to assure his shaken audience that Poe finally did manage to control at least one of his problems.

Catherine Chisholm Cushing's *Edgar Allan Poe: A Character Study* enjoys the distinction of being the first drama about Poe to reach the New York stage.[4] It ran briefly at the Liberty Theatre early in October of 1925. Although the *New York Times* panned the production, it did concede that "the incidents included in [the play] are based plausibly enough upon known biographical facts in the man's unhappy career."[5] One wonders just how familiar the reviewer was with these "known...facts." The play opens

with Poe returning to the Allan home in Richmond from a university in Washington, a university from which he was once suspended but now is expelled by the president for drinking and gambling. His "wild ways" are "the talk of the South," but he can be excused in some measure because he inherited his love of liquor from his father, who was a Virginia aristocrat of the bluest blood destined to have become America's finest actor had he had the strength to resist Demon Rum. Among those present at Poe's return are John and Frances Allan, Elmira Royster and her father, and Virginia and Mrs. Clemm. John Allan banishes his profligate foster son, but before Poe departs, he and Elmira defy both the Allans and the Roysters by announcing that they are engaged to be married. The engagement lasts for three years, terminating only when Elmira discovers that Poe is unable to support her. He is then free to marry his little cousin Virginia, who it turns out has loved him all along and has been encouraged by her conviction that she, and not Elmira, was the inspiration for "Annabel Lee." Because he had to compete with all of America's leading literary figures, Poe's winning both the one hundred dollar prize for fiction and the fifty dollar prize for poetry in the Baltimore *Saturday Visiter* contest is an enormous feat, little short of a Pulitzer. When the prizes are awarded in the early 1830s, Helen Whitman and Frances Osgood are present in Baltimore along with a character named Ludwig Griswold. "Grizzy," as his friends call him, is a vicious little sycophant who hates Poe and proves to be his nemesis. Impressed with Poe's having won both prizes, the "Editor," presumably of the *Saturday Visiter*, offers him a post on his magazine—a post above the wretched and envious Griswold. But Poe's tenure is brief. It ends with a kind of kangaroo court at which Bryant, Longfellow, Willis, and Griswold accuse him of having abused them as a critic. When Poe loses his editorial post, Virginia enters her decline and dies at Fordham, comforted in her last moments by Frances Osgood and Helen Whitman. Deteriorating badly, Poe next puts in an unexpected and madcap appearance at the Richmond home of John P. Kennedy. Among others who just happen to be visiting Kennedy at that moment are Nathaniel Parker Willis, J. H. B. Latrobe, Helen Whitman, Frances Osgood, and Elmira Royster—William Cullen Bryant is expected but fails to appear. At the close of "the man's unhappy career" in Baltimore, Poe is pursued by a raven (which most of the witnesses mistake for a bat) and is summoned by Virginia's spirit voice calling to him in her soft Southern accent, "Ed-gah." Then with the curtain slowly descending and the soft strains of "The Blue Danube" swelling in the background, Poe is heard to murmur, "Lenore...Lenore...."

One may well wonder just how Miss Cushing's play ever managed to

make it as far as any stage, much less a stage in New York. The answer, at least in part, probably lies in the playwright's determination to translate Poe into a character who would appeal specifically to an audience in the 1920s. She lays special emphasis upon Poe's life as the romance of a youth who rebels against convention and then goes down in pathetic defeat. He rebels first against the moral and social conventions represented by the Allans, the Roysters, and the president of that university in Washington. Then he rebels against the American literary establishment. When Willis, Bryant, Longfellow, and Griswold finally succeed in having him removed from his editorial post, he becomes a broken man. In character, then, he is very much a child of the "Roaring Twenties," but not the 1820s. When he confronts John Allan at the opening of the play, he is a typical college hellion right out of the Jazz Age:

John Allan

(On his feet, livid with anger)

Sira? What are you doing home from the University without permission?

Poe

I have permission, sir. Of His Excellency, the President!

All

(Aghast)

The President?

(Royster leaps to his feet)

Mr. Allan

You mean you've been suspended?

Poe

(Smilingly)

Oh, nothing so trivial as suspension, sir.

Allan

My God! You haven't been expelled?

Poe

(Bowing — Smilingly)

I am pleased to say I have had that exalted honor conferred upon me!

(Elmira only laughs....)

Mrs. Allan

Oh, Eddie!

Allan

And why were you expelled, sir?

Poe

Well—there was quite a long list of virtuous reasons tabulated, as I recall—

Allan

Name them, sir.

Poe

For special excellence in branches of higher education not included in the curriculum if I remember rightly.

A rebel against her parents, Elmira is an appropriate companion to Miss Cushing's Poe. Their dialogue is laced with the jargon of "twenty-three skiddoo." When they part at the close of their engagement, for example, Poe bids Elmira farewell with "Goodbye, Golden girl!" to which she replies, "Goodbye, Weaver of Dreams!" Both Mrs. Osgood and Mrs. Whitman suffer gross vulgarization. They are much more like flappers than bluestockings. At the award ceremony in Act II, the Editor of the *Saturday Visiter* politely asks them if they "know Mr. Kennedy and Mr. Miller." "Better than their wives know them," quips Mrs. Osgood. And later in the same scene, when the Editor lets slip an ungentlemanly phrase, he bows to the ladies apologetically, "I beg your pardon," he says. "The hell you do," Mrs. Whitman snaps back. Mercifully, Virginia escapes this kind of treatment. Instead she plays her role as the conventional, sentimental, and sickly heroine. It is, indeed, a testament to at least the minimal good taste of theatre-goers in New York that, in spite of Miss Cushing's efforts at pandering to their interests, they sent her creature to an early grave. It failed to survive opening night.

New York theatre-goers eleven years later were only a little more receptive to Sophie Treadwell's *Plumes in the Dust,* another conventional dramatization of Poe's life.[6] This play survived eleven performances at the Forty-Sixth Street Theatre in November of 1936, with Henry Hull in the leading role. The brevity of its stage career notwithstanding, *Plumes in the Dust* comes closer than any other conventional play about Poe to achieving a successful union of dramatic essentials and biographical fact. The action is built around almost the same episodes in Poe's life that form the basis, though remote, of Miss Cushing's melodramatic abomination. They are Poe's break with John Allan in 1826-27, his winning of the Baltimore *Saturday Visiter* contest in the early 1830s, Virginia's decline and death at Fordham, Poe's relations with the New York literati, his last trip to Richmond, and his death in Baltimore. Both as drama and as biography, the finest

moments in *Plumes in the Dust* occur in the opening scene, which represents Poe's strained relations with John Allan, whom Miss Treadwell characterizes as a hypocrite and a tyrant. Tension in the scene mounts steadily until mutual hostility between Allan and Poe erupts into a heated exchange. "You're a heartless, unprincipled, immoral reprobate," Allan charges; and Poe lashes back, "You dare to talk to me of heart! Of morals! You who keep your mistress—your common vulgar mistress—just around the corner from your home!—preferring your own low convenience to your wife's poor pride!" Unfortunately, *Plumes in the Dust* fails to sustain anything like this level of emotion in spite of Miss Treadwell's heroic measures, especially her jockeying of events in Poe's life. In Act II, Scene 2, for example, she has an inebriated and contentious Poe in the midst of a literary soiree jolted by the news that Virginia has died in his absence. In the following scene, where Poe courts the widowed Elmira Royster Shelton in Richmond, the playwright takes the liberty of having her Poe deliver as speeches to Elmira passages from letters that Poe had, in fact, written to Sarah Helen Whitman.

Although *Plumes in the Dust* is the most nearly successful conventional play about Poe, it does not quite succeed either as biography or as drama. It does not succeed as biography principally because it offers a distorted account of Poe's life. Like Miss Cushing, and Hazelton too, Miss Treadwell has the action of her play leap from Baltimore in the early 1830s to New York after 1845, thereby ignoring the most fruitful period in Poe's literary career. That *Plumes in the Dust* does not succeed as drama was explained by Brooks Atkinson in his review of the 1936 production for the *New York Times.*[7] The play is "an earnest pageant of desolation and melancholy," Atkinson reported. It is difficult, he continued, to dramatize Poe's life without turning it into "a minor 'Hamlet,'" and

> Miss Treadwell and Mr. Hull have rather conspired toward that end. She has done it by putting on his lips opulent literary phrases that sound a little egregious when Mr. Hull speaks them with an actor's exuberant swagger. When he strides masterfully into a polite literary party and lays about him with purple patches and a good deal of rodomontade about his integrity as a critic, the life of letters sounds uncomfortably pompous.

Hollywood's most ambitious venture at dramatizing the life of Poe was a 1942 film released by Twentieth Century-Fox under the title *The Loves of Edgar Allan Poe.*[8] Based upon a screen play by Samuel Hoffenstein and Tom Reed, it starred John Shepperd as Poe and Linda Darnell as Virginia. Publicity described the film as "the unknown side of America's most famous

literary genius, that surpasses his own startling stories of dark emotions and deep passions—[it] is the true drama of [Poe's] life, known only to the women who loved him." Though the studio insisted that there was no need of "doctoring" the facts, the film reduces "the women who loved him" to Virginia Clemm and Elmira Royster and pits them against one another in a struggle for Poe's affections, a struggle to which his literary career is largely rendered subordinate. That they might be suitable contenders for a poet's heart, Elmira is portrayed as "a beautiful brunette" under the influence of whose "spell" Poe "poured out the deepest passions of his heart," and Virginia is cast as a "Baltimore belle" whose "interesting little figure" is at one point displayed "in the pantalettes of the period." Among the episodes in this love story are an angry encounter between Poe and Elmira's husband in which the poet "socks" his antagonist on the jaw and an emotional visit by Elmira to the bedside of the dying Virginia at Fordham Cottage, a visit in which Virginia triumphs so completely over Elmira that the film fails to mention that Poe courted the widowed Mrs. Shelton two years after Virginia's death. Relegated to a desultory subplot, Poe's literary career is reduced to the simple terms of Poe as the champion of international copyright struggling against the exploitative practices of American publishers. In a vain effort to inject some life into this subplot, the picture offers a scene in which Thomas Jefferson counsels Poe to pursue his literary inclinations; it confronts Poe with the dilemma of choosing between editorship of the *Southern Literary Messenger* and editorship of *Graham's Magazine;* it exaggerates the significance of Poe's meeting with Dickens; and it humiliates Poe by having Griswold turn down "The Raven" for publication in the *Broadway Journal.* Just how thrilled the public was with this rendering of Poe is suggested by Theodore Strauss in his review of the film for the *New York Times.*[9] "As an addition to the library of films suitable for grade school edification and instruction," the review begins, "'The Loves of Edgar Allan Poe' may conceivably serve some purpose, particularly in those classrooms where the dull, the prosaic and uninspired is held to be appropriately educational. But as an adult drama about one of America's most complex men of letters it is no more than a postured and lifeless tableau." "Meanwhile," Strauss concludes, "a perceptive drama of an unhappy and greatly gifted man remains to be done."

But Strauss misses the point. The issue is not *when* a successful drama about Poe will be written but whether one *can* be written. And the prospect is not encouraging. As Professor N. Bryllion Fagin pointed out some years ago, the problem is that Poe's biography is unpromising as the stuff of drama, unpromising because it fails to furnish what Professor Fagin calls sufficient

"complication, tension, romantic interest, and emotional appeal."[10] His life was, in Fagin's words, "relatively unadventurous":

> It was neither colorful nor extraordinarily unfortunate, sad, or tragic. Charles Lamb began life in more unadvantageous circumstances; Charles Dickens knew greater poverty, at least in his childhood; Dostoievsky was more cruelly ravaged by spells of ill health; De Quincey, and probably Coleridge, imbided more laudanum; and Robert Burns consumed more alcohol.[11]

Professor Fagin could have gone on: Shelley was a more refractory child and a far less conventional adult; Cooper could boast a much less commendable college career; Melville suffered far more neglect at the hands of the reading public; Thoreau practiced more integrity; Longfellow knew greater domestic tragedy; and even Wordsworth led a sexual life more deserving of censure. What emerges from Poe's biography is not the romantic figure of the legend: that haunted and suffering spirit, victim both of his own genius and of a cruel fate, the high priest of pure beauty raging through the crass, ugly, and hostile world of nineteenth-century America. What emerges instead is the figure of a dedicated and disciplined craftsman, critic, and editor whose life was for the most part one of quiet indigence and domestic harmony. This figure, this "man behind the legend," as Edward Wagenknecht has called him, is appropriate not to tragedy or to melodrama: it is appropriate to documentary. And when playwrights such as Hazelton, Cushing, Hoffenstein, Reed, and even Treadwell, playwrights beguiled by the image of the legendary Poe, have attempted to translate that image into something stageworthy, they invariably collide with the unyielding fact that Poe's life simply does not support the legend.

One way to avoid this collision is to write plays about Poe that steer as clear as possible from the facts of his biography. And this is precisely what some playwrights have been attempting in recent decades. They have turned from Poe's life to his mind, playing out their dramas in what they believe to be the recesses of Poe's own haunted psyche.[12] It is a shift from conventional drama to what we might call "psychodrama" (if we can appropriate that term), and it is nicely illustrated in a work entitled *Poor Eddy*. Written by Elizabeth Dooley and produced in 1953 by the Columbia University Theatre Guild, *Poor Eddy* is what the playwright calls a "ballet-biography."[13] Its format consists of what Mrs. Dooley describes as brief "realistic" scenes taken from Poe's life coupled with what she calls "arabesques," or renderings of the "otherworld" of Poe's "sleeping and waking dreams." These arabesques are ballet pieces which interpret passages recited from Poe's writings, chiefly

passages from his fiction and poetry. Movement from realistic scene to accompanying arabesque is marked by distinctive "threshold" music and by the presence of a scrim behind which the actor-dancer playing Poe passes to indicate that action is moving from outward experience to imaginative or internal states of mind. The entire production consists of two acts, the first made up of three realistic scenes with their accompanying arabesques and the second act made up of five realistic scenes and five arabesques. The second scene in Act I is a good example of how *Poor Eddy* operates. Here the realistic scene is set in Philadelphia in 1840. Poe discovers that Virginia, now in her eighteenth year, is consumptive and that marital relations, which she and Poe have postponed for five years because of her age, must now be postponed indefinitely. In the accompanying arabesque, a narrator recites passages from "Ligeia" while the movements of the dancers express the triumph of love over death. Similarly, the following realistic scene presents the sudden-bursting of a blood-vessel in Virginia's throat, and the accompanying arabesque is based upon "The Masque of the Red Death." Because each of its eight realistic scenes is balanced with its arabesque, *Poor Eddy* stands as a transitional work between dramatizations of Poe's life and dramatizations of his psyche.

Nicholas Argento's opera *The Voyage of Edgar Allan Poe*, produced first in Minneapolis in 1976 and then in Baltimore the following year, goes a good deal further in shifting the balance from life to psyche.[14] Argento and his librettist, Charles Nolte, rest their version of Poe upon only one episode. It is his departure by boat from Richmond on his journey to Baltimore in the closing days of his life. In Argento's hands, this voyage becomes a recapitulatory vehicle, a complex metaphor blending Poe's life as the desperate and futile quest of a Romantic idealist with his works, principally "Annabel Lee," "Eldorado," *Pym*, and "MS Found in a Bottle." The opera represents an hallucinatory experience in which the disturbed psyche of the dying poet is haunted by painful episodes in his past; or as a voice informs him in the first scene of the opening act: he is "on a voyage of Discovery. A heart that hates annihilation like the tomb must gather the past into hallucination." Regrettably, Argento's version of Poe's suffering psyche hovers somewhere between the simple maudlin and the traditional Byronesque. "All I touched turned autumn in my hand," he whines at the close of the opera:

> My youth, a fragile vessel caught upon the waves of a savage sea. My heart, my heart a ravaged garden without a single bloom. Look upon this ruin mocked by starless skies. How else shall I speak, how shall I speak my soul's pain? The buried loves of these sad eyes? I live within the storm. Pity me! I cannot write, I cannot think, I cannot love as others do.

> It is true. It is true! I murdered for my art! I killed all that I most loved, and sacrificed remembered bliss to feed my muse. It had to be. Have mercy on my life.

And opera buffs had mercy on Argento's Poe, indeed, more than mercy. The Minneapolis correspondent to the *New York Times* pronounced the 1976 performance "a rich, mature and substantial creation," and the *Baltimore Sun* not only headlined its review of the 1977 production "A Critical Success," but it hailed the opera a "dynamic" accomplishment.[15] One of the reporters for the *Sun* did note, however, that he found "a few" bewildered members of the audience who confessed to not knowing "enough about Poe's life to follow all the characters associated with him" in the opera. And the same reporter admitted to having overheard Baltimore City Council President Walter S. Orlinsky grumble, "Why do they always sing in Chinese?" With all due respect to the legitimacy of Mr. Orlinsky's grievance, it is the student of Poe and the genuine Poe buff who have the greatest grounds for grumbling. For how are we to countenance such *bizarreries*, as Poe would have called them, such outrages as Argento's having cast Poe's wife Virginia as the Eurydice-like victim of her husband's unquenchable and ungovernable curiosity about death and Argento's having Poe's beloved mother Elizabeth portrayed in her son's hallucinations as a "slut" and a "whore" who consorts with the merged figures of John Allan and Rufus Griswold?[16]

Although Argento has his Poe die in Richmond without having in fact undertaken his voyage, we know, of course, that Poe's death occurred in Baltimore, where, according to one of the most tenacious features of the Poe legend, he was villainously drugged and exploited as a repeater in an election then in progress and subsequently abandoned in a shabby tavern. It is this legend which furnished the setting for Ted Davis's *Poe: A Gathering Darkness*, a drama currently making the rounds of college and university campuses as part of the repertoire of a small professional theatre company based in Boston.[17] Approximately a quarter of the action in Davis's play dramatizes the suffering of Poe at the hands of the scoundrels who seized him in Baltimore. The bulk of the action, however, represents, as in Argento's opera, hallucinations of the drugged, intoxicated, and dying Poe, hallucinations in which he is made to relive painful experiences in his past. But Davis's Poe does not relive these experiences alone. For in the manner of William Wilson's *Doppelgänger*, protagonist Poe is accompanied by an actor in the role of what the script calls "Shadow Poe." He is the protagonist's alter ego, his conscience, mocking, prodding, coaxing, prompting, contradicting, but, above all, compelling Poe to confront those painful realities which he dearly longs to evade. Principal among these realities is Poe's relationship to his

wife Virginia, a relationship which, according to Davis's version, was a legitimate source of deep guilt. Virginia was Poe's "forever child," the innocent victim, à la "Ligeia" and especially "The Oval Portrait," the innocent victim of her husband's quest for ideal love and beauty. "I married her! Loved her! Cared for her," Poe says at one point. You "despised her," the Shadow Poe insists. "You invented a thing to love or rather you loved your own creation—a seduction of the spirit. Your words caressed your lover into existence....But what your hands touched crumbled before you." "Untrue," Poe answers, "I know what love is! I stood by my Virginia in her time of need. I married the ideal—my perfect love." "And all the while," the Shadow reminds him, "your fantasy turned Virginia into someone—something else—your words shaped her, rearranged [her] membranous face, her mewling voice, her leprous skin, her infantile mind, the taste of the dead on her lips. Your marriage was the perfect fantasy—making love to a vision. No touching of mortal flesh." "I will not accept such a thing," Poe protests. "I'll prove you wrong." "Words exalt—flesh corrupts," the Shadow responds. "Think on this fact only....Think on Ligeia...not Virginia...think on Ligeia." And then the mood on stage alters as Poe becomes the narrator in a dramatization of his tale "Ligeia."

Davis makes extensive use of Poe's fiction and poetry, and this is a feature his play shares with Argento's opera and Dooley's ballet-biography. And it seems to have been inescapable. For although Davis, Argento, and Dooley pretend to dramatize Poe's psyche, the fact is that we know precious little about it. Poe was both an extremely private as well as a very elusive person. Beyond the little domestic circle of himself, Virginia, and Mrs. Clemm, a circle into which we have only the fleetingest of glimpses, no one ever came close enough to Poe personally to have left us a record of what he really was like in mind and spirit. And his utterances, including his essays as well as his letters, especially his so-called love letters, are of little help because Poe was an incessant role-player, always the "creative actor," as Professor Fagin has called him.[18] Accordingly, in the absence of any other apparent avenue to his mind, those who would dramatize his psyche have turned to his imaginative works. But just as the unyielding facts of Poe's biography are the Scylla upon which has floundered every attempt to exploit his life and character in conventional drama, so the presumption that Poe's fiction and his poetry somehow constitute a window to his mind and spirit is the Charybdis into which attempts at psychodrama are inevitably drawn. It is an insidious presumption because it is so attractive and compelling, but above all it is an exquisitely ironic one because instead of promoting our apprecia-tion or understanding of the real Poe, it carries us back to the very origins of

the Poe legend, above all, to that feature of the legend as in some respects a hoax perpetrated by Poe himself on a grand scale. For did Poe not contribute immensely to the establishment of the legend by encouraging the notion that many of his poems and his stories are in some obscure way autobiographical documents, encouraging it by creating heroes who look like him, who display the mannerisms he assumed, and who speak from the pages of his fiction and his poetry with what appears to be the authentic voice of the author himself? The inevitable effect has been the conviction that Poe's mind was a haunted palace, that he had lost a Lenore and an Annabel Lee and could find solace only in drink and drug. Ironically, it was Poe's old nemesis Rufus W. Griswold who was one of the earliest and principal victims of this hoax. For was it not Griswold who, when Poe was literally only hours in his grave, solemnly instructed us that if we are really to know Poe's mind and heart, we must read his darkest works as "a reflection and an echo of his own history"?

## NOTES

[1] The number of dramas written about Poe, even an approximation, is not ascertainable because the mortality rate of scripts which have been neither produced nor published is very high and because finding those which have managed to survive is haphazard at best.

[2] George Cochrane Hazelton, *The Raven: A Romantic Play in Five Acts.* Copyright obtained 2 August 1893. Revised for production at Albaugh's Lyceum Theatre, Baltimore, 11 October 1895, as *Edgar Allan Poe; or The Raven.* Revised for printing as *The Raven: A Play in Four Acts and a Tableau* (New York, 1903). Revised for publication as a novel, *The Raven: The Love Story of Edgar Allan Poe ('Twixt Fact and Fancy)* (New York, 1909). *The Raven,* a motion picture by George Cochrane Hazelton copyrighted in 1915 by Essaway Film Manufacturing Company and "based on the poem by Edgar Allan Poe," probably is still another revision of the earlier play. My discussion of the play is based upon the typescript filed for copyright in 1893.

The earliest dramatization of Poe is Lambert A. Wilmer's little verse play *Merlin,* published in the Baltimore *North American,* 18 and 25 August and 1 September 1827, reprinted by Thomas Ollive Mabbott, ed. *Merlin, Baltimore, 1827, Together with Recollections of Edgar A. Poe by Lambert A. Wilmer* (New York, 1941).

[3] *Baltimore Sun,* 12 October 1895, p. 10.

[4] My discussion of this play is based upon a typescript filed for copyright in 1925. I am grateful to the family of the late Miss Cushing for permission to quote from this copy.

[5] *New York Times,* 6 October 1925, p. 31.

[6] *Plumes in the Dust* originally was a four-act play entitled *Poe*, a typescript of which was filed for copyright on 21 January 1920. Miss Treadwell tightened up the action by shifting scenes and by reducing the original four acts to three. She also used information made available through publication of the Poe-Allan correspondence. My discussion of the play is based upon a prompt book on deposit at the New York Public Library. I am grateful to the late Miss Treadwell for permission to quote from this source.

[7] Brooks Atkinson commented upon *Plumes in the Dust* in the *Times* on three occasions: 26 October 1936, p. 21; 7 November, p. 14; and 15 November, xi, 1. The first occasion was to review the premiere performance at Princeton, New Jersey, on 25 October. The second was to review the opening in New York on 6 November. And the third was to offer observations on the dramatic potentialities of Poe's life and character. I quote here from the 7 November review of the opening performance in New York.

[8] A mimeograph of the screenplay is on deposit at the Enoch Pratt Free Library. I am grateful to Twentieth Century-Fox Film Corporation for permission to quote from this copy.

Film makers have by no means neglected Poe. A number of his tales have been made into motion pictures, some of them repeatedly, and there have been a number of original efforts "based upon" Poe. Some of these efforts, notably *The Man With the Cloak* (a 1951 MGM version of John Dickson Carr's short story "The Gentleman from Paris"), have incorporated Poe himself as a character in fictitious settings. For its lively interest in Poe even in its infancy, see Denis Gifford, "Pictures of Poe: A Survey of the Silent Film Era 1909-29," in *The Edgar Allan Poe Scrapbook*, ed. Peter Haining (New York, 1978), pp. 129-132.

[9] *New York Times*, 21 September 1942, p. 19.

[10] N. Bryllion Fagin, *The Histrionic Mr. Poe* (Baltimore, 1949), p. 224.

[11] Fagin, p. 3.

[12] I do not wish to give the impression either that the three dramas I discuss here are the only efforts at what I call "psychodrama" or that this phenomenon is limited strictly to recent decades. The earlier efforts usually were fictions in which Poe himself is cast as a character in his own works, more often than not "The Raven."

[13] My discussion of *Poor Eddy* is based upon a prompt book on deposit at the New York Public Library. I am grateful to Mrs. Dooley for permission to quote from this text.

[14] The libretto to *The Voyage of Edgar Allan Poe* has been published in *Commemorating the World Premiere of "The Voyage of Edgar Allan Poe,"* edited by David J. Speer, et al. (St. Paul, 1976), pp. 41-79. I am grateful to Boosey and Hawkes, Incorporated, of New York, for permission to quote from the text of the libretto.

[15] *New York Times*, 26 April 1976, p. 38; *Baltimore Sun*, 7 June 1977, p. B1.

[16] Having discussed Dooley's ballet and Argento's opera, I should at least mention an "opera ballet" by Byron Stanley Schiffman entitled *The Raven; or, Edgar Allan Poe*, copyrighted in 1952, with new matter added in 1954. When I inquired, the Copyright Office was unable to locate its copy of the script. There is no record of production.

[17] I wish to thank Ted Davis for furnishing me with a copy of the script, from which I quote with his permission, and for his willingness to discuss both his work and Poe at length.

[18] Fagin, p. 16.

# "THAT METAPHYSICAL ART": MYSTERY AND DETECTION IN POE'S TALES

*BRUCE I. WEINER*

## I

Despite some recent challenges, Edgar Allan Poe continues to hold the patent on the invention of the detective story. Scholars trace his inspiration to Scripture and the Classics, to Voltaire's *Zadig* (1748), Godwin's *Caleb Williams* (1794) and the sensational *Mémoires* (1828) of the French detective, Francois-Eugène Vidocq, but most agree that the form Poe gave to his detective tales was original and definitive. Everything since, argues Jacques Barzun, is only elaboration and complication.[1] Some critics maintain, moreover, that Poe's theme in fiction reaches a climax in the solutions of his detective, C. Auguste Dupin. Dupin, they argue, is Poe's ideal projection of himself as artist, the poet-mathematician who combines imagination and reason to achieve transcendental vision.[2]

Poe, however, took a more modest view of his invention. Although he consistently ranked the Dupin stories among his best, he also made light of them as puzzles or hoaxes. Writing to his friend, Philip Pendleton Cooke, in 1846, two years after he had abandoned his detective, Poe admitted that the "hair-splitting" of Dupin "is all done for effect." People think his tales of ratiocination "more ingenious than they are—on account of their method and *air* of method. In 'The Murders in the Rue Morgue', for instance, where is the ingenuity of unravelling a web which you yourself (the author) have woven for the express purpose of unravelling? The reader is made to confound the ingenuity of the supposititious Dupin with that of the writer of the story."[3] Poe complained to Cooke, moreover, that in the last collection of his fiction (*Tales,* 1845), selected by Evert Duyckinck, too much space went to the ratiocinative, misrepresenting the "wide *diversity and* variety" of his tales. Each, Poe protests, "is equally good *of its kind,*" although "the loftiest kind is that of the highest imagination—and, for this reason only, 'Ligeia' may be called my *best* tale."[4]

"Ligeia" (1838) may be Poe's best tale, but it is not altogether a different kind of tale from "Murders" (1841). It too pits a protagonist against a mystery, the solution of which promises the sort of transcendental vision Dupin seems to achieve. The mystery in "Ligeia," however, remains impenetrable. The frantic efforts of the narrator to fathom the strange nature of his

wife ironically anticipate the calm deductions of Dupin. Indeed, so desperate is Ligeia's husband for a solution that he implicates himself in a crime. Similar elements of unsolved mystery are present in other tales Poe published just prior to the advent of Dupin, including "The Fall of the House of Usher" (1839), "William Wilson" (1839) and "The Man of the Crowd" (1840). As Stuart Levine argues, the Dupin stories "should not be considered as an isolated handful of experiments in a totally different genre."[5] Not only do they advance Poe's preoccupation in the tales with the possibilities of transcendental, artistic vision, as Levine suggests, but they do so in the form of mystery and detection.

The theme that links these tales would seem to culminate in the detective stories, Dupin emerging in 1841 as Poe's "Transcendental Hero" or "Detective God."[6] Why, then, does Poe belittle the ingenuity of "Murders" and call "Ligeia" his best tale? We know that he associated "the highest imagination" in poetry with "indefiniteness" and in fiction with an "undercurrent of meaning" that remains submerged.[7] Is the unsolved mystery then the higher art? I would argue that Poe manages the solutions of Dupin at the expense of his artistic convictions. In the unsolved mystery he dramatizes an indeterminate struggle for transcendental vision, such as he suggests in "The Poetic Principle," defines and limits the aesthetic and spiritual aspirations of mankind. In the detective tales he indulges in hoax and fantasy, displacing the struggle for transcendence with the illusion or "air" of success. The human quandaries of the protagonists in the unsolved mysteries give way to the godlike omniscience of Dupin.

## II

Although Poe owes debts to Voltaire, Godwin and Vidocq, the form of mystery and detection he employs in tales as diverse as "Ligeia" and "Murders" may come more directly from unknown tales like Robert Macnish's "Who Can It Be?," in *Blackwood's Edinburgh Magazine* for 1827. There is no mention of Macnish or his fiction in Poe's works, but the American was a careful reader of *Blackwood's* and could not have failed to notice "Who Can It Be?" or tales like it that Macnish published under the pseudonym, A Modern Pythagorean. "Who Can It Be?" is a type of mystery story that was popular in Poe's day. William Blackwood, publisher of the magazine, thought that it owed something to Washington Irving's "The Stout Gentleman," and it has been identified as a source for Poe's "The Man of the Crowd."[8] These are tales in which a narrator tries to discover the identity of a mysterious stranger.

In "Who Can It Be?" Macnish's narrator, nervous and lethargic after a heavy meal on a hot evening, is about to doze off when his curiosity is aroused

by a stranger pacing back and forth outside his dining-room window. There is "apparently nothing remarkable about the man," but the narrator is "irresistably attracted" to him. "What could be the meaning of this? There was something unfathomable about him; his name was Mystery, and the longer I looked at him the more miraculous did his whole appearance seem."[9] As in Irving's tale, the narrator's perplexity is largely comic, spoofing in this case the fashion of anonymous and pseudonymous authorship in magazines like *Blackwood's* and the lack of real distinction in famous men and their ideas. Macnish also seems interested in the drama of his narrator's consciousness. The effect of the heat and the heavy meal, on the one hand, and the mysterious stranger, on the other, divide the narrator's "corporeal and mental functions..., the former inspiring me to sleep, the latter striving to keep me awake."[10] He oscillates between a desire for the release of sleep and a compelling "wish to know" who the stranger is, between nervous reverie and rational observation. He tries, like Dupin, to deduce the stranger's identity from his features, dress and gait, but his detective work produces only greater confusion and a relapse into languorous trance. Waking again to observation, the narrator is further frustrated by his attempt to solve the mystery. Finally, he rushes out in a fit of anger to confront the stranger, only to find him gone.

Poe's narrator in "The Man of the Crowd" is similarly perplexed by a mysterious stranger he observes passing outside the London coffee-house in which he sits convalescing after a long illness. As in "Who Can It Be?" the mystery serves to revive the narrator, to provoke him into consciousness and action. Poe's character is already aroused into excited observation of the crowd when the countenance of a "decrepid old man" arrests his attention and compels him "to keep the man in view—to know more of him."[11] Unlike Macnish's narrator, Poe's must give chase to satisfy his curiosity, but his detective work produces a similar confusion of reason and anxious speculation. After shadowing the old man's lonely pursuit of the London crowd for a night and a day, the narrator is "at a loss to comprehend the waywardness of his actions" (*M*.2: 514). Like Macnish's narrator, he tries at last to solve the mystery by confronting the stranger face to face, but the old man passes him by without noticing him. Macnish's narrator surmises in frustration that his stranger is "neither more nor less than a villain;"[12] Poe's concludes cryptically that the Man of the Crowd is "the type and genius of deep crime" (*M*.2: 515).

In these tales and Irving's "The Stout Gentleman" too, mystery seems to induce consciousness, to provoke a semi-conscious, solipsistic narrator into awareness and action. All three narrators are aroused from some listless

state—Macnish's narrator from his after-dinner drowsiness, Poe's from his convalescence, Irving's from boredom—into a state of wakeful observation, and they are all compelled by a desire for knowledge. The mystery in each case, however, proves impenetrable and the narrators become increasingly bewildered, frustrated, aggressive and preoccupied with a sense of evil or crime. Thus the pattern of the tales is ironic. The mystery that brings the narrators to life serves also to define their mortal limitations, literally reducing Macnish's narrator at one point to a state of unconsciousness. Poe's tale, however, takes seriously what is only comically suggested in its sources. In "The Man of the Crowd" we are made conscious of some horrible mystery of the human condition and, in the narrator's attempt to solve it, some profound limitations of human understanding.

Ellery Queen was the first to recognize "The Man of the Crowd" as a detective tale, seeing in Poe's narrator a prototype of both the "armchair detective" and "gumshoe" (he dons caoutchouc overshoes to pursue the old man).[13] Significantly, in time of publication and probably composition, "The Man of the Crowd" immediately precedes "Murders." Although Poe shifts the focus of mystery in "Murders" from the type and genius of deep crime to the type and genius of crime detection, the pattern of mystery is much the same. Dupin too is drawn out of a listless and dreamlike retirement from the world by a mystery that exercises his powers of observation and reason. "Observation," Dupin tells his companion—echoing the narrator of "The Man of the Crowd"—"has become with me, of late, a species of necessity" (*M*.2: 535). Dupin's attention is fixed not by the sight of a mysterious person but by newspaper reports of a brutal murder, committed apparently by some mysterious person or persons possessing unusual strength and speaking a strange tongue (I should note that the mysterious stranger in Irving's tale also remains out of sight). The obvious difference between these tales is that Dupin solves the mystery. Although some of the bewilderment and frustration of the narrators of "Who Can It Be?," "The Stout Gentleman," and "The Man of the Crowd" survives in Dupin's companion, who tells the tale, the mystery in "Murders" serves primarily to evoke the extraordinary acumen of Dupin.

Dupin, however, is an anomaly. The puzzled protagonist and unsolved mystery are far more prevalent in Poe's fiction. "The Man of the Crowd" is not the only tale in which a mysterious stranger frustrates a desire for knowledge. Finding his own wife a stranger, whose mysterious nature he cannot explain, the narrator of "Ligeia" exclaims: "What was it—that something more profound than the well of Democritus...What *was* it? I was possessed with a passion to discover" (*M*. 2: 313). The narrator of "Usher"

asks the same question when he unwittingly observes in the facade of Usher's mansion an image of his estranged friend: "What was it...what was it that so unnerved me in the contemplation of the House of Usher? It was a mystery all insoluble" (*M.* 2: 397). The narrator of "William Wilson" is similarly perplexed by a mysterious person who looks like him and bears his name: "Were these,—*these* the lineaments of William Wilson?...What *was* there about them to confound me in this manner?" (*M.*2: 437). There is no Dupin to solve these mysteries, perhaps because, though they lead us to suspect the commission of crimes, they call for an investigation of metaphysical problems. We may wonder whether the narrator of "Ligeia" has murdered his second wife Rowena to effect Ligeia's return from the dead, whether Roderick Usher has knowingly buried his sister alive, or whether William Wilson actually kills his double, but these questions are subsumed by the profounder mysteries of the characters' suffering. Crime in these tales is symptomatic of a fallen human condition; as in "Who Can It Be?" and "The Man of the Crowd," some mysterious evil or iniquity seems at once to provoke and limit consciousness. This kind of mystery becomes even more explicit in tales Poe published after the invention of Dupin, such as "The Black Cat" (1843), "The Imp of the Perverse" (1845) and "The Cask of Amontillado" (1846), which, like "William Wilson," take the form of a condemned man's confession. We read these tales wondering not who done it but why. They recall the narrator's opening remarks in "The Man of the Crowd" about men "who die nightly in their beds, wringing the hands of ghostly confessors...die with despair of heart and convulsion of throat, on account of the hideousness of mysteries which will not *suffer themselves* to be revealed." It is a burden of conscience "so heavy in horror that it can be thrown down only into the grave" (*M.* 2: 506-507).

Poe's unsolved mysteries may have their source in tales like "Who Can It Be?" but they aspire to the metaphysical significance of *The Scarlet Letter, Moby-Dick,* and *Billy Budd,* which also draw us into investigations of mysterious persons or things that are "types" of deep crime. The Romantics, we know, were disposed to see the world as a mystery, having rejected the rational and mechanistic view of the previous age. Emerson, for one, welcomed the challenge of a mysterious universe because he believed that it would arouse his listless and retrospective age, much as a mystery arouses Dupin, into a wakeful sense of its own vital capacities. In the view of some, Dupin embodies an Emersonian faith in the power of human intellect and will to penetrate the mystery of experience, to discover a correspondence between the real and the ideal.[14] The metaphysics of the unsolved mysteries of the Romantic age, however, follow the more skeptical line of works like

Byron's verse-drama *Cain,* subtitled *A Mystery.* As Paul Cantor argues, Byron's aim in investigating the first murder was to demonstrate more radically than Milton had in treating Adam's fall that "the human condition is one of exile and alienation."[15] Byron's Cain is a model for Romantic protagonists like Hester Prynne, Ahab and Billy Budd, whose crimes are a response to their inability to solve the mystery and correct the apparent injustice of their existence.[16] The Man of the Crowd, apparently, is an even more radical version of Cain, one who has lost all consciousness of Eden and become, as Genesis predicts, a creature of the city. His deep crime, so far as we can tell, is not an act but a condition of profound alienation and despair. William Wilson too, that "outcast of all outcasts most abandoned," is a type of Cain, driven paradoxically by his own conscience, as Byron's Cain is by his sense of justice, into a life of crime.[17]

## III

According to W. H. Auden, the psychological appeal of detective stories is precisely to the sense of guilt we inherit from Cain. They are parables, he argues, of innocence restored, of an ideal world of order disrupted by a murder and set right again by the detective god. As such, however, they are a literature of fantasy and escape, less significant as art than, say, *Crime and Punishment* because less accurate concerning the mystery of human suffering.[18] Poe's Dupin stories, however, have long been ascribed the high artistic purpose Auden would deny them. For example, one of the earliest admirers of Poe's detective tales, the French journalist E. D. Forgues, believed that the ultimate aim of Poe's use of the Calculus of Probabilities to describe the methods of Dupin was "to subdue an obstinate unknown quantity by the power of induction, to neutralize the resistance it offers to reason, and to gain mathematical certainty in regards to moral problems" and "eternal Principles."[19] Forgues observes a similar purpose in much of the fiction of the day:

> There are as many enigmas as there are tales and all of them take diverse forms and guises. Whether wearing the fantastic livery of Hoffman or the grave and magisterial costume of Godwin renovated by Washington Irving or Dickens, it is always the same combination which sets Oedipus and the Sphinx by the ears—a protagonist and a puzzle...an impenetrable mystery of the intellect, which irritated...by the veil stretched before it, solves the enigma after incredible operations of the mind rendered in the most minute detail.[20]

In Forgues's view the solved mystery predominates, and he prefers Poe's ratiocinative tales because they contain a logic that "has all the appearance, if

not the reality," of subduing the unknown. In these tales, Forgues argues, Poe is the logical master of cosmic mysteries, whereas in tales like "The Man of the Crowd" and "The Black Cat" he is merely a poet, "an inventor of objectless fantasies, of purely literary whims."[21] As Sidney Moss noted in bringing Forgues's essay to light, he fails to see the connection between these two kinds of tales.[22] The confrontation between protagonist and puzzle is present in both, but logic and minute detail prove no match for the mysteries in "The Man of the Crowd," "The Black Cat" and "Ligeia."

The metaphysical purpose Forgues attributes to the tales of ratiocination really belongs to the unsolved mysteries. Dupin's success, in fact, results largely from a shift to mysteries of a lower order. It may be, as Edward Davidson suggests, that crime in the Dupin stories disrupts the ostensible order of things to permit a glimpse of an ideal world beyond,[23] but Dupin is not directly engaged with the ideal. He is as ardent a student of Transcendentalism as the narrator of "Ligeia," but the mysteries he solves are material. They are *outré* but not occult, brutal or clever but not, like the mystery of the Man of the Crowd, deep. Indeed, the paradox upon which Poe builds his detective tales nullifies the problem of the unsolved mysteries. "Truth is not always in a well," Dupin tells the narrator in "Murders," but "as regards the more important knowledge, I do believe that she is invariably superficial" (*M*. 2:545). So much for the mystery of Ligeia's eyes, "more profound than the well of Democritus." Contrary to what Dupin suggests when he scoffs at the police for holding the object of their investigation too close, or failing to realize that a star is more clearly seen when looked at askance, this is more than a difference of how we look at truth. The cosmic mystery in "Ligeia" is reduced in "Murders" to the dimensions of the typical whodunit. Dupin circumscribes the mystery himself when he dismisses the possibility of the occult: "It is not too much to say that neither of us believe in praeternatural events. Madame and Mademoiselle L'Espanaye were not destroyed by spirits. The doers of this deed were material, and escaped materially" (*M*. 2:551).

Still Poe tries to have it both ways with Dupin. By confining him to an investigation of material crimes, Poe satisfies those doubts about the power of human understanding that prevail in the unsolved mysteries, but he characterizes Dupin's analysis as a "moral activity which disentangles," which partakes of the reciprocal laws of physics and metaphysics (*M*. 2:528; 3:989). The true analyst displays "a degree of *acumen* which appears to the ordinary apprehension praeternatural. His results, brought about by the very soul and essence of method, have, in truth, the whole air of intuition" (*M*. 2:528). In these propositions about the faculty of analysis, Poe attempts to bridge the distinction, current in the psychology of his day, between the

rational and imaginative faculties, between the discriminating powers that tie us down to the material world and the creative intuition that elevates us to the ideal.[24] The method of the true analyst, according to Poe's narrator in "Murders," is the converse of the artist's creative process. The question remains, though, whether Dupin's analysis in practice is the "metaphysical acumen" it is supposed to be in theory. Donald Stauffer maintains that it is. Dupin's solutions "are actually flashes of intuition" which "approach that vision of the ultimate unity of all things which [Poe] was to set down in its final form in *Eureka*."[25]

Stauffer asks us to suspend our disbelief, however, in an illusion that Poe himself discredits. In "The Mystery of Marie Roget" his narrator admits that Dupin's solution of the Rue Morgue murders "was regarded as little less than miraculous" only because the "simple character of those inductions by which he disentangled the mystery" were never explained to the police or the public. Although Dupin's "analytic abilities acquired for him the credit of intuition," his "frankness would have led him to disabuse every inquirer of such prejudice" (*M.* 3:725). Ironically, the narrator himself is guilty of promoting such prejudice, for he functions chiefly to convey the impression that Dupin's solutions are miraculous flashes of intuition.[26] Poe's strategy in the detective tales, to paraphrase the narrator of "Murders," is to make Dupin's solutions *appear* preternatural to the ordinary intellect, to give them the whole *air* of intuition, while revealing that they are, in fact, brought about by the very soul and essence of logical method. The effect is achieved by Dupin's unexpected announcement to the bewildered narrator that he has solved the mystery, making it seem like clairvoyance. Then Dupin backtracks to explain the chain of reasoning that led to his conclusion. Not preternatural, Dupin's analysis seems no less marvelous, for even when explained it appears abstruse to ordinary intellects like the narrator.

In "Murders" the narrator offers his tale "in light of a commentary upon the propositions" he has advanced regarding the faculty of analysis, propositions that link analysis to intuition and imagination. He then tells of his acquaintance with the eccentric Dupin, who has withdrawn from the world to dwell in the gloom of "a time-eaten and grotesque mansion." The narrator reinforces the suggestion of his initial propositions by connecting Dupin's "rich ideality" with "a peculiar analytic ability" that he exercises in reading men's thoughts. The first example of Dupin's analysis is thus presented by the narrator as an act of clairvoyance. Strolling with the narrator one night near the Palais Royal, Dupin suddenly breaks in upon his companion's thoughts as if to read his mind. Astonished, the narrator asks for an explanation and Dupin traces his interruption back to the last remarks they

exchanged by a series of inferences he drew from the narrator's movements and mumblings. The method is inductive, although the accuracy of Dupin's inferences does some violence to the calculus of probabilities. But the anecdote establishes the pattern for the murder mystery to follow. What seems preternatural to the narrator turns out to be quite rational, though no less astonishing.

Dupin's solution to the murders is more strictly logical than his mind-reading. This time he follows up and verifies conclusions drawn initially from newspaper accounts of the murders by visiting the scene of the crime, making sure that his "deductions are the *sole* proper ones, and that the suspicion arises *inevitably* from them as the single result" (*M.* 2:550).[27] Still his solution comes as a surprise to the narrator and the reader. Having shared with us the newspaper accounts of the murder of Madame L'Espanaye and her daughter, the narrator tells briefly of Dupin's investigation of the scene, carried out "with a minuteness of attention for which I could see no possible object" (*M.* 2:546). Just at this point, when the narrator is about to throw up his hands at the peculiar circumstances of the crime, Dupin reveals that he has solved it. Again, his acumen seems uncanny, but only because his method has not been fully revealed to us.

Dupin reaches his conclusion not in a flash of intuition but by means of inductive reasoning and some careful detective work. He explains that he began with a suspicion, engendered by the newspaper reports of the murders and "sufficiently forcible to give a definite form—a certain tendency—to my inquiries in the chamber" of the victims (*M.* 2:550). His sleuthing at the scene of the crime, where, the narrator tells us, he "scrutinized everything—not excepting the bodies of the victims" (*M.* 2:546), may seem hypocritical in light of his ridicule of the "vast parade of measures" employed by the police, but it serves actually to point up the logical nature of his investigation. Whereas the methods of the police are "ill adapted to the objects proposed" (*M.* 2:545), Dupin's are adjusted to the circumstances of the crime. His investigation is directed by logic rather than routine. He goes to the scene of the crime having already inferred from the newspapers that the assailant is "absolutely alien from humanity." How else to explain the horrible brutality of the crime, the apparent lack of motive and means of escape, and the shrill utterances that several witnesses of different nationalities all describe as sounding "foreign"? Guided by a reasonable suspicion, Dupin can uncover evidence that the police overlook and explain circumstances that they cannot.

The logical method that governs Dupin's investigation at the scene of the crime becomes evident when he asks the narrator to consider first the

problem of the "hermetically sealed" room. Having dismissed the possibility of preternatural causes, Dupin reveals that he eliminated all the means of egress except two fourth-story windows, apparently nailed shut, which overlook the rear courtyard where the body of Mme. L'Espanaye was found. The police are stymied when the windows resist their efforts to open them, but Dupin reasons that "all apparent impossibilities *must* be proved to be not such in reality" (*M.* 2:552). He discovers that the windows are fastened not only by visible nails but by hidden springs. If it were not for the nails, one of the windows could have been open, enabling the murderer to enter and escape, tripping the spring as he went. Dupin tries the nails and finds that one of them has long been broken in place. Reasoning, as he says, *a posteriori,* from effect (the murderer was material and escaped materially) to cause, Dupin can explain the "impossible" and narrow his suspicion. The extraordinary agility required to scale the wall to enter or leave by the window confirms his idea of the alien nature of the criminal.

Dupin's explanation of how he solved the problem of the sealed room brings the narrator only slightly nearer the truth. Finally Dupin must produce a key piece of evidence, a tuft of coarse hair from the grasp of the mutilated Mme. L'Espanaye, which even the narrator can see is "no *human* hair" (*M.* 2:558). Dupin confirms that it belongs to "the large fulvous Ourang-Outang of the East Indian Islands" (*M.* 2:559). That the police could overlook this clue and others noticed by Dupin seems unlikely, but it is the literary license Poe exercises to keep us guessing and to emphasize his point. The clues are missed and consequently withheld from us because the police and the narrator cannot logically adjust their investigation to fit the crime. Proceeding *a priori,* from the assumption that the murderer is human, they are blind to evidence of the inhuman.

According to G. R. Thompson, Poe's strategy in "Murders" typifies "the basic ironic technique" of his fiction. The rational and supernatural are kept in tension by Dupin's reasoning, which works in effect to bring the narrator and the reader to a "flesh-creeping sense of the uncanny." Just when we are unnerved by the realization of "a *grotesquerie* in horror absolutely alien from humanity" (*M.* 2:558), Dupin calmly provides further evidence and explanation of his solution. In Thompson's view, "the sense of grotesque horror is momentarily increased by Dupin's matter-of-fact tone and then dissolved abruptly by the rational explanation" in the end.[28] The irony, I would suggest, however, is of a different sort. The rational explanation does not so much *dissolve* the sense of the uncanny as *displace* it. Poe wants us to accept finally the legitimacy of Dupin's reasoning, but he wants us to regard it with awe. To the ordinary intellect, it should appear preternatural. Poe antici-

pates here what Jacques Barzun takes to be the defining characteristic of detective fiction: an intense interest in the material world, in the "inescapable necessity in the workings of physical nature."[29] In the detective story, the real and rational are marvelous. Surely Poe means to evoke our wonder at Dupin's unravelling of physical circumstance:

> "To use a sporting phrase, I had not been once 'at fault.' The scent had never for an instant been lost. There was no flaw in any link of the chain. I had traced the secret to its ultimate result,—and that result was *the nail* ....'There *must* be something wrong,' I said, 'about the nail.' I touched it; and the head, with about a quarter of an inch of the shank, came off in my fingers (*M*. 2:553)."

Detective fiction, Barzun claims, is "the romance of realism."[30] Poe's narrative strategy in "Murders" makes for precisely this kind of romance. The narrator's propositions about the faculty of analysis and the tale he offers to illustrate them work to produce an ironic verisimilitude, making the matter-of-fact seem wonderful, the rational appear preternatural.

David Ketterer suggests that Dupin is a "viable Usher," living in the gloom of a "time-eaten and grotesque mansion...tottering to its fall" (*M*. 2:532) yet able to avoid the universal disintegration that overcomes Usher by "the potent combination of intellect and imagination."[31] Dupin, however, is not confronted by the kind of occult mystery that haunts Roderick Usher. "If he is a seer," David Halliburton contends, "he is a seer of circumstances."[32] Unlike the protagonists in the unsolved mysteries, who draw us into an investigation of metaphysical problems, Dupin limits us to a consideration of physical crimes. His detective work is only loosely connected to the metaphysical by analogy. In "Marie Roget," for example, Poe suggests that his attempt in fiction to solve an actual crime demonstrates an analagous parallel between real and ideal events, between the physical and metaphysical realms—clearly a faulty logical extension. There is nothing metaphysical about this tale, just painstaking and sometimes fallacious "deduction."[33] That he did not pursue the connection between the physical and metaphysical further in the Dupin stories, Halliburton suggests, "indicates Poe's recognition that the detective tale had boundaries that it could not cross without becoming another kind of work."[34]

I do not mean to minimize Poe's accomplishment in the detective tales. They are ingenious and they endure, as Philip Van Doren Stern once observed, because they are more artful and probing than much of the detective fiction they spawned.[35] Viewed in relation to the broader pattern of Poe's mystery and detection, though, they cannot be called his best tales or even his

best mysteries. "Ligeia," "Usher," "William Wilson" and "The Man of the Crowd" are more compelling because more akin to our experience of mystery in the world. In tales like "William Wilson" and "Usher," according to S. K. Wertz and Linda L. Wertz, we find "genuine mystery." This is to be distinguished from the "problem" in "Murders" or the "puzzle" in "The Gold-Bug," solved respectively by acquiring new knowledge or clarifying what we already know. For "genuine mystery" there is no objective solution because the inquirer finds himself involved in, or part of, the mystery he investigates. His inquiry leads to a preternatural encounter with the terms or limits of his own existence. Such is the experience, as we have seen, of the narrators in Poe's unsolved mysteries. Whereas "genuine mystery," according to the Wertzes, "provides the basis for a more comprehensive understanding of human existence," the detective tales smack of "a bogus act of abstraction" from existence, a pretense to objectivity and control that falsifies experience.[36]

Poe's own sense of the bogus pretension of the detective tales informs his letter to Cooke and may explain why he abandoned the form in 1844, parodying it in "The Oblong Box." In this tale the narrator's comic ineffectiveness as a sleuth "illustrates the speciousness of an intellectual system out of touch with the problems of human fallibility and mortality."[37] Thus, just four years after the invention of Dupin, Poe returns by means of irony to the point of "The Man of the Crowd." The narrator here is no better a detective than the narrator in "The Oblong Box," but his perplexity is a response to the genuine human mystery his decadent counterpart does not even see.

## IV

There is some evidence in Poe's criticism of the mystery and detection genre that he regarded the unsolved mystery as the work of higher imagination. Just a month after "Murders" appeared, Poe published a "Prospective Notice" of Charles Dickens's *Barnaby Rudge,* then only partially serialized. He followed up a few months later with a full review of the completed novel, claiming to have solved Dickens's murder mystery in the earlier notice. The real value of the review, however, lies in Poe's perception of the disadvantages of mystery writing.[38] Dismissing the historical pretext of the novel and reading it primarily as a mystery, Poe observes that in narratives like *Barnaby Rudge,* where "every point is so arranged as to perplex the reader and whet his desire for elucidation," the author arouses an interest in many points that would otherwise be dull but only at the expense of obscuring those points which are most interesting, those which enable us to see how and why the

mystery came about. According to Poe, this is why mysteries like *Barnaby Rudge* are better reread. He contends, moreover, that the mystery writer is not likely to satisfy the curiosity he arouses; "the anticipation [of the denouement] must surpass the reality," especially where there is, as in *Barnaby Rudge*, "a skilful intimation of horror held out by the artist....These intimations—these dark hints of some uncertain evil—are often rhetorically praised as effective—but are only justly so praised, where there is *no denouement* whatever—where the reader's imagination is left to clear up the mystery for itself—and this is not the design of Mr. Dickens."[39] Poe articulates here a rationale for the unsolved mystery of deep crime or evil. In criticizing Dickens for failing to resolve his mystery effectively, Poe perhaps justifies his own method in "Murders" of initiating Dupin's solution halfway through the tale, balancing anticipation with explanation, but he also seems to define a mystery of higher imagination. Dickens, Poe claims, is no mystery writer at all; he is best at "tales of ordinary sequence. He has a *talent* for all things, but no positive *genius* for *adaptation*, and still less for that metaphysical art in which the souls of all *mysteries* lie."[40] By "adaptation" Poe means the art of *mimesis* in complex narrative, of ravelling and unravelling a sequence of events so as to maintain an illusion of truth or probability. This art, he suggests to Cooke, accounts for the ingenuity of his detective tales. Yet this he relegates to "the metaphysical art in which the souls of all *mysteries* lie." Poe is evidently distinguishing between those webs of plot the mystery writer weaves for the express purpose of unravelling and those mysteries of the human condition, those "dark hints of some uncertain evil," which cannot be explained.

Poe had not only a talent but a positive genius for both kinds of mystery. His genius for both, however, reflects a sharply divided view of the human condition. Man's fate in the unsolved mysteries is to become conscious of his mortal limitations; in the detective tales it is to transcend them in the exploits of Dupin. As Auden suggests of all detectives in fiction, however, Dupin is the product of fantasy. He answers to our wish for escape from the reality of human suffering and uncertainty. Poe could not sustain Emerson's faith that "we have no questions to ask which are unanswerable...that whatever curiosity the order of things has awakened in our minds, the order of things can satisfy."[41] The correspondence between real and ideal events, between the human and divine, that Emerson perceived by means of an intuitive "Reason" eluded Poe's imaginative ratiocination. Still, when he abandoned his detective in 1844, he did not forsake the faculty of analysis but continued to use it in tales like "Mesmeric Revelation" (1844) and "The Power of Words" (1845) to address more directly the ultimate questions of life, death and the

hereafter. In his late work, *Eureka,* Poe sought by means of ratiocination to solve the metaphysical mystery of the origin and destiny of the universe. He offers *Eureka* as a "Prose Poem" or "Romance," a work of imaginative analysis in which the artistic unity is to make manifest the divine order of things. Poe aims for the ultimate *mimesis,* but he is forced to admit, even as he tries to convince us to the contrary, that the artist's skill at "adaptation" must fall short of unravelling the plot of God.[42] Despite the sometimes prophetic wisdom of *Eureka,* it seems to me to confirm finally the vision of the unsolved mysteries. His cosmogony describes a universe whose inexorable movement towards annihilation intimates some horrible, uncertain evil and whose mysteries remain all insoluble.

## NOTES

[1] *The Delights of Detection* (New York, 1961), p. 12. Others acknowledging Poe as inventor of the detective story are Arthur Conan Doyle, *Through the Magic Door* (London, 1907), p. 114; Dorothy L. Sayers, *The Omnibus of Crime* (New York, 1929), pp. 9-10; Ellery Queen, *101 Years' Entertainment: The Great Detective Stories, 1841-1941* (Boston, 1941), p. vi; Howard Haycraft, *Murder for Pleasure: The Life and Times of the Detective Story* (New York, 1941), p. 12; A. E. Murch, *The Development of the Detective Novel* (1958; rpt. New York, 1968), p. 83; Julian Symons, *Mortal Consequences: A History—From the Detective Story to the Crime Novel* (New York, 1972), p. 27; Benjamin Franklin Fisher IV, "Blackwood Articles á la Poe: How to Make a False Start Pay," *RLV,* 39(1973), 418-432. The most serious challenge to Poe's patent is R. F. Stewart's *'...And Always a Detective': Chapters on the History of Detective Fiction* (North Pomfret, VT, 1980), ch. 2.

[2] See Edward Davidson, *Poe: A Critical Study* (Cambridge, MA, 1957), pp. 217-222; Stuart Levine, *Edgar Poe: Seer and Craftsman* (Deland, FL, 1972), pp. 166-167; and David Ketterer, *The Rationale of Deception in Poe* (Baton Rouge, 1979), pp. 221-222, 238.

[3] *O.* 2:328.

[4] *O.* 2:329. In the same year Poe wrote Evert Duyckinck that "Ligeia" is "undoubtedly the best story I have written" (*O.* 2:309). Two years earlier, in a letter to James Russell Lowell, Poe listed his "best tales" in the following order: "Ligeia," "The Gold-Bug," "The Murders in the Rue Morgue," "The Fall of the House of Usher," "The Tell-Tale Heart," "The Black Cat," "William Wilson," and "A Descent into the Maelstrom" (*O.* 1:258).

[5] *Edgar Poe: Seer and Craftsman,* p. 166.

[6] The characterizations belong to Levine, p. 162, and Robert Daniel, "Poe's Detective God," *Furioso,* 6(1951), 45-54.

[7] See for example Poe's "Letter To B——," *H.* 7:xxxv-xliii and his reviews of Thomas Moore's *Alciphron,* 10:65-67; Longfellow's *Ballads and Other Poems,* 11:73-80; and "Tale Writing...Hawthorne," 13:148-149.

[8] *Tales, Essays, and Sketches by the Late Robert Macnish, LL.D.* (London, 1844), 2:56. J. Lasley Dameron was the first to notice the similarity between "Who Can It Be?" and "The Man of the Crowd," *Popular Literature: Poe's Not So Soon Forgotten Lore* (Baltimore, 1980), pp. 8-10. Macnish and Irving were in fact parodying a fashionable genre. Irving classifies "The Stout Gentleman" with those stories "greedily sought after at the present day" about "mysterious personages that have figured at different times, and filled the world with doubt and conjecture; such as the Wandering Jew, the Man in the Iron Mask, who tormented the curiosity of all Europe; the Invisible Girl, and last, though not least, the Pig-faced Lady" — *Bracebridge Hall* in *The Works of Washington Irving* (New York, 1909), 3:47.

[9] *Blackwood's Edinburgh Magazine,* 22(1827), 433.

[10] Ibid. Macnish, a doctor, was well known for his interest in unusual states of consciousness, having authored popular treatises on *The Anatomy of Drunkeness* and *The Philosophy of Sleep.*

[11] *M.* 2:511. Further references to Poe's tales will be to this edition.

[12] *Blackwood's* 22(1827), 437.

[13] *Ellery Queen's Poetic Justice...* (New York, 1967), p. 86.

[14] See n. 2.

[15] "Byron's *Cain:* A Romantic Version of the Fall," *KR,* n.s. 2(1980), 52.

[16] Hester and Billy are explicitly compared to Cain in chapter 5 of *The Scarlet Letter* and chapter 3 of *Billy Budd,* although Ahab perhaps more obviously bears his mark.

[17] The first murder is also suggested by Montresor's killing of Fortunato in "The Cask of Amontillado." Seeking revenge for the "thousand injuries" Fortunato has done him, Montresor seems to strike out like Cain against a capricious fate. His revenge recalls the jealous motive of Cain's crime. "For the love of God," Fortunato cries out as Montresor walls him up in the wine cellar. "Yes," Montresor replies, "for the love of God!" (*M.* 3:1263).

[18] "The Guilty Vicarage," *The Dyer's Hand* (New York, 1962), pp. 157-158. Cf. Daniel, "Poe's Detective God," p. 54 and Daniel Hoffman, *Poe Poe Poe Poe Poe Poe Poe* (Garden City, 1973), p. 129.

[19] Forgues's essay, entitled *"Etudes sur le Roman Anglais et Americain,"* appeared in *Revue Des Deux Mondes,* n. s. 5(1846), 341-366. I quote the translation of Sidney P. Moss in "Poe as Probabilist in Forgues' Critique of the *Tales," New Approaches to Poe: A Symposium,* ed. Richard P. Benton (Hartford, 1970), p. 4.

[20] Ibid.

[21] Ibid., p. 10. Forgues was reviewing the edition of the *Tales* (1845) that Poe characterized the next year in his letter to Cooke as too full of the ratiocinative.

[22] Ibid., p. 11.

[23] *Poe*, p. 217.

[24] Donald B. Stauffer, "Poe as Phrenologist: The Example of Monsieur Dupin," *Papers on Poe: Essays in Honor of John Ward Ostrom*, ed. Richard P. Veler (Springfield, O, 1972), pp. 118-119.

[25] Ibid., pp. 121-122.

[26] Daniel—"Poe's Detective God," p. 49—observes of Dupin that his "success seems intuitive, but really results from the methodical analysis of data" (p. 48).

[27] Poe uses the terms "inductive" and "deductive" loosely. Although parts of Dupin's investigation proceed deductively, his conclusions following necessarily from certain premises, he is at the scene of the crime to narrow his suspicion about the murderer. Verifying, or making more certain, a suspicion or inference is part of the process of inductive reasoning. Even when Dupin announces to the narrator that he has solved the crime, he is not wholly certain of his conclusions (*M.* 2:548).

[28] *Poe's Fiction: Romantic Irony in the Gothic Tales* (Madison, WI, 1973), p. 119.

[29] "From Phaedre to Sherlocke Holmes," *The Energies of Art* (New York, 1965), pp. 307-308.

[30] *The Delights of Detection*, p. 11.

[31] *The Rationale of Deception in Poe*, p. 243. Cf. Daniel, "Poe's Detective God," p. 46.

[32] *Edgar Allan Poe: A Phenomenological View* (Princeton, 1973), p. 239.

[33] For the fallacies in Poe's tales of ratiocination, see William K. Wimsatt, Jr., "Poe and the Mystery of Mary Rogers," *PMLA*, 55(1941), 230-258 and J. Woodrow Hassell, Jr., "The Problem of Realism in 'The Gold-Bug'," *AL* 25(1953), 179-192.

[34] *Poe: A Phenomenological View*, p. 245. There are readings that take the detective tales to be a different kind of work than I am suggesting. See for example Richard Wilbur's "The Poe Mystery Case," *New York Review of Books*, 13 July 1967, pp. 16, 25-28; Daniel Hoffman's *Poe Poe Poe Poe Poe Poe Poe*, pp. 103-133; Jacques Lacan's "Seminar on 'The Purloined Letter'," trans. Jeffrey Mehlman, *YFS*, 48(1972), 38-72; and David I. Grossvogel's *Mystery and Its Fictions: From Oedipus to Agatha Christie* (Baltimore, 1979), pp. 96-105. These readings tend to emphasize, in fact, the *unsolved* mysteries in the detective tales—the submerged identification of Dupin with the perpetrator or victim of the crime, especially the cunning Minister D—— and the Queen in "The Purloined Letter," or the undivulged contents of that letter—uncovering in the tales a metaphysical, psychoanalytic, or semiotic significance. Although provocative and often plausible, these readings seem to me to miss the central point of the Dupin stories. Man's metaphysical aspirations, his fragmented psychology, and the failure of his understanding and language to comprehend the mystery of his condition are more squarely addressed in "Ligeia," "Usher," "William Wilson" and "The Man of the Crowd." These themes are submerged in the Dupin stories not so that we might uncover them in a kind of allegory but so that Dupin's faculty of analysis might prevail. Poe is not so much concerned with mystery in the detective tales, strange as that may seem, as with solutions. The operation of Dupin's reason in the solution of a crime is what Poe wants to hold our attention. The suggestion of unsolved mystery in

"The Purloined Letter" is especially rich, perhaps signalling the end of Dupin, but the elaborate, subtlety of some of the psychological and semiotic readings calls to mind Dupin's parting shot in "Murders" at the Prefect of Police, who, "somewhat too cunning to be profound...has *'de nier ce qui est, et d' expliquer ce quin n' est plas'* " (M. 2:568).

[35] "The Case of the Corpse in the Blind Alley," *VQR*, 17(1941), 227-228.

[36] "On Poe's Use of 'Mystery'," *PoeS*, 4(1971), 7-10.

[37] J. Gerald Kennedy, "The Limits of Reason: Poe's Deluded Detectives," *AL*, 47(1975), 195.

[38] J. Brander Matthews, "Poe and the Detective Story," *Scribner's Magazine*, 42(1907), 287-293; *The Recognition of Edgar Allan Poe*, ed. Eric W. Carlson (Ann Arbor, 1966), p. 84.

[39] *H.* 11:49-50, 58.

[40] Ibid. p. 64.

[41] *Selections from Ralph Waldo Emerson*, ed. Stephen E. Whicher (Boston, 1957), p. 22.

[42] *H.* 16:291-292.

# EDITH WHARTON AND "THE CASK OF AMONTILLADO"

*ELEANOR DWIGHT*

During Edith Wharton's childhood, New York society condemned "that drunken and demoralized Baltimorean"[1] as an atheist and blasphemer; consequently, the books of Edgar Allan Poe were banned from her father's library. Still we can be confident that she read them sooner or later, although, says R.W.B. Lewis, "Poe resonated less in her imagination" than Whitman.[2] Because Wharton tended to avoid acknowledging authors who influenced her, Americans in particular, one must seek clues in what she wrote.[3] Such clues suggest that her attitude towards Poe was ambiguous. Poe is "a Great Poet" to Lewis Raycie, the hero of *False Dawn* (1924), who is ahead of his time in appreciating Italian "primitives."[4] In "Telling a Short Story" (1924) Wharton calls Poe "sporadic and unaccountable" but praises him as an originator of the modern short story. She puts his original stories in "that peculiar category of the eerie which lies outside of the classic tradition."[5]

They both wrote stories of the supernatural, but Wharton's differed in that she aimed for a more restrained effect. She once deplored those who wrote about "the pathological world" where the action takes place "between people of abnormal psychology" and does not "keep time with our normal human rhythms"—a description that fits what she called the "awful hallucinations" of Poe's stories.[6] Wharton's plots aim to frighten the reader with just a glimpse into Poe's world, but she used his techniques—most remarkably in "The Duchess at Prayer." (1902).

In an 1899 letter Walter Berry, Wharton's life-long friend and literary mentor, discussed a story she was writing, "The Duchess at Prayer." "I'll be delighted to hear the whyness of La Grande Bretèche. How about the Cask of Amontillado?"[7] They had been reading ghost stories, for two months before Berry wrote: "I'm crazy about *The Turn of the Screw*. Have read it twice and isn't it creepyness besides all the rest."[8] And in December, 1898: "I'm delighted that you have loosened the first stone in your cell toward an escape... Meantime I see you de- and re-articulating Pelican, thrusting old bones under the pillow whenever there's a rattling at the door handle."[9] Obviously Wharton had read "The Cask of Amontillado," and she uses it for "The Duchess at Prayer."

As Blake Nevius has pointed out, "The Duchess at Prayer" is "unmistakably a reworking of Balzac's plot"[10]—which may have reduced what Wharton was paid for it. Berry wrote in November, 1899: "If the whole atmosphere individualizes the story so completely as to differentiate it from the Grande Bretèche, the fact that there *is* a resemblance should not be reason for a cut in rates."[11] Although the plot is adapted from "La Grande Bre-

tèche, aspects of the dialogue and setting must be attributed to "The Cask of Amontillado." The ending is also Poesque: the serene face of a marble statue becomes distorted by a grimace of horror.

In Balzac's story the narrator had often visited a deserted house near Vendome called "La Grande Bretèche," where he would pass the time alone in "debauches of melancholy."[12] Three people from Vendome eventually tell him the story of the house. It had once belonged to Conte de Merret. The notary describes how he was summoned to the deathbed of the Count's widow: Her "fleshless hands resembled bones covered by a stretched skin, their veins, their muscles were perfectly visible...Never had a living creature attained to such thinness without dying."[13] Madame's will left the house to the notary, but he was charged to leave it for fifty years as it was the day of her death "forbidding the entrance into the apartments to anyone whatsoever, prohibiting the slightest restoration, and even allowing an annual sum to secure guardians, if they should be necessary, to insure the complete execution of her intentions."[14] From the innkeeper our narrator hears about a lodger who once stayed there, a young Spanish prisoner of war, small, handsome, with "black hair, great eyes of fire"[15] and the finest linen Mère Lepas had ever seen. Every night he would go out to return at midnight, until one night he failed to return and was never seen again. Mère Lepas suspected his disappearance had something to do with Madame de Merret, for Rosalie, Madame's maid, once told her that the crucifix she loved and was buried with was of ebony and silver, and the Spaniard had an ebony and silver crucifix with him when he came to stay at the inn. Rosalie, who now works there, tells the heart of the story.

The Count's custom was to go to his club after dinner, but one evening he returned home two hours later than usual and instead of retiring to his upstairs bedroom, he decided to visit his wife's room on the ground floor and tell her how he lost at billiards: "His foot steps, easily recognisable, resounded under the archway of the corridor."[16] As he approached he thought he heard someone shut the closet door, but on entering he found his wife alone before the fire. When he demanded if there was someone in the closet, his wife denied it, swearing on a crucifix of silver and ebony. The Count then ordered the wardrobe to be walled up with plaster and bricks, despite his wife's efforts to distract him so her lover could escape—for at one point the maid caught a glimpse inside and saw his anguished face, with dark hair and eyes. For twenty days the Count refused to leave: "During the first moments when some sounds would be heard in the walled-up cabinet and when Josephine wished to entreat him for the dying unknown, without permitting her to say a single word: 'You have sworn on the cross that there was no one there.' "[17]

"The Duchess at Prayer" is also set in a large old house, a villa near Vicenza in the seventeenth century. Neglected by her husband the Duchess Violante had spent a long lonely winter there. She prayed frequently in the chapel and had taken to visiting the crypt, where the bones of Saint Blandina were kept. Her husband's lively cousin Ascanio, with whom she shared many interests, had not been seen at the villa for some time. When her husband returned unexpectedly from Rome with a statue of her by Bernini, she became horrified at his plan to use it to block the entrance to the crypt. In vain she tried to dissuade him from his project, to coax him to leave her alone. The statue was emplaced; they dined together; and the Duchess swooned when the Duke toasted the absent cousin. After suffering dreadfully all night, she died. When the servant girl went to the chapel to pray for her mistress, she heard a "low moaning"; "coming in front of the statue she saw that its face, the day before so sweet and smiling, had the look on it that you know—and the moaning seemed to come from its lips."[18]

Balzac's tale does not lack for atmosphere. Hearing about the disappearance of the Spanish prisoner the narrator says: "My hostess left me a prey to vague and shadowy thoughts, to a romantic curiosity, to a religious terror sufficiently like that profound feeling that takes possession of us when we enter at night into some somber church where we perceive a feeble, distant light under the lofty arches; an undecided figure slips along, the rustle of a robe or of a cassock is heard—we shiver."[19] The wasted, dying countess lying in her enormous bed in the chamber hung with brown tapestries is a scene worthy of Poe: "icy, and more than that, funereal."[20] Wharton duplicates Balzac's house of mystery, the motivation, a jealous husband's revenge, and method of telling the story, but for her ending and other chilling details, she goes to Poe.

Although the crisis of Balzac's story takes place in the bedroom, Wharton choses the chapel and its crypt, an underground setting like that of "The Cask of Amontillado." In Poe's story the vengeful but outwardly genial Montresor coaxes his victim Fortunato, pathetically dressed in carnival costume, with bells jingling, down through the long dark passageway, dripping with moisture, and littered with the bones of the dead, into the inner recesses of the crypt. There he chains him to the granite and entombs him by walling up the passageway. In "The Duchess at Prayer" the characters reach the entrance to the crypt, where the Duke and Duchess pause and converse. But the details of dampness, bones and cold stone are all there, as is the dominating horror, a victim buried alive.

Like Poe, Wharton uses dialogue to advance the action. In "The Cask of Amontillado" Montresor and Fortunato discuss business while they descend

into the vault, ostensibly to taste a rare sherry. The reader knows that Montresor plans to avenge himself on Fortunato; thus the dialogue is filled with irony. In Wharton's story, because the Duchess' lover is hiding in the crypt and the Duke plans to trap him there, the reader is also aware of the irony in their conversation.

When Montresor presents his victim with a bottle of Medoc from the cellar and says "drinks":

> He raised it to his lips with a leer. He paused and nodded to me familiarly, while his bells jingled.
>
> "I drink" he said, "to the buried that repose around us."
>
> "And I to your long life."[21]

When the Duke and Duchess dine together they toast to Ascanio, who is dying in the crypt:

> "Here's to the cousin," she cried, standing, who has the good taste to stay away when he's not wanted. I drink to his very long life—and you, Madam?"
>
> At this the Duchess, who had sat staring at him with a changed face, rose also and lifted her glass to her lips.
>
> "And I to his happy death," says she in a wild voice; and as she spoke the empty goblet dropped from her hand and she fell face down on the floor.[22]

Another borrowing is Wharton's use of the word "pleasantry" as Poe used "joke" and "jest." Early in their confrontation when the Duchess recognizes her husband's purpose in blocking the crypt with Bernini's statue, she says:

> "I recognize there one of your excellency's pleasantries—"
>
> "A pleasantry?" the Duke interrupted....
>
> "You will see," says the Duke "this is no pleasantry, but a triumph of the incomparable Bernini's chisel."[23]

When Fortunato realizes Montresor's purpose he says desperately:

> "Ha! ha! ha!—he! he! he!—a very good joke, indeed—an excellent jest. We will have many a rich laugh about it at the palazzo—he! he! he!—over our wine—he! he! he!"
>
> The Amontillado!" I said.[24]

After Montresor finishes the first tier of masonry he senses that Fortunato's intoxication is wearing off, for he hears "a low moaning cry from the

depth of the recess." Wharton's servant girl also hears "a low moaning," as if coming from the statue. Poe ends his story:

> Against the new masonry I re-erected the old rampart of bones. For the half of a century no mortal has disturbed them. *In pace requiescat!*[25]

And Wharton's ending:

> "And the crypt?" I asked. "Has it never been opened?"
> "Heaven forbid, sir!" cried the old man, crossing himself. "Was it not the Duchess' express wish that the relics should not be disturbed?"[26]

In both stories the murder has been successfully concealed. Poe graphically describes the fate of Fortunato and horrifies readers with the cool and calculating way Montresor has lured his prey to a ghastly death. Wharton lets us imagine the victim's agony, once he has been trapped in the crypt. In Wharton's story the wife replaces Fortunato, for the effect of her husband's revenge must be observed from how she behaves, with readers conscious of her guilty secret.

The motives for revenge differ, and, like Balzac, Wharton introduces a second victim, the mistress of the murdered lover, where Poe's story focuses on two characters, the murders and his intended victim, with the murderer himself explaining how he has succeeded. Fortonato's innocence makes the reader want to cry out a warning, but particularly in the Wharton story we identify with the women bereft, more than with her murdered lover, whom we scarcely get to know. A theme common to the three stories, however, is the way the murderer exploits weakness: Fortunato is vain and greedy; the Duchess and the Countess are both paralyzed by a guilty conscience.

Montresor tells us at once that Fortunato "had a weak point." Unlike Balzac, who suggests nothing about the personality of the Countess and her attraction to the Spanish prisoner, Wharton makes it easy to imagine why the flighty and fun-loving young wife succumbed to her cousin's charm. The process whereby the stronger character identifies and plays on his advantage over the other is the same in the Poe and Wharton stories. The avenger is in control of the dialogue, as he is in control of the situation, but his victim is handicapped—Fortunato by his gullibility and the Duchess by the enormity of her adultery. In Balzac's story the ironic verbal duel is missing. The Count immediately confronts his wife: "Madame, there is someone in your cabinet![27] When she denies it, he begins his revenge, and the only hint of irony flows from his pretending to believe is wife's denial because she has sworn on the crucifix.

Although the Poe and Wharton stories share the elements noted, the atmosphere of each story is distinctive. The world of Wharton's story is neat and tidy and the murder is never mentioned; the world of Poe's is bizarre and terrible, and the murder is described in exquisite detail. Because they hear the tale from the murderer, Poe's reader is forced into this highly-charged atmosphere. Wharton's narrators, on the other hand, are not emotionally connected to the action, and at first do not even recognize its deadly nature. The story reaches the reader third-hand: the caretaker of the villa learned it from his grandmother, who was the Duchess' maid, and he tells it to a visitor, so that the reader remains distanced from the horror. Outwardly all is well in Wharton: the Duchess is beautifully dressed, the fastidious order of Wharton's world is maintained, husband and wife keep up the pretense of normality (as one must in front of the servants). Horror is evoked by the reader's imagination.

Only in the ending do we get a glimpse of the fantastic. Like a living being, the face of Bernini's statue of the Duchess has recorded the dreadful murder it alone witnessed. A not uncommon nineteenth-century literary conceit was the concept of the art work that comes alive or reflects human behavior. An example is Poe's own "Oval Portrait." In other Poe stories, like "Ligeia" and "Morella," a spirit is transferred between bodies. When the statue lives for an anguished moment in which a ghastly grimace replaces its smile, Wharton is using a Poesque device to surprise the reader into acceptance of the fantastic, unreal and impossible.

Wharton clearly borrowed from Poe for "The Duchess at Prayer." She wrote eleven other stories of the supernatural, which draw on her personal horrors, as Lewis has explained.[28] On the surface they seem very different from Poe's tales, but do they owe something to Poe? In Wharton's ghost stories a woman is almost always the central character and the setting a large and gloomy house remote from the rest of the world. The woman is unhappy, abandoned, or sick. All that takes place is generally logical and consistent with everyday life. In each story, however, one strange event surprises the reader: the appearance of a ghost or an apparition, the mysterious disappearance of characters, or the control of living characters by those already dead.

Wharton's stories differ from Poe's in that they are understated and less obviously frightening. There are no crazed narrators or decomposing bodies, few settings like that of "The Fall of the House of Usher." In Poe's world of nightmare, strange images act according to the laws of the subconscious. Wharton's world is usually conventional. Her technique was first to gain readers' confidence, then to lure them into an incredible adventure:

> When the reader's confidence is gained the next rule of the game is to

avoid distracting and splintering his attention. Many a would-be tale of horror becomes innocuous through the very multiplication and variety of its horrors. Above all, if they are multiplied they should be cumulative and not dispersed. But the fewer the better: once the preliminary horror is posited, it is the harping on the same string—the same nerve— that does the trick. Quiet iteration is far more racking than the diversified assaults; the expected is more frightful than the unforeseen.[29]

This technique is the antithesis of Poe's. At critical moments, however, Poe's presence emerges in her tales. In "The Eyes" a man who has out of vanity promised to help someone, and then failed to follow through, is haunted at night by the apparition of a pair of ghastly eyes:

They were the very worst eyes I've ever seen: a man's eyes—but what a man! My first thought was that he must be frightfully old. The orbits were sunk, and the thick red-lined lids hung over the eyeballs like blinds of which the cords are broken. One lid drooped a little lower than the other, with the effect of a crooked leer; and between these folds of flesh, with their scant bristle of lashes, the eyes themselves, small glassy disks with an agate-like rim, looked like sea pebbles in the grip of a starfish.

But the age of the eyes was not the most unpleasant thing about them. What turned me sick was their expression of vicious security.[30]

Was Wharton inspired by "The Tell-Tale Heart": "I think it was his eye! yes, it was this! He had the eye of a vulture—a pale blue eye, with a film over it. Whenever it fell on me, my blood ran cold."?[31] Or was it by the teeth in Poe's "Berenice"?

The teeth!—the teeth!—they were here, and there, and every where, and visibly and palpably before me; long, narrow, and excessively white, with the pale lips writhing about them, as in the very moment of their first terrible development.

...and still I sat buried in meditation, and still the *phantasma* of the teeth maintained its terrible ascendancy as, with the most vivid and hideous distinctness, it floated about amid the changing lights and shadows of the chamber.[32]

Was the strangling of the dogs in "Kerfol" suggested to Wharton by the strangling of the cat in "The Black Cat"? Other Poe-like details Wharton used were ghosts who are only seen by one person, mournful settings, moans and shrieks, all stock Gothic details, but wonderfully developed by Poe.

In her ghost stories, therefore, as in "The Duchess at Prayer," Wharton seldom leaves the everyday world for Poe's world of the raving and obsessed where logic disappears. When bizarre or ghastly circumstances appear in a Wharton story, they occur off-stage, like the death of the Duchess' lover. The reader's imagination must provide the graphic details, but Wharton knew her. Poe and she borrowed from him in her own way. Except for "The Duchess at Prayer," how much is a matter of conjecture.

## NOTES

[1] Edith Wharton, *A Backward Glance* (New York, 1934), p. 68.

[2] R.W.B. Lewis, *Edith Wharton, A Biography* (New York, 1975), pp. 236-237. Professor Lewis sees Poe's influence in Edith Wharton's short story, "The Bolted Door."

[3] See R.W.B. Lewis, *Edith Wharton, A Biography*, p. 237.

[4] Edith Wharton, *False Dawn* (New York, 1924), pp. 28-33.

[5] Edith Wharton, "The Writing of Fiction," *Scribner's Magazine*, 77(1925), 344.

[6] Edith Wharton, "The Writing of Fiction," *Scribner's Magazine*, 76(1924), 576-577.

[7] Walter Berry, Letter to Edith Wharton, 9 January 1899. Permission to publish Berry's letters has been graciously granted by the Collection of American Literature, in the Beinecke Rare Book and Manuscript Library, Yale University.

[8] Walter Berry, Letter to Edith Wharton, 2 November 1898.

[9] Walter Berry, Letter to Edith Wharton, 7 December 1898. "Pelican" is another story she was then writing.

[10] Blake Nevius, *Edith Wharton, A Study of Her Fiction* (Berkeley, 1961), p. 154.

[11] Walter Berry, Letter to Edith Wharton, 6 November 1899.

[12] Honoré de Balzac, "The Grande Bretèche," *Another Study of Woman*, trans. William Walton, *The Human Comedy* (Philadelphia, 1897), 22: 264.

[13] "The Grande Bretèche," p. 271.

[14] "The Grande Bretèche," p. 273.

[15] "The Grande Bretèche," p. 278.

[16] "The Grande Bretèche," p. 285.

[17] "The Grande Bretèche," p. 293.

[18] Edith Wharton, "The Duchess at Prayer," *The Collected Short Stories of Edith Wharton* (New York, 1968), 1: 244.

[19] "The Grande Bretèche," p. 281.

[20] "The Grande Bretèche," p. 271.

[21] "The Cask of Amontillado," *M.* 3: 1259.

[22] "The Duchess at Prayer," p. 243.

[23] "The Duchess at Prayer," pp. 239-240.

[24] "The Cask of Amontillado," *M.* 3: 1263.

[25] "The Cask of Amontillado," *M.* 3: 1263.

[26] Edith Wharton, "The Duchess at Prayer," p. 244.

[27] "The Grande Bretèche," p. 286.

[28] See R. W. B. Lewis, "Powers of Darkness," *Times Literary Supplement*, 13 June 1975, pp. 644-645.

[29] Edith Wharton, "The Writing of Fiction,," *Scribner's Magazine*, 77(1925), 344.

[30] Edith Wharton, "The Eyes," *The Collected Short Stories of Edith Wharton*, 2: 120.

[31] "The Tell-Tale Heart," *M.* 3: 792.

[32] "Berenice," *M.* 2: 215-216.

# KILLIS CAMPBELL (1872-1937)

*D. M. McKEITHAN**

Killis Campbell, son of Robert C. and Alice (Hawes) Campbell, was born on 11 June 1872, at Enfield, nineteen miles northeast of Richmond, in King William County, near the center of Tidewater Virginia. He attended the public schools of his native township until his sixteenth year. In the fall of 1888 he became a student at the College of William and Mary at Williamsburg and remained there for two sessions. Having secured a Peabody scholarship in 1890, he transferred to the University of Nashville in the fall of 1890 and studied there until June, 1892. He was awarded the Bachelor of Arts degree in 1891 and the Bachelor of Letters degree in 1892.[1] Neither the short autobiography at the end of his doctoral dissertation nor the brief biography in the *Alumni Directory of Peabody College, 1875-1909* throws any light on his whereabouts or activities during the academic year of 1892-1893. Possibly he was earning money to continue his education.[2] In the fall of 1893 he enrolled a second time in the College of William and Mary and graduated with a second Bachelor of Arts degree in June, 1894.

For the next four years (1894-1898) he was a graduate student at Johns Hopkins University, where his mentor was James Wilson Bright, Professor of English. He took courses in English language and literature under Professor James Wilson Bright and Professor William Hand Browne, in German under Professor Wood and Dr. Learned, and in French under Drs. Menger, Marden, and Rambeau. During his first three years at Johns Hopkins he held a Hopkins scholarship, and during his fourth year he held a fellowship in English. He graduated with the Ph.D degree in 1898.

His doctoral dissertation, *A Study of the Romance of The Seven Sages with Special Reference to the Middle English Versions,* appeared in *Publications of the Modern Language Association of America,* 1899 (XIV, No. 1), but the printers, John Murphy & Company of Baltimore, had issued it separately in the summer of 1898 as a publication of the Modern Language Association of America, indicating on the back of the title page that it had been "Reprinted from the *Publications of the Modern Language Association of America,* Vol. XIV, No. 1."

The main purpose of the dissertation was to "investigate thoroughly the relations of the Middle English versions" of the collection of popular stories known as *The Seven Sages of Rome.* A preliminary section, however, reviews the history of the romance, its origin in the Orient, its transmission to the Occident, and its popularity in France and Italy. In this first part, Campbell says, he depends mainly on the investigations of other scholars, especially Gaston Paris of France.

In the second and major portion of the study Campbell relies mainly on original study of the eight Middle English versions, in as many different manuscripts, all in verse, which he analyzes and collates in an attempt to establish relationships. He has much to say about authorship, dialects, and sources and adds an account of sixteenth-century and chap-book versions. To examine manuscripts and rare books he had spent the summer of 1897 in Britain reading in various libraries, including those at the British Museum, Balliol College and Cambridge University. It is an admirable scholarly study, written in an eminently readable style. It received favorable notice in *Romania* (Gaston Paris), in the *Beiblatt zur Anglia,* and in the *Revue Critique.*

After one year, 1898-1899, as English Master at Culver Military Academy in Indiana, he joined the staff of the "School of English" at the University of Texas. In 1899-1900 there were only four members of the staff:

Professor Liddell
Professor Callaway
Instructor Campbell
Tutor Heard

The catalogue for 1900-1901 lists six:

Morgan Callaway, Jr., Professor of English
Killis Campbell, Instructor in English
Pierce Butler, Instructor in English
Mary B. Heard, Tutor in English
Cora Waldo, Tutor in English
Edgar E. Townes, Fellow in English

In an announcement in October, 1899, concerning new members of the faculty the University of Texas *Record* (I, No. 3, p. 351) stated: "He [Killis Campbell] brings with him strong recommendations both in respect to character and scholarship, and an enthusiasm which will certainly bear rich fruit in his teaching." The editor prophesied better than he knew, and every year for over a generation Killis Campbell was admired more and more for his character, his scholarship, and his enthusiasm for teaching. He remained at the University of Texas until he died in 1937. He began as instructor, became adjunct professor in 1906, associate professor in 1911, and professor in 1918. In 1912-1914 he served as chairman of his department, still known as the School of English.[3]

In 1902 Killis Campbell married Mary Hogg Aitken of Baltimore. To them were born five children—a girl, twin girls, and twin boys. Alice,

Katherine and Mary, Hawes and Killis. All the children graduated from the University of Texas and all of them, together with their mother, survived him.

He delighted in literature and in teaching it but considered it his duty to teach students how to write. For twenty years after he arrived at the University, no one in his department gave more time than he to teaching composition. During the whole of that period he taught Freshman English every year, and in the years 1919-1921 he was in general charge of the course, as he had often been in earlier years. Thereafter he taught it from time to time until 1925.

He established English 3, English composition for sophomores, and taught it every year from 1899 to 1920. In 1909 he set up a course in composition for juniors and seniors. English 25, and taught it every year until 1925, at which time he turned it over to Miss Erma Gill and Mrs. Annie Irvine. Thereafter he continued to give much attention to composition in his courses in literature. Even in his graduate seminars he assigned a ten-page essay to be handed in at the end of the first two weeks, and his graduate students soon learned that he expected them to be writers as well as scholars.

When Professor Campbell came to Texas, the sophomore survey of English literature was called English 2: Outline History of English Literature, and the catalogue lists him as a teacher of the course every year from 1902 to 1919. Thereafter he taught it occasionally until 1926.

One of his favorite courses for a decade was the poetry of Milton, which he began teaching in 1904-1905. In 1914-1915 he turned the course over to Evert Mordecai Clark but taught it one more time in 1917-1918. The catalogue for 1906-1907 announced that Killis Campbell would teach English 7: Outline History of the English Novel. It came down to and included Meredith. It also included one American, Nathaniel Hawthorne. In 1912-1913, when he served as chairman of the School of English, he gave the course to James Blanton Wharey but began teaching it again next year although he was still chairman. In 1916 he relinquished the course to Professor Wharey, who taught it thereafter until he retired.

Although trained as a specialist in Anglo-Saxon and Middle English language and literature, Killis Campbell began moving into American literature at the very beginning of his teaching at the University of Texas. The catalogue for 1899-1900 lists as one of his courses English 11: The Literature of the South. The next year the number was changed to English 8. In 1903-1904 he began teaching English 11: American Poetry. Both courses were for juniors and seniors. The course in the literature of the South was discontinued after 1906, probably because he was especially interested in poetry and

because Poe and Lanier were included in the poetry course. The numbers of these and other courses were changed from time to time. Eventually the American poets were given in two one-semester courses, English 337 and 338, and Professor Campbell continued teaching them with enthusiasm and pleasure until his final illness began, in the fall of 1936. In 1915 a course in American prose was set up with his assistance and taught for the next twenty years by Leonidas Warren Payne, Jr. After Professor Campbell's death the poetry and prose courses were combined.

Killis Campbell became a professor in 1918, and in 1918-1919 for the first time began giving a graduate seminar, English 138: Studies in American Literature. The number of the seminar remained 138 until 1924, it was 238 for the next two years, and after that his seminars were 388 and 389. The topic was Lowell from 1918 to 1925 by which time he had decided that Lowell was not substantial enough for a graduate seminar. Other writers, including Emerson, became the topic from time to time until he settled down to three and gave them in turn—Hawthorne, Poe (short stories), and Whitman.

In the same year, 1918-1919, his assignment included English 20, which by this time had become a course for students writing a thesis for the Master of Arts degree.[4] In those days only professors were permitted to direct M. A. theses; and there were only three professors in the department—Callaway, Campbell, and Royster[5]—although Griffith, Law, and Payne became professors the following year.

In the years 1919-1936 master's theses were completed under the direction of Killis Campbell on Willa Cather, Dickens, Emily Dickinson, Emerson (5), Rufus Wilmot Griswold, Bret Harte, O. Henry (2), Hawthorne (3), Lafcadio Hearn, Irving, Charles Kingsley, Lanier, Vachel Lindsay, Longfellow, Amy Lowell (2), William Vaughn Moody, Frances Sargent Osgood, Poe (5), Maurice Thompson, Mark Twain (3), Edith Wharton, Whitman (6), and Whittier.

He also directed master's theses on the following topics: The Beginnings of the Short Story in America, Birds in American Poetry, Birds in American Prose, Blank Verse in American Literature Before 1850, Farm Life in Early American Fiction, The Gothic Element in American Literature, The Indian in American Poetry of the Nineteenth Century, Industrialism in American Poetry, Literary Fads and Fashions in America in the 1830s, Literary Fads and Fashions in America in the 1840s, Orientalism in American Poetry up to 1900, The Origin of Transcendental Thought in America, The Sea in American Poetry, Sectionalism in American Poetry, Society Verse in American Literature, The Sonnet in American Literature, Symbolism in American Literature, and Tradition in American Literature. Eight of these theses were

completed in 1936, in Professor Campbell's last year of teaching (1935-1936).

In 1927 Floyd Stovall received the first degree of Doctor of Philosophy in English ever conferred by the University of Texas. He wrote his dissertation on Shelley with Reginald Harvey Griffith, but he had been a student of Killis Campbell, specialized thereafter in Poe and Whitman, dedicated his edition of the poems of Poe to Killis Campbell, and ended his career as Poe Professor at the University of Virginia.

The first dissertation directed by Killis Campbell was on Whitman's debt to Emerson. Arlin Turner, known for his writings on Hawthorne and Cable, as well as his years as Editor of *American Literature*, wrote his dissertation on Hawthorne under the direction of Killis Campbell. Characteristically, Turner's "Acknowledgements" to *Nathaniel Hawthorne: A Biography* (1980), completed long years after his original training, reveal gratitude to his former teacher: "First, I would name Professor Killis Campbell, who guided my first study of Hawthorne and who, by precept and his own example, made responsible literary research and effective writing seem to be goals worth pursuing" (p. ix). Arlin Turner's first publications and his last professional address—to the Poe Studies Association: 28 December 1979, in San Francisco—centered upon Poe. These, and his entire career, demonstrated that Killis Campbell's precepts were well heeded. Campbell also directed Mrs. Alice Cooke's dissertation on Whitman's background in the life and thought of his time. Subsequently Mrs. Cooke taught Whitman at the University of Texas until she retired. He directed other dissertations on Whitman, began several on Poe that were completed after his death, and many articles written in his Poe, Hawthorne, and Whitman seminars were later published.

The teaching of a variety of courses and reading of countless student papers did not prevent his serving on committees at all levels or working in other ways for the good of the University. A former colleague, Professor A. L. Bennett, told me recently that he took a course in Anglo-Saxon taught by Professor Killis Campbell one summer in the late 1920s. It was very characteristic of him to volunteer to teach the course when no regular teacher of the course was available. "Al" said that he and the other students thought their teacher knew the subject thoroughly.

From 1902 until 1908 he was a member of the Catalogue Committee of the General Faculty and had a share in the editing and proofreading of numerous University catalogues. Almost every year from 1903 until his death he was a member of the Committee on University Publications. At times there was no separate committee on catalogues, so his work on them might have continued for a long time, as indicated in the next paragraph.

His assignment as a member of the Committee on University Publications varied. In March, 1904, he was listed as editor of the "Official Series" of University of Texas publications, which was explained thus: "A fourth series [of bulletins] is the *Official,* which is to contain such Bulletins as the catalogues, the Reports of the Board of Regents, the catalogues of the Summer Schools, etc., etc."[6] He was editor of the Official Series at least until June, 1906.[7] He was a member of the Committee on Official Publications from time to time as long as he lived.

He became editor of the University of Texas *Record* with Volume VI, No. 3, February 1906. This bulletin was a quarterly containing detailed information about nearly all affairs of the University—growth and development, new construction, enrollment, additions to the faculty, resignations, deaths, publications of the faculty, directories of faculty and students, commencements, alumni news, the Library, meetings on the campus, public addresses (sometimes printed in full), actions of the Regents, annual reports of the president and faculty, student life, athletics, literary societies, student publications, student organizations, and other matters. Killis Campbell edited No. 3 and No. 4 of Volume VI and all numbers in Volume VII and Volume VIII. Each of the volumes contained well over 300 pages.

Inside the front cover of the *Record,* Volume X, No. 4, 22 April 1911, he is listed as "Editor-in-Chief of Publications of The University of Texas." University publications were issued four times a month, arranged in series: Record, Mineral Survey, General, Humanistic, Medical, Scientific, Reprint, University Extension, Official and Press. If there were giants in the earth in those days, Killis Campbell must surely have been one of them. When his health finally broke down in September, 1936, his colleagues Griffith and Law were sure that the cause was his overworking for the good of the University. Fortunately, he did not remain editor-in-chief very long, for he had a conscience which required him to do his work with thoroughness and care, and his health might have broken down sooner than it did.

In several numbers of the *Record* issued in 1909-1911, I found reports on the Fortnightly Club signed R. A. L. (Robert Adger Law). One report named Killis Campbell as treasurer of the club and two gave the titles of two papers he had read at club meetings, "The Widow of Ephesus" and "Poe and Plagiarism Once More."

Killis Campbell founded the University of Texas *Studies in English,* as a bulletin of the University of Texas, in 1911 and edited it until the fall of 1936. At first it followed no time schedule. The first three numbers were monographs by single authors: No. 1 (8 April 1911), *English Elements in Jonson's Early Comedy* (328 pages), by Charles Read Baskervill; No. 2 (15 November

1914), *A Study in Shirley's Comedies of London Life* (68 pages), by Hanson T. Parlin; No. 3 (15 July 1915), *Joseph Dennie and His Circle: A Study in American Literature from 1792 to 1812* (285 pages), by Milton Ellis. The last sentence in Parlin's Preface reads: "In the work of getting it through the press, it would be hard for me to express what I owe to my friends Professor Killis Campbell and Mr. R. W. Fowler of the University of Texas." Baskervill, Parlin, and Ellis were members of the School of English at Texas. Baskervill moved to the University of Chicago, Ellis moved to the University of Maine, Parlin remained at the University of Texas and became Dean of the College of Arts and Sciences.

No. 4 of *Studies in English* was dated 15 March 1924. It was a volume of scholarly articles by Frank F. Covington, Jr., Robert Adger Law, James Blanton Wharey, Reginald Harvey Griffith, Fannie E. Ratchford, Evert Mordecai Clark, and Killis Campbell. Similar volumes appeared annually thereafter.

Between No. 3 and No. 4 of *Studies in English* there was a gap of nine years, but Editor Campbell was not idle. During the period of 1915-1922 he edited the first ten numbers of *The English Bulletin*, "an organ for the expression of opinion by teachers of English in Texas concerning pedagogical and other problems that arise in their work." The ten numbers were dated December 1915, March 1916, November 1916, December 1917, November 1918, November 1919, December 1919, September 1920, November 1921, and December 1922.

Many numbers of this publication, a bulletin of the University of Texas, contained four articles totaling about thirty-five pages. No. 1 contained articles by Morgan Callaway, Jr., Robert Adger Law, Killis Campbell, and Gates Thomas. Articles for No. 2 were written by Thomas Ewing Ferguson, Mary Johnson, Alexander Corbin Judson, and Earl Lockridge Bradsher. Authors who appeared in No. 3 were James Finch Royster, Pauline Belle Warner, Leonidas Warren Payne, Jr., and Robert Adger Law. In his writing for this bulletin Killis Campbell insisted that English teachers in the Texas public schools should be well qualified, that they should not be overburdened with other assignments, and that stress should be placed on student writing.

From 1909 to 1916 he was chairman of the Committee on Admission and Condition Examinations. From 1913 until his final illness he was chairman of the Committee on Attendance at Professional Meetings. From 1914 to 1916 he was a member of the Faculty Council. But it would be pointless to continue the catalogue. All the committees mentioned above were committees of the General Faculty, and Killis Campbell was always willing to do a

fair share of work on committees of the Department of English, the College of Arts and Sciences, and the Graduate School.

After he reached the rank of professor in 1918, he was a member of the Budget Council of the English Department, the largest department in the University and constantly growing. Many of its problems were the business of the Budget Council, including recruitment, promotions, and salaries, and the number of hours required to do its work was often incredible.

Over the years Killis Campbell was a faithful member of the Modern Language Association of America and often attended its annual meetings and participated in the discussions. He presided as chairman at the first meeting of the American Literature Group, which he had helped to establish, at the annual meeting of the MLA, at Johns Hopkins in 1921. The secretary was elected for another term, but according to the minutes, "Professor Campbell asked to be excused from continuing as Chairman on account of ill health." He was not especially robust, but he remained active and continued working as hard as ever for the next fifteen years. He was a member of the Executive Council of the MLA for the years 1924, 1925, and 1926 and served the association as Vice President in 1934.

It often happens that the best teachers and committee workers are also the best scholars, though it is a mystery how they find the time for all these activities. Killis Campbell did. Moreover, he was devoted to his wife and children and gave them more time than most men give their families.

Mary and Hawes Campbell compiled *A Bibliography of the Writings of Killis Campbell* from their father's notes soon after his death. It covers five magazine pages.[8] The items are arranged chronologically from 1898 through 1936, and the only intervening years not appearing in the list are 1900, 1906, and 1932. In 1899-1900 he was getting settled in Austin with new courses to teach, in 1906 he was seeing a book through the press, and in 1932 he was preparing research lectures for publication.

The bibliography begins with an article and a book published in 1898: "The Sources of Davenant's *The Siege of Rhodes*"[9] and his doctoral dissertation, previously mentioned. At the end appear these items under 1936, his last year of work:

"A Word of Explanation," *American Literature,* 8:463-464 (January)

"Recent Additions to American Literary History: A Collective Estimate," *Studies in Philology,* 33:534-543 (July)

"A New Life of Irving" (a review of S. T. Williams' *The Life of Washington Irving), Sewanee Review,* 44:372-377 (July)

"Poe's Treatment of the Negro and of the Negro Dialect," The University of Texas *Studies in English,* 16:106-114 (July)

Review of David K. Jackson's *Poe and the Southern Literary Messenger*, *Modern Language Notes*, 51:487-488 (November)

A Facsimile of the 1831 Edition of *Poe's Poems*, Facsimile Text Society, pp. viii, 124

Nearly half of the notes and articles listed are on Poe (23), and another discusses Poe, Longfellow, and Lowell. His edition of the poems of Poe (1917) was the most scholarly edition of the work of any American poet. He wrote the chapter and compiled the bibliography on Poe for the *Cambridge History of American Literature* (1918). Seventeen of the book reviews were on Poe, and half a dozen others were on Poe and other writers.

The notes, articles, and reviews appeared in the *Dial* (19), *Modern Language Notes* (17), the *Nation* (10), the *Sewanee Review* (7), Texas *Studies in English* (7), *American Literature* (7), *Publications of the Modern Language Association of America* (5), *Studies in Philology* (4), the Dallas *News* (4), the *Journal of English and Germanic Philology* (3), *The English Bulletin* (2), The New York *Evening Post Literary Review* (2), the *Alcalde* (2), and one each in the *University of Texas Bulletin* (No. 156), the *Weekly Review*, *Modern Language Review*, the *Texas Outlook*, the *William and Mary Quarterly Historical Magazine*, and the *Dictionary of American Biography*. Although Killis Campbell's major scholarship dealt with Middle English romances and the life and writings of Poe, his notes, articles, and reviews indicate wide reading in English and American literature.

In his dissertation on the Middle English versions of "The Seven Sages of Rome" he had expressed his hope of bringing out an edition of the poem. To study the manuscripts he had spent the summer of 1897 at the British Museum, Oxford, and Cambridge. To continue his research he returned to Britain in the summers of 1902 and 1904 and worked mainly in the British Museum, the Bodleian Library at Oxford, and the Library of the University of Edinburgh.

His edition of *The Seven Sages of Rome*, published by Ginn & Company (Boston, New York, Chicago, London) in 1907, was fourth in the Albion Series of Anglo-Saxon and Middle English Poetry. The series was intended to comprise the most important Anglo-Saxon and Middle English poems, each volume to contain a single poem, critically edited, and provided with an introduction, notes, and a "full" glossary. The first three in the series were *The Christ of Cynewulf*, edited by Albert S. Cook of Yale, *The Squyr of Lowe Degre*, edited by William E. Mead of Wesleyan University, and *Andreas and the Fates of the Apostles*, edited by George Philip Krapp of Columbia. The general editors of the series were J. W. Bright of Johns Hopkins and G. L. Kittredge of Harvard. In his Preface Campbell says he has been "generously

aided by others" and acknowledges his debt to Professors Bright, Kittredge, and Callaway, all of whom had read the book in manuscript or in proof and had offered valuable suggestions.

In his exhaustive Introduction he discusses the Oriental versions of *The Seven Sages* and the transmission of the story to Western Europe, classifies the redactions made in France, Italy, Spain, Germany, Holland, Scandinavia, and Russia, and considers in detail the English versions, especially the two manuscripts (Cotton, and Rawlinson) represented in the text. After the Introduction he gives a long list of variants and analogues of the stories contained in *The Seven Sages*. The text of the poem covers pages 1-145. The notes cover 38 pages, the glossary covers 17, and the index covers 11. The index is detailed, the glossary is full, and the notes are generous. That it is a work of thorough scholarship was recognized by Professors Bright and Kittredge, who accepted it for publication in the Albion Series, by Professor Callaway, who read it before publication and reviewed it in the University of Texas *Record* [8 (1908), 49-50], and by reviewers in the *Athenaeum* (London: 4 May 1907) and the *Nation* [New York: 16 May 1907].

In an article entitled "Vacation Activities of the Faculty," in the University of Texas *Record* [8 July 1911] appears this item: "Dr. Campbell delved into libraries at Baltimore, Richmond, Washington, Philadelphia, New York, and other Eastern cities, for a similar purpose [i. e., "for research work"]."[10] What may be a related item appears in the *Record* for May 1912 (p. 313): "In the April *Sewanee Review* Professor Killis Campbell publishes some notable documents relating to the early life of Edgar Allan Poe, which have escaped the eyes of all Poe's biographers." He spent many summers in libraries in these and other cities, including Boston, doing spade work for future biographers[11] and gathering material for his edition of Poe's poems.

*The Poems of Edgar Allan Poe,* edited by Killis Campbell, was published by Ginn & Co. of Boston in 1917. I quote from the Preface:

> This edition of Poe's poems includes all the poems collected either by the poet himself or by his literary executor, Rufus W. Griswold. I have endeavored to give also a complete and accurate record of the multifarious revisions made by the poet in republishing his verses...; and I have departed from former editors in presenting these at the foot of the page along with the text to which they refer, where alone they may be easily consulted. In the Notes—and here, again, I have departed from former editors—I have given a full and detailed commentary on each of the poems. From the vast body of material, biographical, historical, critical, and interpretative, that has been written about Poe, I have endeavored to garner whatever will contribute to a truer understanding of his poems or to a juster appreciation of them. And where comment from others was

> wanting or seemed inadequate, I have attempted to supply the deficiency by researches of my own.

The Introduction (pp. xi-lxiv) contains six sections: The Main Facts in the Life of Poe, The Canon of Poe's Poems, The Text of Poe's Poems, Poe's Passion for Revising His Text, Poe's Indebtedness to Other Poets, and The Clash of the Critics with respect to Poe's Poems. The text of the poems, covering pages 1 through 135, is followed by four uncollected poems and other poems attributed to Poe. The voluminous notes cover 158 pages, 14 of which deal with "The Raven." Campbell tells us where the poem was first published and lists all places of republication up to 1850. He discusses the date and place of composition, the text, the origin and circumstances of composition, and critical estimates. Finally there are four pages of comments on particular lines, words, and phrases. The Appendix contains a collation of the editions published by Poe (1827, 1829, 1831, 1845), prefaces and prefatory notices, and "The Philosophy of Composition." There is an index of first lines and an index of titles, the latter referring both to the text and to the notes.

Killis Campbell's edition of Poe's poems is a superb work of editing and of scholarship. Moreover, in all his evaluations of Poe as man or writer he was fair and just. He fully recognized Poe's genius and his many gifts and virtues. On the other hand, nobody knew better than he all his weaknesses and shortcomings, and he made no effort to conceal them. The reviewer in the Boston *Transcript* was enthusiastic about it as the most important scholarship on Poe in years, used the descriptive words "admirable" and "excellently presented," and conjectured that its sobriety and sanity might be its greatest merit.

*Poe's Short Stories,* edited by Killis Campbell, was published in the American Authors Series by Harcourt, Brace & Company in 1927. In a prefatory notice the general editor, S. T. W. (Stanley T. Williams), states that in the series "the emphasis will be upon the text of a book rather than upon annotation or critical apparatus. Aside from footnotes essential to an understanding of the text, and a brief selected bibliography, editorial comment, for reasons of space, will be limited to a comprehensive introduction." With such limitations, Killis Campbell was prevented from doing as much for the stories as he had done for the poems. Nevertheless, he manages to get into the volume an impressive amount of information that only a first-rate scholar could have provided. The Introduction of seventeen pages, written in clear and graceful but compact style, contains criticism and analysis of a high order and a biographical sketch. The selected reading list gives the collected editions of Poe's works, the chief biographies, and books and articles relating

to Poe's stories. A "Note on the Text" signed K. C. states that "the text adopted for each of the stories is that of the latest known publication or revision which received the author's supervision and sanction." The "Bibliography of Poe's Stories and Sketches" (p. xxxiii) "includes the date and place of first publication of each of Poe's stories and sketches, and of each subsequent publication authorized by Poe, so far as is now known."

The catalogue of the University of Texas Graduate School for 1930-1931 states: "The University Research Professor for the session of 1930-1931 is Killis Campbell, Ph.D., Professor of English." He was elected by his colleagues on the faculty of the Graduate School. According to custom, he was relieved of all teaching during the year to do research, and he delivered a series of public lectures in the spring. I attended the lectures, remembered many of Professor Cambell's ideas and some of the phaseology as well as the hall where the lectures were delivered. I did not recall, however, how many lectures there were or when they were delivered, so I decided to check with the student newspaper, the *Daily Texan*. I found a file in the Barker History Center. April, I thought, would have been the best time for the lectures, so I began my search with the issue of 1 April 1931.

Almost immediately I began to feel entirely at home back in the early thirties, for I was reading about friends and neighbors of long ago. Edmund Quereau, Tutor in English, who had been my office mate for a time, had just won a scholarship to study at the University of Bordeaux. I haven't seen him since he left for the University of Bordeaux, but heard of him from time to time—teaching French at Westmoorland College in his home town, San Antonio, United States Consul at Dakar, married to a countess and living in the South of France. There were references to Professor Starnes, my colleague and neighbor on Park Place, and to Judge Stayton, Professor of Law, who lived across the street from us on Grandview. There was a column of University history by President Benedict and announcements of available scholarships by Dean Parlin. Dr. Floyd Stovall, who had been scheduled to read a paper on Whitman at the Fortnightly Club, had to be out of town, so Professor Robert Adger Law traded dates with him and read a paper on Shakespeare. Professor Slover, another friend in the English Department, had just been awarded a Guggenheim fellowship to study abroad.

I shook my head, scrambled back to the present age, went on with the search, and soon found, in the issue of Sunday, 5 April 1931, an announcement concerning Professor Campbell's lectures. The "daily" *Texan* did not appear on Monday, but another preliminary announcement of the lectures occupied a spot on page one on Tuesday, the day on which they were to begin. There were four lectures, all delivered in Garrison Hall Auditorium,

where meetings of the General Faculty were often held. Here is the schedule:

Tuesday, 7 April; 8 P.M. "Poe Myths and Their Makers"
Wednesday, 8 April; 5 P.M. "The Mind of Poe"
Thursday, 9 April; 5 P.M. "The Background of Poe"
Friday, 10 April; 10 A.M. "The Origins of Poe"

The lectures were well attended by faculty and students. Each lecture was reported next day on Page One of the *Daily Texan.*

Killis Campbell's *The Mind of Poe and Other Studies* was published by the Harvard University Press in 1933. In the Preface he does not mention his research professorship or public lectures. The volume contains seven studies: "The Mind of Poe," "Contemporary Opinion of Poe," "The Poe-Griswold Controversy," "The Backgrounds of Poe," "Self-Revelation in Poe's Poems and Tales," "The Origins of Poe," and "The Poe Canon." In his Preface and footnotes Professor Campbell states that the second, third, and seventh were reprinted with revisions and additions from *Publications of the Modern Language Association of America* and that the fourth had appeared in part in *Studies in Philology* under the title "Poe in Relation to His Times."

As in the case of each of his earlier books, the critics were much impressed by the thoroughness of Professor Campbell's scholarship. The reviewer in the Boston *Transcript* thought "Professor Campbell's estimates and comparisons are founded upon the rock of such careful and comprehensive research that it would seem no dispute of its criticisms could overturn it." Percy H. Boynton of the University of Chicago wrote in *Modern Philology* (31:101) that "in his seven studies he has included a sounder body of fact than I know where to look for in any other single work on Poe."

In the catalogues and announcements of courses for 1936-1937 Professor Campbell was scheduled to teach his usual courses: 337f (American Poets), 388f (Studies in American Literature), 338s (American Poets), 389s (Studies in American Literature), 98 (thesis), 99 (dissertation). In September 1936, however, he suffered a stroke from which he never fully recovered and teaching and research came to an end. He died early on the morning of Sunday, 8 August 1937, at the age of 65. He was buried in Oakwood Cemetery in Austin. In 1947 his wife Mary was buried at his side.

His oldest friend in the English Department, Professor Morgan Callaway, Jr., had died during the preceding year. I once heard him say of Professor Campbell, "I love him like a brother." Professor Reginald Harvey Griffith and Professor Robert Adger Law had joined the staff of the English Department in 1902 and 1906, respectively, and through the years they had been true and tried friends of Killis Campbell. They also loved him like a brother.

The University of Texas *Studies in English,* 17 (1937), was dedicated to Killis Campbell:

Dedicated
to
Killis Campbell
June 11, 1872 - August 8, 1937
Professor of English in The University of Texas
Founder and Editor of *Studies in English*
Teacher, Scholar, Gentleman

For the volume Professor Robert Adger Law wrote a sketch and a tribute, "Killis Campbell, 1872-1937," from which I quote these passages:

> Campbell was above all else a teacher and a scholar. Moved by a conscience worthy of his Scottish ancestry, he never shirked a teaching duty or allowed it to become burdensome. With ceaseless patience he would explain difficulties to the humblest of his students, or would assist through correspondence any distant scholar begging help in the solution of a baffling bibliographical problem....
>
> Few teachers in this institution have been more beloved of their disciples; none have, by sheer nobility of character, better deserved to be....
>
> But the list [of his publications] does not touch upon hours of labor spent in committee rooms to compile reports on military training, on faculty attendance at professional meetings, on the teaching of English composition in school and college, or more delightful hours indulged in fishing, in gardening, and, best of all, in companionship with his children and grandchildren....
>
> Genuine vacations, which he so much enjoyed, because fewer and briefer as the years went on, and were too frequently interrupted by the encroachments of students, who besought his aid, and the meticulous reading of proof for this periodical. Finally, Nature asserted her rights to a rest long denied, and in September, 1936, all work really ceased.

At a meeting of the General Faculty of the University of Texas on 9 November 1937, a resolution on the death of Killis Campbell was read by Reginald Harvey Griffith and adopted unanimously by the faculty. From it the following passages are quoted:

> As a teacher he was successful in an unusual measure, winning both the respect and the very deep affection of his students, and inciting them to an eagerness to learn....
>
> When Professor Campbell began teaching American literature here, about thirty years ago,[12] the subject was not in much repute among

colleges anywhere; he himself felt apologetic about it then. But his enthusiasm grew. Other colleges began offering similar courses. And he lived to see the subject spread out like a banyan tree. It came to be deemed a field worthy of 'investigation,' and therein Doctor Campbell was a leader....

As a colleague, neighbor, friend, Campbell possessed generous and endearing qualities. Wide, rich, tender in his sympathies, he was a support in endeavor, a counsellor in perplexity, a comforter in trials and sorrows. Never raucous, never a seeker after the applause of the mob, he was quiet, modest, dependable—a good companion. His sense of duty was stern, to his own cost in the end, for, driving himself in his labors for the University, he overtaxed his strength and shortened his life.

A gentleman, a scholar, and a Christian:—the fragrance of his memory will linger in the minds of those who knew him long after his voice is stilled in his last sleep.

D. B. Casteel
C. C. Glascock
R. A. Law
L. W. Payne, Jr.
J. B. Wharey
R. H. Griffith, Chairman

"In Memoriam Killis Campbell, 1872-1937," by Floyd Stovall and Tremaine McDowell, appeared in *American Literature* in March 1938. I quote these passages from it:

With the death of Killis Campbell, American literature lost one of its most distinguished scholars, and the Modern Language Association one of its most faithful members....

He was on the first Advisory Board of *American Literature* and served on the Editorial Board from January, 1933, until May, 1935....

His four books and his frequent contributions to the leading journals of the country bear witness to his great wealth of ideas and his tireless ability in research. As editor and critic of the writings of Edgar Allan Poe, in particular, his work is recognized as pre-eminent....

Distinguished though he was as a scholar, those who knew him personally valued him most as a teacher and as a man. For thirty-eight years, he was a member of the Department of English at the University of Texas, where he was loved and respected until his death....

In his dealings with colleagues and students, he was unfailingly courteous and fair....

With all the virtues of the traditional Southern gentleman, Professor Campbell was nevertheless the most democratic and the most beautifully simple of men. He loved animals and growing things, and was an enthusiastic gardener. More than ordinary men he cherished his friends, his family, and his home. His influence in America has been wide and deep, and it will not soon nor willingly be lost.

When I first arrived in Austin in June 1928, I had a greeting for Professor Campbell from Professor Lancelot Harris of the College of Charleston, who had been his classmate in the seminars of Professor James Wilson Bright at Johns Hopkins, where they graduated together as learned doctors in 1898. I also knew pretty well his edition of Poe's poems, though in the years that I knew him as teacher and colleague, neither he nor I ever mentioned that volume. After a conversation of half an hour, his welcome to Texas was so cordial that I felt, and never afterward had occasion to doubt, that he had taken me into his circle of friends.

I was a full-time instructor but took one graduate course each semester. During my first two long sessions in Texas I was studying Anglo-Saxon and Middle English with Professor Callaway, but the following semester I began taking Professor Campbell's seminars in Hawthorne, Poe, and Whitman, which were the only courses I ever had in American literature. He was on my doctoral committee and on the final oral examination—which in those days included everything from Gothic and Anglo-Saxon down to John Masefield and Robert Frost—he quizzed me at length on American literature but asked nothing about Hawthorne, Poe, or Whitman. He explained later, "I knew you had heard of those writers. I wanted to find out what you knew about others."

In his seminars he stated his opinions freely and clearly, but never dogmatically, and encouraged students to express opposing points of view, which he always considered with great courtesy, even when he found it necessary to point out how illogical and indefensible they were. He never employed ridicule or sarcasm in his relations with students or colleagues. His standards were high, and his will was like steel in defense of principles, but he never failed in kindness, courtesy, or generosity. Despite his superb gifts and achievements, he never had the slightest touch of arrogance, which he considered pitiful and inexcusable in a dean, a professor, or a bishop, though he might find it amusing in an instructor or a traffic cop.

I was never in a position to observe his relations with undergraduates, but his graduate students admired him fervently and eagerly sought to win his approval through study and hard work. He never seemed concerned about getting anything for himself but unselfishly sought to be of service to others. This was obvious in his relations with colleagues and students and at home with his wife, children, and grandchildren, all of whom adored him. In a long career most energetic and vigorous people have occasion to feel that they have at least one or two enemies, but Killis Campbell might very well have been an exception. At any rate, I never heard anyone speak of him except with great respect or admiration. He was an unselfish, generous, and lovable man.

## NOTES

*For permission to publish this sketch of Killis Campbell, gratitude to the Jay B. Hubbell Center for American Literary Historiography, Duke University, for which it was originally prepared, is acknowledged.

[1] Catalogues of the University of Nashville, Peabody Normal College, for the years 1890-1891 and 1892-1893 list graduates. Peabody Normal College operated under the charter of the University of Nashville from 1889 until 1909. George Peabody College for Teachers was incorporated under its own charter on 5 October 1909. On 1 July 1979, Peabody College was merged with Vanderbilt University as The George Peabody College for Teachers of Vanderbilt University. In a letter dated 1 August 1979, Evelyn Stephenson, Secretary, Archives Office, George Peabody College for Teachers, sent me this information about Peabody College and Killis Campbell's degrees, together with xerox copies of relevant pages in catalogues and the *Alumni Directory of Peabody College, 1875-1909.*

[2] This conjecture was correct. Mary and Hawes Campbell informed me on a visit in our home (19 January 1980) that their father spent the year as a salesman traveling with a friend who later practiced medicine in Texas. They were selling stereoscopic views, going as far west as Colorado, where they did a thriving business in mining camps. Hawes and Mary have a pedlar's permit for which Killis Campbell paid three dollars to do business in a town in Alabama.

[3] It remained "School" through the year 1919-1920 and became "Department" in the year 1920-1921.

[4] The course number was changed to 80 in 1926, to 98 in 1933.

[5] James Finch Royster.

[6] The University of Texas *Record,* V, No. 3, March 1904, p. 277.

[7] See the *Record,* VI (February, 1905 - June, 1906).

[8] The University of Texas *Studies in English,* 17 (1937), 10-14.

[9] *MLN,* 13 (June), 353-363.

[10] Vol. XI, No. 1, p. 68.

[11] In the Preface to his *Israfel: The Life and Times of Edgar Allan Poe* (1926) Hervey Allen expresses his appreciation to George E. Woodberry, James A. Harrison, Killis Campbell, and Thomas Ollive Mabbott "for the benefit of their labors in the Poe field, without which no competent comment on Poe would now be possible." In the Preface to his one-volume edition of *Israfel* (1934) Allen writes: "In particular I wish to thank Professor Killis Campbell, Thomas Ollive Mabbott, and S. Foster Damon for their emendations."

[12] In the session of 1899-1900.

# THOMAS OLLIVE MABBOTT

*HENRY W. WELLS**

I cannot refrain from a brief, unsolicited statement for the Jay B. Hubbell Center for American Literary Historiography concerning my friend, Thomas Ollive Mabbott, deceased, but still vivid in memory. I wish especially to emphasize the conclusion, so often to be drawn, that persons of high attainments have been to the manner born. Tom was from his early years clearly destined to be a research scholar and to dedicate his efforts to Poe. He persisted in his course virtually from youth to his final year, even leaving much of his work to be posthumously completed. I knew him best when he seemed scarcely passed boyhood; he certainly appeared unmistakably youthful. I saw relatively little of him during the many years of his distinguished teaching at Hunter College. Thus I knew him best as a fellow-student, not when he was a teacher, well-known and widely recognized in the scholarly world. For this very reason I may be in a position to add items of reminiscence or biography that few others can now supply, depicting him as I knew him intimately over half-a-century ago. He was one of the rarest of men, at least one of the rarest among us in his own times. I have often thought that it would take a Balzac to do him justice.

I first met Tom socially in an extremely old-fashioned and conservative hotel on Fifth Avenue, around the corner from Washington Square. I never had the opportunity really to know his parents, but in those early years he was to all appearances living with two elderly aunts. Henry James would have been hard put to imagine the formality of this social setting. Politically the climate was entirely Republican, a form of secular piety. I recall it best in terms of starched table napkins and a dining room hushed, even solemn. Even at that time Tom was completely entranced by Poe, with whom he had been joined in a child-marriage destined to last through a lifetime. There was no question about it; the two had met, never to part. I myself was of a totally different temperament where such orientation was concerned, but at least no one of my own inclinations could fail to love and admire Tom.

Although Poe was at the core of Tom's intellectual life, there was much more to him than that, though possibly it would better be said that into his studies of Poe he poured an extraordinary wealth of knowledge, richness of sensitivity and humanity. It is not, I trust, improper to describe him as a strange man; so was Poe, and Tom was peculiarly, possibly uniquely qualified to be the charioteer of that eccentric and romantic genius. There was genius there, even if of a secondary order. Tom was a virtuoso in scholarship no less than Poe in poetry, but you could not thrust Tom into any category; he was himself. Although unabashed in his many violently held opinions,

which an unsympathetic observer might term prejudices, he possessed a far-reaching mind, acquisitive and curious to explore—as did Poe—infinite corners in both light and shade.

Tom was a classicist as well as a romantic. This accorded with his chief hobby, numismatics. He possessed coins of virtually all the Roman emperors, several of his rarest pieces not duplicated even in the collections of the British Museum. With the meticulous care of a devoted collector, he kept his treasures in a cabinet of considerable elegance, exhibiting them to his friends as another collector might jewels. No one was less mercenary or less avaricious. He became a distinguished member of the Numismatic Society. He himself seemed as much at home in a great library as a plant in a botanical conservatory. His true home in New York was not that which I have attempted to describe in the Washington Square area but in his beloved library at Forty-Second street. Still dearer to him was the British Museum, with which he was in frequent correspondence. It was of interest to me that he also showed an admiration for the thoroughness and systematic procedure of so much German scholarship in the fields that especially attracted him. All his enthusiasm for learning notwithstanding, there were other sides to him. He enjoyed the company of people of many types and conditions; I recall his really warm friendship with an Irishman prominent in Tamany Hall and the New York Police Department. Although he certainly was himself a rare bird, it is just as certain that he was no snob. By no means was he a castrated chicken locked in an academic coop. He loved lyric poetry; truth to tell, he was at least normally inclined to the erotic. You could hardly decide whether he enjoyed more the odes of Sappho or Broadway musical comedy, where he frequently sat among the rows nearest the stage.

Devoted as he was to the man as well as to the book, he showed a natural admiration for distinguished scholars whom he met. None stood higher in his esteem nor was held more warmly in his heart than the Editor-in-chief of *The Cambridge History of American Literature* and specialist in Daniel Defoe, William P. Trent, his teacher at Columbia. Trent, as we knew him during his latter years as teacher, had some physical infirmities. It seemed altogether natural that Tom should carry the heavy cluster of books and papers that Trent invariably transported to his lecture hall. I, too, admired Trent. It is a pleasure as I think of the two in my mind's-eye trudging together slowly up and down the extensive flights of ceremonious steps at Columbia between Philosophy Hall, a building in the high Renaissance style, and that monument in the Neoclassical manner, Low Memorial Library, in its imposing architecture seemingly less a library than a mausoleum.

If Tom remained remarkably faithful to his promise in youth and to his

intellectual commitments and ideals, he nonetheless altered radically in physical condition. The young man I knew best was tall, slender, willowy in his movements—endowed with an appetite equally prodigious and that of an acutely refined gourmet. When at the height of his academic career—owing, perhaps, to sitting overlong in library chairs—he became stout, slightly awkward, with more than a slight zest for the bottle. Others will know him best and speak best of him as a mature scholar. For several years he was one of my three or four most intimate friends, and he had a pronounced talent for friendship. Just why for so many years we drifted apart is a perplexing question. We should not have done so, for physically only Central Park stood between us. Tom seemed, however, not greatly in favor of cultivating his relations with the Columbia folk, who had not, I fear, at the time recognized his superior talents, while he gave the greater part of his attention to new friends promptly acquired through his teaching at Hunter College. I was myself no Poe specialist but, truth to tell, most deliberately a specialist in not being a specialist. I always felt affection for him, however, and I had scarcely ever met a woman whom I admired more than his wife, Maureen, distinguished in her own right as hostess, friend of poets and scholars and, ultimately, a devoted assistant and collaborator in her husband's studies. I would surely have been much the gainer had I seen more of Tom in his mature years. I am not at all sure, though, that he was really more noteworthy or engaging in the flower, so to speak, than in the bud. As it now seems to me, all that was to be was at least implied when I first caught sight of him, which, as I recall, was in W. P. Trent's class on seventeenth- and eighteenth-century literature. This is a happy occasion for me to lift a glass to an old friend, one of the most extraordinary and richly endowed persons I have ever known.

## NOTE

*For permission to publish this reminiscence of Thomas Ollive Mabbott, gratitude to the Jay B. Hubbell Center for American Literary Historiography, Duke University, for which it was originally prepared, is acknowledged. Special thanks go to Maureen Cobb Mabbott, who first called my attention to this sketch, and to her daughter, Jane Mabbott Austrian, for their assistance.

# THERE, BUT FOR THE GRACE OF GOD, GO I: ELIOT AND WILLIAMS ON POE

*LAURA JEHN MENIDES*

T. S. Eliot and William Carlos Williams disagreed on so much in their personal and artistic lives that it is not surprising that they should differ in their response to Poe. Williams' chapter on Poe in *In the American Grain* and Eliot's "From Poe to Valéry,"[1] to take their most substantial statements on Poe, seem worlds apart in their assessments of his influence and place in literature.

Eliot finds Poe longing for Europe, an expatriate at heart; Williams finds Poe the quintessential American, "more American" than Hawthorne, or as one critic puts it, a real "local boy."[2] Eliot's Poe has drawn virtually nothing from his American roots; Williams' Poe is definitely "in the American grain," a hero in the line of Columbus, DeSoto, Sam Houston and Daniel Boone. Eliot's Poe is "adolescent" and incapable of skepticism; Williams' Poe makes mature judgments and is often satiric. Eliot criticizes, and Williams applauds, Poe's use of words. Eliot says that the important Poe founded a French literary tradition, which, however, is now "exhausted" and useless to modern artists; Williams insists that "on Poe is founded" an American literary tradition that must be respected and continued, as Williams himself aims to continue it. Williams whole-heartedly approves of Poe's emphasis on form and technique; Eliot's approval is muted, for he fears that in the concentration on form, meaning is lost.

Readers of these two essays could go on with differences, but it would be profitable to stop and ask: Why the differences? Two reasons, I think. First, Eliot and Williams find very different Poes because they look in different places in the Poe canon. Williams concentrates on Poe's voluminous magazine criticism and the prose tales but slights the poetry; Eliot emphasizes the poetry and poetic theory and slights the fugitive criticism.[3]

A more important reason for their difference is that each is so personal in his response to Poe; each seems to see his own merits and concerns reflected in Poe. Eliot looks at Poe from the perspective of the expatriate who has found in the Anglo-Catholic tradition all that was missing in America; he has found, in other words, what Poe, who stayed in America, could not find. Williams views Poe from the perspective of the stay-at-home American; he sees Poe as an American Adam, a writer who willingly forgoes European influences and responds to the difficult American challenge to be original, a writer, however, whose originality is continually threatened. The point to be made and investigated further is this: both Eliot and Williams reveal a profound and disturbing kinship with Poe. Each seems to discover in Poe a

model or version of himself—and also a dire warning. Each, however, finds a different model, a different warning.

Williams' Poe chapter in *In the American Grain* is not an academic essay but instead a highly charged paean, in which, gradually, Williams reveals his intense identification with Poe. Williams describes the earlier writer as so original, so accurate in expressing himself and his condition in America, that he becomes his century's best expression of America. If Poe's true merits were better known, Williams insists, he could be a valuable model for other American artists and the basis of an American artistic tradition; if Poe's defects were better understood, he could provide a valuable warning. Williams seeks to set the record straight about Poe, but at the same time he reveals his own most serious concerns.

The Poe (and penultimate) chapter of *In the American Grain* is the best demonstration of Williams' thesis and also an important key to the method and message of *Paterson*. *In the American Grain* is Williams' attempt to understand the sources of his own urges, repressions and contradictions. He finds those sources in the two major—and contradictory—strains in American culture, strains apparent in all his heroes, including Poe, including himself. The book's heroes—Columbus, Boone, Sam Houston, Lincoln, and Poe—are all original men; all understand that the New World demands new response and expression, that it challenges them to be new. All of these heroes, however, are hounded and thwarted by another American strain—a littleness, a fear of newness and originality, a terrible, ruinous repression. Faced with this opposition (in American culture and often in themselves) most of the book's heroes, like Poe, are destroyed.

In allying himself with these heroes, especially with Poe, Williams seems determined to recognize and name these strains for what they are, to separate them, and then to absorb and foster American originality, and to overcome American repression. Thus, Williams insists that the repressed, self-destructive Poe is not the *essential* Poe. Williams iterates and reiterates that the essential, important Poe is the original American artist, meeting the New World with newness of his own.

This essential, important Poe is a worthy model. The comment in the *Literary History of the United States* that no modern American poet has yet proclaimed Poe's "living value" in terms equal to Valéry's is simply untrue. It reveals either that Spiller et al. have not read Williams' Poe chapter or that *In the American Grain* continues to be misunderstood or unappreciated.[4] Repeatedly, Williams' Poe chapter proclaims Poe's living value: he is, Williams insists, "a genius intimately shaped by his locality and time"; "a light in the morass." "On him is FOUNDED A LITERATURE." "In him American

literature is anchored, in him alone, on solid ground." Poe is "more American" than Hawthorne; he "heed(s) more the local necessities, the harder structural imperatives." And Williams insists, "The value of Poe's genius to OURSELVES must be uncovered." These quotations refer to Poe's prose works—his critical articles and tales—for it is in the prose that Williams finds his positive model. In fact, seven-eighths of Williams' chapter is devoted to Poe's prose works, and more than half to the criticism.

Williams shares many critical attitudes with Poe; in fact he selects from Poe's volumes of criticism those passages that make his own favorite critical appeals. For example, Williams states that although Poe "slights" the notion of a "nationality of letters," his "constant focus of attention" in one essay is "the preeminent importance, in letters as in all other branches of imaginative creation, of the local."[5] Here is Williams' point, made often in his work, that art must express its own local place in order to express universals. As other examples of shared critical concerns, Williams also notes that Poe deplores "plagiarism," especially the slavish "copying" of European stylistics, that Poe insists upon high-quality, original American literature, and not "colonial imitation," that Poe urges American writers to find American idiom and to experiment with form.[6]

Critical affinities between Poe and Williams are easier to discern than artistic affinities, but Williams' essay suggests the latter as well. In fact, the critical and artistic are linked by the special definitions that Williams gives to the words "local" and "original" (definitions that, as mentioned earlier, he finds in Poe). Williams writes that Poe has "the firmness of INSIGHT into the condition upon which our literature must rest, always the same, a local one, surely, but not of sentiment or mood, as not of trees and Indians, but of original fibre." Poe expresses the local, that is, not by copying American landscape or other features (that would be a form of plagiarism), but by honestly and accurately expressing himself and his situation in America. As Williams asserts, "the whole period, America 1840, could be rebuilt psychologically...from Poe's 'method'." The whole period, and Poe's situation in that period are expressed, Williams continues, throughout Poe's tales, especially in their images. Williams points to the many images of "broken" people (as, for example in "Loss of Breath") and to "the recurrent image of the ape" in "Hop-Frog," "Dr. Tarr and Professor Fether," and "Murders in the Rue Morgue." Perhaps, Williams suggests, it is Poe's "disgust with his immediate associates and his own fears, which cause this frequent use of [the ape]...to create the emotion of extreme terror."

As in this quotation, throughout his essay Williams praises Poe's ability to "create"—to give artistic form and expression to his particular situation at

a particular time and place in America. Williams must have had this attribute of Poe in mind when he himself was writing *Paterson,* when, that is, he was attempting to express *him*self and *his* America, for there are significant parallels between Poe's "broken" characters in the tales and Williams' "divorced" ones in *Paterson,* and between Poe's ape as an image of disgust and fear and Williams' images of dwarfs and other grotesques in *Paterson.* In fact, what Williams says of Poe is equally true of himself when he was writing *Paterson*—that the "grotesque inappropriateness of the life around him forced itself in among his words."

Throughout his account of Poe's prose works, Williams notes Poe's insistence on method—on finding the proper artistic form and imposing it on the enormous "formless mass" of America. Once more, Williams sees in Poe his own major concern, voiced repeatedly in *In the American Grain* and *Paterson*—the need to express America. Williams says of Poe's "method" in the tales:

> The significance and the secret is: authentic particles...taken apart and reknit with a view to emphasize, enforce and make evident the *method.* Their quality of skill in observation, their heat, local verity...the detached, the abstract, the cold philosophy of their joining together; a method springing...freshly from the local conditions which determine it.

These words of praise for Poe actually describe Williams' own method in *In the American Grain* and *Paterson,* both of which feature "authentic particles"—quotations from historical and contemporary sources—which are then "reknit," emphasizing the "method" of the works. Similarly, Williams' *Paterson* and *In the American Grain* reveal the very qualities he discovers in Poe: "skill in observation," "heat," "local verity." And significantly, Williams' art finds its inspiration exactly where he says Poe's was found: in "the local conditions which determine it."

Perhaps the most interesting parallel between what Williams finds in Poe's art and what he accomplishes in his own involves the American writer's use of non-American materials. Again, Williams is full of praise, for, he says, even when Poe uses foreign cultures, he is original, and American:

> Poe could look at France, Spain, Greece, and NOT be impelled to copy. He could do this BECAUSE he had the sense within him of a locality of his own, capable of cultivation....Poe's use of the tags of other cultures than his own manages to be novel, interesting, useful, *unaffected,* since it succeeds in giving the impression of being not in the least dragged in by rule or pretence but of a fresh purpose.

Williams, too, has "fresh purpose" when in his very American *Paterson* he quotes Sappho, or when he describes in loving detail in Book 5 the medieval unicorn tapestries. What the speaker of *Paterson* finds exciting is that he is able to make these medieval Flemish tapestries live—live in America. In a literal as well as a symbolic sense, the tapestries in *Paterson* have become American. Literally, they have come to America, to the Cloisters in New York; more importantly, *Paterson*'s speaker finds in them an imaginative expression of himself and his America. To read Williams' words on Poe, to understand what Williams sees in Poe, is to understand Williams' own artistic aims. Poe has indeed provided a model.

If Williams finds his model primarily in Poe's prose, he finds his warning primarily in the poetry. If in the former he discovers American artistic originality, in the latter he discovers that originality thwarted and destroyed. As Williams explains, certain heroic souls, like Poe, can comprehend, and can meet, the New World's challenge to be new themselves; other Americans, most Americans Williams would say, can not meet the challenge to be new and so fall back on old patterns (that is, they plagiarize) and actually become fearful of and destructive towards originality.

This conflict—between originality and its opposition—is, according to Williams, found to some extent in all of Poe's work, for it is part of Poe's situation in America. It finds its way into the criticism, Williams says, when Poe becomes "ill-tempered" and "monomaniacal" in his drive to expose plagiarists. Similarly, in the tales the "gross inappropriateness" of the opposition finds expression among Poe's words—and thus the ugly and terrifying images cited earlier. But, Williams says, it is in the poetry that the full and ultimately destructive effects of the opposition are revealed. In the poems, according to Williams, Poe exposes his intense, unrelieved yearning for agreement and support, his recoil from those who fail to give support, and finally, his terrible, ruinous isolation. "In his prose," Williams says, Poe "could still keep a firm hold, he still held the 'arrangement' fast and stood above it, but in the poetry he was at the edge—there was nothing." These charges about Poe's poetry are made without much evidence or detail, Williams perhaps reinforcing his point that the essential Poe is to be found in the prose, not in the poetry. In fact, while he discusses the prose at length, he rather dismisses the poetry: "there are but five poems," he says, "possibly three."

Williams apparently reads in Poe's poems an expression of his own tendencies towards recoil and isolation. Throughout his chapter he seems resolved not to let the forces of repression and denial destroy him as they destroyed Poe. Those forces may come, Williams suggests, from within as

well as from without, for if the drive to originality is in the American grain, so too is the drive toward repression of originality. With the image of Poe before him, Williams seems determined to continue his own fight against the plagiarists, but to temper the anger, to guard against the recoil and the destructive isolation—to put himself in the line, not of the destroyed Poe, but of the local and original artist.

Unlike Williams, whose identification with Poe pervades his essay, Eliot is reticent and uneasy about admitting kinship with Poe (he can "never be sure," he says, whether he was influenced by Poe). The influence—the kinship—can be discerned, however, in Eliot's poetry (especially in the early poems written in the symbolist mode)[7] and in what I would like to consider: Eliot's many articles on and references to Poe written over five decades, especially "From Poe to Valéry." Eliot wrote the latter in 1949, when he had left America and become, as he said, a British citizen, a classicist, and an Anglo-Catholic,[8] when, as evidenced by the *Four Quartets,* he was reassessing his own early years and recovering from what he considered poetic and spiritual failings. It seems that at least part of the reason why Eliot is so uneasy, so qualified in his praise, and often so negative in his reactions to Poe is that he sees Poe as an early version of himself, an Eliot who never left America, an Eliot that might have been.

Thus many virtues and defects that Eliot finds in Poe are the same qualities that he describes in his early, pre-*Four Quartets,* work. Let me discuss four of Eliot's observations. First is the two-sided effect, for the artist, of being born an American: artistic isolation and rootlessness on the one hand and, on the other, artistic originality. Eliot says of Poe: "There can be few authors of such eminence who have drawn so little from their own roots, who have been so isolated from any surroundings." Poe is "not at home where he belongs, but cannot go anywhere else"; he is a "kind of displaced European," a "wanderer with no fixed abode." Eliot, it seems, sees Poe as he saw himself during his early career when he was similarly a "kind of displaced European," a "wanderer." In 1909, for example, Eliot writes of the "sacrifice" of those Americans "retained" to America "while their hearts are always in Europe,"[9] and in his early poems, the biting, humorous "Mélange Adultère de Tout" and the sardonic "Gerontion," his speakers have no "fixed abode," but either flit from place to place or are blown hither and yon. Throughout his early years in America, Eliot admitted later, he never felt that he belonged: in St. Louis, he said, he always felt the Easterner, and at Harvard he was always the Southerner.[10] Like the Poe described in his essay, Eliot was "isolated from any surroundings."

Living in the isolating and "starved environment" of America made Poe

a "pathetic" creature, Eliot writes, but it also may have accounted for his genius—his "originality."[11] The suggestion is that a place so starved, so lacking in the traditional materials of art "forces" the artist to be original. The term "originality" does not carry Eliot's unqualfied approval (as it does Williams'), but, as it is used, rather reveals Eliot's ambivalence towards America and the possibilities for the American artist. As he writes in "Tradition and the Individual Talent," "no poet, no artist of any art, has his complete meaning alone." Eliot seems to be warning himself against what he sees in Poe—an originality that signals isolation from artistic roots. Instead, Eliot seems determined to display his own originality by his new, his original, interaction with a traditional community of art.

Eliot's second observation about Poe concerns the misapplication of Poe's intelligence, and it recalls Eliot's own fear, expressed in "Mr. Eliot's Sunday Morning Service," "Gerontion," and elsewhere, that intelligence, unless exercised in the proper context and tradition, is empty and frustrating. The point is made in one of Eliot's essays in which he acknowledges Poe's fine intellectual and critical abilities, but charges that the intelligence and critical acumen are misspent. Poe, Eliot writes, was "the directest, the least pedantic, the least pedagogical of the critics writing in his time in either America or England" but, he says, "it is not a point of vast importance, as most of the writers whom Poe criticized are embalmed only in their coffins and in Poe's abuse."[12] The implication here is that the artist/critic should channel his intelligence toward worthier, more lasting subjects—those perhaps in what Eliot elsewhere calls the "main current" of tradition.

Related to the above complaint is Eliot's third major observation about Poe, again an observation about his own early self. Poe, Eliot says, lacks consistency; his vision of life is "limited."[13] The charge is expressed throughout the essays; each time Eliot, in effect, exposes Poe's "dissociation of sensibility." Although the term, examined at length in "The Metaphysical Poets," does not appear in any of his Poe essays, it is clear that Eliot sees Poe as a victim of this dissociation, this split between the faculties. According to Eliot, Poe is missing "a consistent view of life"; he is "adolescent"; he has not developed conviction and commitment. He simply "entertains" theories, but doesn't "believe" them. "What is lacking," Eliot says, "is not brain power, but the maturity of intellect which comes only with the maturing of the man as a whole, the development and coordination of his various emotions." What is lacking, in short, is just what Eliot found lacking in himself and was later able to recover, according to the *Four Quartets*, in the Christian tradition—the ability to unite the intellectual with the emotional and spiritual aspects of life.

To Eliot, Poe's inability to write a long poem stems from this lack of maturity and coordination of human faculties. As Eliot writes of Poe:

> He himself was incapable of writing a long poem. He could conceive only a poem which was a single simple effect: for him, the whole of a poem had to be in one mood. Yet it is only in a poem of some length that a variety of moods can be expressed; for a variety of moods requires a number of different themes or subjects...A long poem may gain by the widest possible variations of intensity. But Poe wanted a poem to be the first intensity throughout.

Eliot charges that even "The Bells," which may seem "a deliberate exercise in several moods," is actually "as much a poem of one mood as any of Poe's."

Much the same charge has been levelled against Eliot's *The Waste Land,* which, for all its variety, has been seen as a poem of one mood—a single, sustained cry of near despair.[14] Eliot himself, later in life, dismissed *The Waste Land* as a "piece of rhythmical grumbling."[15] Eliot was aware, of course, that *The Waste Land* was considered a masterpiece, but his comment signals his reassessment, his belief that the poem lacks mature perspective, the perspective of other moods. Again, Eliot seems to have found in Poe a problem that he himself had faced and, in his later years, had worked to overcome. What Eliot in "From Poe To Valéry" says he prefers in poetry—a long poem of many moods, a poem of commitment—is exactly what the reader finds in *Four Quartets.* The essay on Poe, in fact, not only reveals important aims of *Four Quartets,* but also justifies several unpoetic passages in the poem. Eliot writes in the Poe essay about the requirements of a long poem: "In a long poem some parts may be deliberately planned to be less 'poetic' than others; these passages may show no lustre when extracted, but may be intended to elicit, by contrast, the significance of other parts, and to unite them into a whole more significant than any of the parts."

Perhaps the most important observation in Eliot's "From Poe to Valéry" relates to Poe's self-conscious attention to form and to the process of composition. It relates, too, to what Eliot admits is Poe's "immense" influence on Baudelaire, Mallarmé and Valéry. Eliot suggests that Poe's focus on technique—part of his "originality"—was encouraged by his American "starved" environment. According to Eliot, that is, America provides so little "subject" that the artist tends to concentrate on form. As he says of Poe's work, the "material" is "tenuous" and "the treatment is everything." Once more, we can read into Eliot's remarks the kinship between Poe and his early self, for wasn't Eliot, in "Rhapsody on a Windy Night" and in "Prufrock," for example, similarly starved for material, similarly absorbed self-

consciously in treatment? Once more, we can see Eliot's need to extricate himself from Poe and from the tradition Poe founded. Once more Poe provides a warning that Eliot has heeded. And in this case the warning is not for Eliot alone, but for all of modern poetry, for after carefully tracing Poe's profound influence on Baudelaire, Mallarmé and Valéry, and after admitting that some of the poetry he most admires is to be found in this symbolist tradition, Eliot charges that this tradition "has ended." It has "gone as far as it can go" and cannot be "of any help to later poets" because two ideas of Poe's—that the poem should be a self-conscious act of creation and that the poem is an end in itself—were taken to the extreme limit by Valéry. At that limit, Eliot says, subject matter all but vanishes. That is, when the poet's attention is devoted excessively to *how* the poem is created, *what* is said is forgotten. The poem thus divorces itself from meaning, belief and commitment, the very things that Eliot, in his later years, in *Four Quartets* especially, sought to restore to poetry.

*Four Quartets* records Eliot's final personal and poetic effort to correct the defects of his early career—the very defects that he analyzes in his essays on Poe. The isolation and rootlessness that Eliot found in Poe and in himself (and that is described throughout the "Prufrock" volume) were corrected by his joining a literary and spiritual community, a "Little Gidding." The "hypertrophy of intellect" (Allen Tate's term)[16] and the dissociation of sensibility that he shared with Poe (and that is so hauntingly depicted in "The Hollow Men" and "Gerontion") were cured, according to Eliot, by his going back to before that dissociation began—seventeenth-century England—and by reconnecting with all that had been severed. In short, by finding coherence—unity of intellect and emotion—in Anglican Christianity. Eliot could thus place himself in the "main line" of tradition, the line which links Eliot to other Anglo-Catholic writers, and thereby to Dante, to Virgil and Homer. In *Four Quartets* also, Eliot corrects the excessive attention to technique which he finds in Poe and in his younger self. (As Matthiessen notes, readers of the early Eliot had to concentrate on his poetic technique; in *Four Quartets,* that concentration must be given to content.)[17] And finally, *Four Quartets,* in its length and complexity, and in its recognition of life's lows and highs, redresses another early fault: the poem attempts to reconcile, through Christian tradition and theology, life's many moods and paradoxes.

The "tradition" from Poe to Valéry, then, is in Eliot's view a short-lived tradition, an interesting development, but it is outside the "main current," a rather fascinating poetic by-way. Eliot himself travelled on it, but—and here is the warning heeded—left it in order to resume his journey toward the main road.

One might ask whether there are any affinities between Poe and this later Eliot, the Eliot who had joined the main road and found unity and coherence. Eliot, I feel certain, would say no. The French may have found something philosophically pleasing about Poe's *Eureka* (as a possible parallel to *Four Quartets*), but Eliot thinks that the French improved Poe. To the French, Eliot says, Poe provided important hints and suggestions, which they then, with the depth and understanding and maturity in their background, formed into something more profound than was in Poe originally. Eliot, I think, looks at Poe as the self he left behind in America. He sees Poe as he did his early self—rather like Dante at the beginning of the *Divine Comedy*: confused, lost in the dark, seeking, vaguely, some lost love, some ideal. I think Eliot would say that, like Dante, he himself has found his Beatrice and his lost love (that is, Divine Love), but that Poe has not. Poe, Eliot writes in 1943, "lives in a world of dreams, shadows, and regrets for a lost, unpossessed, and unattainable love."[18]

That evaluation of Poe is repeated ten years later in 1953 in "American Literature and the American Language," one of Eliot's final essays on Poe. Again Eliot mentions Poe's "dream world"—Poe's reaction to the actual, American world he knew and to the European world he longed for but visited only in his imagination. Although the essay praises Poe's artistic power and originality, it also reiterates Eliot's uneasy and ambivalent feelings about Poe, especially about Poe's isolation from the main line of tradition. Eliot's essay can be read as a version of what Harold Bloom analyzes in *The Anxiety of Influence*—a writer's need to overcome the affinity which he may have felt for a literary forebear. As Eliot writes:

> The writers of the past, especially the immediate past, in one's own place and language may be valuable to the young writer simply as something definite to rebel against. He will recognize the common ancestry; but he needn't necessarily *like* his relatives. For models to imitate, or for styles from which to learn, he may often more profitably go to writers of another country and another language, or of a remoter age.[19]

One can read in that statement Eliot's personal decision to leave America and to ally himself with a broader literary tradition—and thus to achieve what he says eluded Poe.

Consequently Eliot, like Williams, sees his own merits and problems reflected in Poe, his own answers confirmed by Poe's failure to find similar answers. When each of these modern writers looks at Poe, he seems to find first himself, and second, the self he might have been. Each considers Poe from his own perspective and says, in effect (Eliot more literally than Williams): "There, but for the grace of God, go I."

## NOTES

[1] William Carlos Williams, "Edgar Allan Poe," *In the American Grain* (New York, 1925), pp. 216-233. All quotations from Williams are from this chapter. T. S. Eliot, "From Poe to Valéry," *To Criticize the Critic* (New York, 1965), pp. 27-42. Unless otherwise noted, all quotations from Eliot are to be found in this essay.

[2] Reed Whittemore, *William Carlos Williams: Poet from New Jersey* (Boston, 1975), p. 205.

[3] In "From Poe to Valéry," Eliot *says* that he is considering Poe's work as a whole, but he actually refers to only one essay on poetic theory and ignores the magazine criticism.

[4] Robert E. Spiller, Willard Thorp, Thomas H. Johnson, Henry Seidel Canby, Richard M. Ludwig, William Gibson, eds. *Literary History of the United States*, 4th ed., rev. (New York, 1974), p. 321. The Poe essay was written by F. O. Matthiessen. See Benjamin T. Spencer, "Doctor Williams' American Grain," *TSL*, 8 (1963), 1-16.

[5] Williams refers to Poe's essay on Frederick Marryat—*H.* 10:197-202.

[6] For a discussion of Williams' affinities with Poe, and with Whitman, see E. P. Bollier, "Against the American Grain: William Carlos Williams Between Whitman and Poe," Donald Pizer, ed. *Essays in American Literature in Memory of Richard P. Adams* [*Tulane Studies in English, 23*] (New Orleans, 1978), 123-142. See also Paul Mariani, *William Carlos Williams: A New World Naked* (New York, 1981).

[7] F. O. Matthiessen, in *The Achievement of T. S. Eliot*, rev. ed. (New York, 1958), p. 8, writes: "it is not to be forgotten that the symbolist movement has its roots in the work of the most thoroughly conscious artist in American poetry before Eliot, Edgar Poe."

[8] In the preface to *For Lancelot Andrews* (New York, 1929).

[9] T. S. Eliot, Review of Van Wyck Brooks's *The Wine of the Puritans, Harvard Advocate:* 7 May 1909, p. 80.

[10] Robert Sencourt, *T. S. Eliot: A Memoir* (New York, 1971), p. 15.

[11] These remarks about "originality" in the "starved environment" of America appear in Eliot's review of the second volume of *The Cambridge History of American Literature, The Athenaeum:* 25 April 1919, pp. 236-237. For comments on this essay, see B. R. McElderry, "T. S. Eliot on Poe," *PoeN*, 2 (1969), 32-33.

[12] *The Athenaeum* review, p. 237, and McElderry, p. 33. Poe's "intelligence" is mentioned also in Eliot's discussions of Poe's detective fiction in *The New Criterion*, 5 (1927), 139-143, 362. For commentary on Eliot's analysis, see Judy Osowski, "T. S. Eliot on 'Poe the Detective'," *PoeN* 3(1970), 39.

[13] See, for example, "A Dream Within a Dream," a BBC talk, published in *Listener*, 24: 25 February 1943, pp. 243-244 and quoted in McElderry, p. 33.

[14] See, for example, Richard Ellman, "The First Waste Land" in *Eliot in His Time*, ed. A. Walton Litz (Princeton, 1973), pp. 51-66, and James E. Miller, *T. S. Eliot's Personal Waste Land* (University Park and London, 1977).

[15] T. S. Eliot, *The Waste Land: A Facsimile and Transcript of the Original Drafts* (New York, 1971), p. 1.

[16] Allen Tate, "The Angelic Imagination," *The Recognition of Edgar Allan Poe*, ed. Eric W. Carlson (Ann Arbor, 1966), pp. 238-239.

[17] Matthiessen, p. 193.

[18] In "A Dream Within a Dream." See also McElderry, p. 33.

[19] *To Criticize the Critic*, p. 56.

# FITZGERALD'S HOMAGE TO POE: FEMALE CHARACTERIZATION IN *THIS SIDE OF PARADISE* AND *TENDER IS THE NIGHT*

*KENT LJUNGQUIST*

F. Scott Fitzgerald's fascination with the life and works of Edgar Allan Poe is well documented. Biographical evidence suggests that Fitzgerald was exposed to Poe's works at an early age in the form of his father's reading aloud "The Raven" and "The Bells."[1] His affection for Baltimore stemmed partially from his knowledge of Poe's burial there, an association reflected in a 1935 letter to Laura Guthrie: "I have stopped all connections with M. Barleycorn....Baltimore is warm and pleasant. I love it more than I thought—it is so rich with memories—it is nice to look up the street and see the statue of my great uncle and to know that Poe is buried here and that many ancestors of mine have walked the old town by the bay."[2] Study of Fitzgerald's indebtedness to Poe has progressed beyond Maxwell Geismar's somewhat fatuous comment: "Fitzgerald's work, like Poe's, is colored by the imagery of incest."[3] His apprentice story "The Mystery of the Raymond Mortgage" burlesques, almost certainly, the nineteenth-century ratiocinative tales of Poe and others.[4] Fitzgerald may have incorporated Poe's use of symbolic imagery for horrifying effects into his early stories "The Cut Glass Bowl" (1920) and "The Ice Palace" (1920).[5] He reveals his most elaborate homage to Poe, however, in *This Side of Paradise* and *Tender is the Night,* the latter marking a much more subtle interweaving of Poesque allusions and images than the former. In particular, female characterization in these novels reveals Fitzgerald's kinship with Poe in presenting the dual nature of woman as elevating and terrifying.

James W. Tuttleton plausibly demonstrates how the numerous references to Poe's works in *This Side of Paradise* indicate that horror and beauty are inextricably linked in Amory Blane's mind.[6] This collocation of terrifying but beautiful images is embodied in Eleanor Savage, whose physical appearance and awesome intellect recall Poe's Ligeia. Furthermore, her troubled mental state is reminiscent of the constitutional and family disease that haunts Madeline Usher and her line. In short, Eleanor reminds us of the host of female presences that dominate the minds of Poe's male protagonists. Although her name calls forth associations with Lenore, as Tuttleton suggests, it more closely resembles a somewhat lesser heroine in the Poe canon, the title character of "Eleonora." One might legitimately ask if Eleanor is a palpable, physical presence in the novel or a dream-like being called forth by Amory's mind during his progressive disillusionment. In the latter guise, she

is more akin to the ethereal and fairy-like Eleonora than to Ligeia or Madeline Usher.

Upon investigation, significant parallels present themselves between Poe's "Eleonora" and complementary chapters in *This Side of Paradise*. The theme of adolescent love permeates both works. Just as Eleanor's eyes entrance Amory Blane, Poe's protagonist fixes on Eleonora's "bright eyes."[7] In both works there is an interpenetration of the physical landscapes, refulgent colors, and musical effects. The river in Poe's "Eleonora" utters "a lullaby more divine than the harp of Aeolus—sweeter than all save the voice of Eleonora" (*M:* 2:641). The setting of *This Side of Paradise* is a "fairyland with Amory and Eleanor, dim phantasmal shapes, expressing eternal beauty and curious elfin moods. Then they turned out of the moonlight into the trellised darkness of a vine-hung pagoda, where there were scents so plaintive as to be nearly musical."[8] The peace of Poe's Valley of Many-Colored Grass is matched by Fitzgerald's landscape in which "No Wind is stirring in the grass; not one wind stirs...the water in the hidden pools, as glass fronts the full moon and so enters the golden token in its icy mass" (p. 234). The haunting quality of Eleonora's voice parallels the "half rhythm, half darkness" (p. 280) of Eleanor's voice. Eleonora's ghostly presence, which survives after her supposed death, is matched by Eleanor's "shadowy and unreal" (p. 234) fading like a ghost. As if in imitation of Poe and Swinburne, to whom Fitzgerald also alludes (p. 232), Amory and Eleanor pay homage to an irrecoverable dream world that is destroyed by the ravages of time. In both works, time may triumph over physical love, but the heroines Eleonora and Eleanor respectively live on in the protagonists' minds.

The chapters marking Amory's confrontation with the terror and beauty of Eleanor display a thorough assimilation of Poesque imagery and themes, but little aesthetic distance on Fitzgerald's part from Poe's materials. Allusions to "The Fall of the House of Usher" and "Ulalume" are obvious and explicit, and Poe's name is invoked directly when the indolent Amory recites Poe's poetry "to the corn fields...congratulating Poe for drinking himself to death in that atmosphere of smiling complacency" (p. 223). Fitzgerald's use of Poe in *This Side of Paradise* seems self-consciously literary, almost as if he were seeking a famous figure of romantic dissolution to parallel his protagonist's youthful disillusionment.

In *Tender is the Night* occur allusions to a specific poem by Poe, "To Helen," but more subtle and less heavy-handed weaving of this tissue of allusions goes into this later and more mature novel. A reliance on Poe is also suggested by the complicated textual history of the novel. Revisions in *Tender is the Night* reveal that the earliest draft concerned a figure of

youthful dissolution from the South, Francis Melarky, who is dismissed from West Point for insubordination and who tours Europe with his mother. Melarky becomes involved in a drunken brawl in Rome and is beaten up by police.[9] Fitzgerald later transformed the Melarky story into that of Dick Diver and Rosemary Hoyt, but Melarky's connections with the South, West Point, and alcoholism perhaps kept the figure of Poe in Fitzgerald's mind as he detailed Dick Diver's disintegration. The twentieth-century writer may have found in Poe's example a precedent for Diver's victimization by internal and external forces.

Fitzgerald's most explicit reference to Poe occurs when Rosemary announces the title of the film she is making, "The Grandeur That Was Rome."[10] This allusion to "To Helen" is replete with irony because the Roman episodes of *Tender is the Night* suggest corruption and decadence rather than the inherited glories of the classical past.[11] Nevertheless, the allusion calls attention to a host of other associations with "To Helen," some ironic, some straightforward, which permeate the novel. This matrix of associations recalls the vaguely Odyssean elements of Poe's poem and thereby provides a Romantic version of the heroic quest that serves as a backdrop to Diver's emotional and psychological deterioration.[12]

Fitzgerald incorporates qualities of Poe's Helen into a gallery of female characters in *Tender is the Night*. Foremost among these is Nicole Diver, whose physiognomy and bearing initially recall the "classic face" and "statue-like" demeanor of Poe's idealized heroine. Although Nicole's name may have been chosen because of its associations with the hardness of money ("nickel"),[13] his descriptions also stress her austere, statuesque features. The result is a riveting "effect" on the observer, a term reflecting a thoroughly Poesque absorption in female beauty:

> her face could have been described in terms of conventional prettiness, but the effect was that it had been made first on the heroic scale with strong structure and marking, as if the vividness of brow and coloring, everything we associate with temperament and character had been molded with a Rodinesque intention, and then chiseled away in the direction of prettiness to a point where a single slip would have diminished its force and quality. (p. 17)

An emotional hardness underlies the aesthetic appeal of her beauty. As Nicole subsequently comments to Rosemary: "I'm a mean, hard woman" (p. 21). Fitzgerald, through Nicole's conversation and physical descriptions, has followed Poe's technique of connecting physiognomy and character, internal temperament and outward demeanor.[14]

Several other pictorial qualities of Poe's goddess-like figure become incorporated into Nicole's appearance. As Poe describes Helen's "hyacinth hair," Fitzgerald regales Nicole, aboard the Swiss funicular, with "fine-spun hair...fluffed into curls" (p. 148). The "classic face" of Poe's Helen finds an analogue in Dick's lavish appreciation for his future wife's facial beauty, "delight in Nicole's face" (p. 149). In concert with these lyrical, poetic descriptions of Nicole in the Alps, Fitzgerald apparently appropriates other images from "To Helen." In a passage reminiscent of Poe's female figure bearing an "agate lamp" in a frozen pose, Fitzgerald describes Nicole amid the beautiful mountains: "On the horseshoe walk overlooking the lake Nicole was the figure motionless between two lamp stands" (p. 153). Even after she and Dick part that evening, she remains a haunting presence like Poe's figure in the "window niche." Unable to sleep and thinking of Nicole, Dick goes "to the window. Her beauty climbed the rolling slope, it came into the room, rustling ghost-like through the curtains..." (p. 156).[15]

As a modern counterpart to Helen's, Nicole's face is cast on a heroic scale, its beauty associated with classical voyages of the past. Whereas in Poe's poem Helen's beauty is linked cryptically with "those Nicean barks of yore," Nicole's face is associated with sea voyages of mythic stature. At one point, in fact, she imagines herself on a boat's prow as a sculptured figure with flowing hair:

> Sitting on the stanchion of this life-boat I look seaward and let my hair blow and shine. I am motionless against the sky and the boat is made to carry my form into the blue obscurity of the future, I am Pallas Athene carved reverently into the front of a galley. The waters are lapping the public toilets and the agate green foliage changes and complains about the stern. (p. 160)

Here Fitzgerald adapts several elements of "To Helen," including the motionless face of a woman with striking hair and the effect of "agate" coloration.

If such connections seem conjectural even in view of Fitzgerald's interest in Poe's poem, it is perhaps no coincidence that one of the boats occupied by Nicole is T. F. Golding's ship, which temporarily anchors in "Nicean" waters: "It was the yacht of T. F. Golding lying placid among the little swells of the Nicean Bay, constantly bound upon a romantic voyage that was not dependent upon actual motion" (p. 260). Interestingly, Fitzgerald changed the geographical reference when he transformed source material from an early story "One Trip Abroad." In the earlier tale—passages of which were later incorporated into *Tender is the Night*—Golding's craft is positioned in

"Monacan" rather than "Nicean" waters: "Before the maid drew the curtains to shut out the glare, Nicole saw from her window the yacht of T. E. Golding, placid among the swells of the Monacan Bay, as if constantly on a romantic voyage not dependent on actual motion."[16]

Fitzgerald was undoubtedly oblivious to the controversy concerning the meaning of Poe's epithet "Nicean barks," which has been ascribed to such varied sources as Milton, Coleridge, Vergil, and the mythological stories of Helen, Bacchus, Psyche, and Ulysses.[17] Fitzgerald may have used "Nicean" for purely geographical reasons or for its evocative sound. Probably, however, he associated the adjective with the ancient Ligurian town of Nicaea, now Nice in France.[18] Less likely but worthy of conjecture is the possibility that Fitzgerald knew that "Nicean" was the adjective form of the Greek word "Nike," a traditional figure in Greek art that represented "victory." In Greek sculpture and numismatics, a "Nike" was usually represented as a beautiful woman standing on a boat prow.[19] As he pondered the choices of his proper names, Fitzgerald's imagination may have shifted among an array of mythic, artistic, and literary references, perhaps including Poe's "Nicean barks." Whatever his possible knowledge of the sources of Poe's poem, there seems little doubt that Fitzgerald invited comparison, often using serious puns, among the following variants: "Nicole," "Nice," "Nicean," and "nice." It is also clear that Fitzgerald connects Nicole's facial features and flowing hair with the onward thrust of seagoing craft, as for example, with the movement of Golding's yacht: "Since dinner the yacht had been in motion westward. The fine night streamed away on either side, the Diesel engines pounded softly, there was a spring wind that blew Nicole's hair abruptly when she reached the bow...." (p. 273). Adrift in the Nicean bay, Dick comments, supposedly in innocuous fashion, but furthering Fitzgerald's serious wordplay: "It's a nice night" (p. 273).[20]

If Fitzgerald intended Nicole as a modern analogue to Poe's Helen, he was not alluding unambiguously to Poe. If her statue-like features connect her with the grandeur of the classical past, they also reflect an emotional hardness that can easily turn into ruthlessness. If she temporarily fashions herself a goddess of wisdom, she also displays the most uncontrollable emotional instability. If she sees herself as a goddess calling brave men to board ships bound for adventurous seas, hers is also a siren song of madness luring potential heroes to destruction. Although handled more dextrously than in *This Side of Paradise*, the combined terror and beauty of Fitzgerald's heroines in *Tender is the Night* hold the vulnerable Diver in their unremitting thrall.[21]

Fitzgerald further illustrates the ambiguous nature of the Helen figure

in *Tender is the Night* in his characterization of two of Diver's female patients at the Zugersee, both of whom serve as foils to Nicole. The first is the thirty-year-old American painter who suffers from nervous eczema but who discovers that emotional suffering is never skin deep. Her exchange with Dick on the instability of the modern world carries heroic echoes, perhaps suggestive of the first Helen who sent men into battle:

> "I'm sharing the fate of the women of my time who challenged men to battle."
> "To your vast surprise it was just like all battles," he answered, adopting her formal diction.
> "Just like all battles." She thought this over. "You pick a set-up, or else win a Pyrrhic victory, or you're wrecked or ruined—you're a ghostly echo from a broken wall." (p. 184)

These echoes may be too faint for the reader to discern their provenance in grand, ancient battles since the heroic ideal has been so devalued in modern society. Nevertheless, Dick takes leave of the American painter and enters the room of another foil to Nicole, an "American girl of fifteen who had been brought up on the basis that childhood had been intended to be all fun" (p. 186). This adolescent girl suffers from a variant of the "Daddy's Girl" syndrome. She has been spoiled by her "normal and conscientious" but overprotective father, a more benign version of Devereux Warren. But the relevance of her role to those of the other female characters is made certain when we learn that her name is Helen.

Poe's "To Helen" provided Fitzgerald with a text that incorporated traditional elements of the classical quest with somewhat vague, evocative suggestions of Romantic longing. Moreover, the poem embodied a serious heroic statement against which he could measure Dick Diver's deterioration and his failure with a gallery of women. Fitzgerald's keen awareness of the ambiguous nature of Poe's heroines also allowed him, in both *This Side of Paradise* and *Tender is the Night,* to portray female characters who were equally daunting in their physical beauty and in their emotional instability. In the latter novel in particular, the ambiguous Helen figure became the object of Diver's quest as well as the proximate cause of his emotional disintegration. Yet this latter-day Helen, whether in the guise of Nicole or of the minor female characters surrounding her, remained the sustaining force behind Diver's imagination, even if she became merely a "ghostly echo from a broken wall." From Poe's "To Helen," Fitzgerald learned much about man's yearning for a world of dreams, often embodied in a female figure of compelling beauty. From Poe's works overall, Fitzgerald learned much

about possible ambiguities in female characterization and so achieved a partial education in Romantic agony.

## NOTES

[1] See Andrew Turnbull, *Scott Fitzgerald: A Biography* (New York, 1962), p. 15. For other references to Poe, see pp. 96 and 187.

[2] *The Letters of F. Scott Fitzgerald*, ed. Andrew Turnbull (New York, 1962), p. 531. See also p. 513 and Turnbull's biography, p. 267.

[3] Maxwell Geismar, "A Cycle of Fiction," *The Literary History of the United States*, ed. Robert Spiller et al. (New York, 1953), p. 1299.

[4] See John Kuehl, ed. *The Apprentice Fiction of F. Scott Fitzgerald* (New Brunswick, NJ, 1965), p. 18. For Poe's works in Fitzgerald's library, see Kuehl, "Scott Fitzgerald's Reading," *PULC* 22(1961), 58-89.

[5] See Sergio Perosa, *The Art of F. Scott Fitzgerald*, trans. Perosa and Charles Matz (Ann Arbor, 1965), p. 35. For affinities between emotional qualities in Fitzgerald's and Poe's works, see also Perosa, pp. 58, 185, 191-193. For a suggestive discussion of the legacy of Poe's dream world as inherited by Fitzgerald and Nabokov, see Martha Banta, "Benjamin, Edgar, Humbert, and Jay," *YR*, 60(1971), 532-549. I am indebted to Richard Kopley for alerting me to a possible Fitzgerald borrowing from Poe in *The Great Gatsby*. During his interrogation of Gatsby, Tom Buchanan inquires about Oxford, as a waiter enters the room:

> Another pause. A waiter knocked and came in with crushed mint and ice, *but the silence was unbroken* by his "thank you" and the soft closing of the door—*The Great Gatsby* (New York, 1953), p. 86.

Stanza 5 of "The Raven" reads:

> Deep into that darkness peering, long I stood there
>     wondering, fearing,
> Doubting, dreaming dreams no mortal ever dared to
>     dream before;
> But the silence was unbroken, and the stillness gave no
>     token
> And the only word there spoken was the whispered word,
>     "Lenore!"
> This I whispered, and an echo murmured back the word
>     "Lenore!"
>                                         Merely this and nothing more.

Whether Fitzgerald borrowed the line consciously or unconsciously, his language, if not unique, is identical to Poe's. In both works, the phrase appears after a door opens. As Kopley pointed out to me in a letter: "The similarity in language suggests a possible relation between Daisy and Lenore, and between Gatsby's dream and 'the dreams no mortal ever dared to dream before' of the narrator of 'The Raven.' "

[6] Tuttleton, "The Presence of Poe in *This Side of Paradise,*" *ELN,* 3(1960), 284-289. Tuttleton mentions "Ligeia," "Usher," and "Murders," but not "Eleonora," in his discussion of Poe's influence.

[7] *M.* 2:642. Subsequent references to Poe's fiction will be noted in the body of my essay by volume and page number.

[8] Fitzgerald, *This Side of Paradise* (New York, 1920), pp. 233-234. Subsequent references to this novel will be noted in the body of my essay by page number. Fitzgerald's phantasmagorical lighting, pungent scents, and musical effects also recall the oppression of the senses in "The Assignation," in which Poe presents an "overpowering sense of splendor and perfume, and music" (*M.* 2:159) in the eccentric visionary's chamber.

[9] See Matthew Bruccoli, *The Composition of Tender is the Night* (Pittsburgh, 1963), pp. 26-28 ff.

[10] *Tender is the Night* (New York, 1933), p. 207. All other references will be noted in the body of my essay.

[11] Robert Roulston briefly notes that Fitzgerald's borrowing from Poe is a grim commentary on Dick's moral disintegration in "Dick Diver's Plunge in the Roman Void—The Setting of *Tender is the Night,*" *SAQ,* 77(1978), 85-97.

[12] Fitzgerald connects Poe's poem and *The Odyssey* when Rosemary announces the title "The Grandeur That Was Rome." Rosemary is then described as "the person for whom [Dick] had made the Mediterranean crossing" (p. 207). In this passage Dick is a Romantic wanderer à la Ulysses. Epic and heroic elements in *Tender is the Night* have been discussed, with varied conclusions, by Edwin Mosely, *F. Scott Fitzgerald, A Critical Essay* (Grand Rapids, 1967), pp. 36-41; Richard Foster, "Time's Exile: Dick Diver and the Heroic Idea," *Mosaic,* 8(1975), 89-108; and Maria Di Battista, "The Aesthetic of Forbearance: Fitzgerald's *Tender is the Night,*" *Novel,* 11(1977), 26-39.

[13] Bruccoli, p. 97.

[14] Poe's most famous example of connecting by analogy physiognomy and psychology is "The Fall of the House of Usher." For comments on Poe's physical shapes or outlines and internal temperament, see John T. Irwin, *American Hieroglyphics: The Symbol of the Egyptian Hieroglyphics in the American Renaissance* (New Haven, 1980), pp. 52 and 55.

[15] Fitzgerald may have also had in mind the Marchesa Aphrodite in "The Assignation," whose "statue-like form," "classical head," "large lustrous eyes," and "curls like those of the hyacinth" recall Poe's Helen. The Marchesa also looks out from her chamber window on a "dark, gloomy niche" (*M.* 2:153).

[16] "One Trip Abroad," *The Bodley Head F. Scott Fitzgerald* (London, 1963), 6:254.

[17] An informative survey of Poe's sources is Edward D. Snyder, "Poe's Nicean Barks (A History of Attempts to Interpret the Cruces)," *CJ,* 48(1953), 159-169.

[18] A hypothesis first suggested by F. V. N. Painter, ed. *Poets of the South* (New

York, 1903), p. 217—that Poe may have had a French locale in mind—has been generally discredited. See Snyder's comments, p. 167.

[19] See Mario L. D'Avanzo, " 'Like Those Nicean Barks': Helen's Beauty," *PoeS*, 6(1973), 26-27. That Poe meant "Nicean" to be an adjectival form of "Nike," that is, "victory," is convincingly argued by Thomas Ollive Mabbott— *M*.1: 167.

[20] Fitzgerald's manipulations of these variants—"Nicole," "Nice," "Nicean," and "nice"—are legion, as just a few passages indicate. See *Tender*, pp. 12, 99, 143, 152-156, and 273.

[21] The dual nature of Fitzgerald's women, "sources of delight and admiration" as well as "forces of destruction," is capably highlighted by Sister Mary Verity McNicholas, "Fitzgerald's Women in *Tender is the Night*," *CollL*, 4 (1977), 40-70. An insightful study connecting the novel to the Gothic tradition but not to Poe is Judith Wilt, "The Spinning Story: Gothic Motifs in *Tender is the Night*," *Fitzgerald/Hemingway Annual*, ed. Matthew Bruccoli (1976), 79-95.

# POE, STEPHEN KING, AND JOHN DICKSON CARR; OR, HOW TO RECREATE A POPULAR AUTHOR IN YOUR OWN IMAGE

*BENJAMIN FRANKLIN FISHER IV*

The topic of this study is the image of Edgar Allan Poe among writers of popular fiction in the twentieth century, particularly of his impact upon Stephen King and John Dickson Carr. The pages of this century's horror and detective stories, or, just as significant, those in histories of such varieties of writing (latter-day Gothics), highlight the ironies that seem perennially to dog Poe's footsteps. A veritable barrage of novels and tales has boiled the pot of sensationalism, whence emerges a Poe inclined to alcoholism, drug addiction, and titillating sexuality—all facets of a captivating, but entirely imaginary personality. The intriguing sexuality, moreover, is altogether absent from his own sketch appropriately titled, in this context, "The Imp of the Perverse." Imps or perversity, in varying proportions, certainly sound keynotes in many biographical and other accounts of Poe's personality and literary intentions, as I hope to demonstrate in the following pages. Among novels that feature Poe as a character, the most outlandish is perhaps Anne Edwards's *Child of Night* (1975). All of Poe's supposedly negative and sensational traits are reincarnated in hot young Eddie Polk, the incestuously-inclined hero in a mawkish plot. John Ball's edited collection of essays, *The Mystery Story* (1976), also does Poe's art no favors by means of inaccurate bibliographical data concerning publications of "The Murders in the Rue Morgue," surely a title deserving better treatment from experts in detective and terror fiction. With decided relief one turns from such materials to a fine detective story like Frederick Irving Anderson's "Beyond All Conjecture," the opening selection in *The Book of Murder* (1930), a Haycraft-Queen "Cornerstone" title, wherein Poe receives just dues. Remembering that the epigraph to "Murders" is the famous passage about the sirens from Sir Thomas Browne's *Urn-Burial,* we go on to discover in Anderson's title (a phrase of Browne's) and in the story itself a conscious acknowledgement of Poe's artistry rather than the repetitions of a frequently, and erroneously, held notion that he was an excrescence disfiguring the profile of American literature.[1] One wonders, after the forty-odd-years' "standard" position of Arthur Hobson Quinn's biography, how such wrong-headedness about Poe persists, recalling that the book bristles with factuality.

Turning to King and Carr as exemplars of twentieth-century views of Poe, we readily perceive differing attitudes implicit in the writings of these two noteworthy names in modern mystery, horror, and detective fiction. Carr's sense of Poe's accomplishments and his own employment of Poesque

characters and motifs are to me far more sound and canny than King's. A good case for this opinion takes shape if we look now to these twentieth-century writers' debts to Poe's famous "The Masque of the Red Death," and, in Carr's work, to certain other tales. King's *The Shining* and Carr's *Corpse in the Waxworks* ([also known as *The Waxworks Murders*] 1932) bear unmistakable signs of Poe's influence, although each novel takes a different tack with that influence.[2]

"Masque" embodies a wealth of those undercurrents of suggestion so dear to Poe, most notably in its richly symbolic life-to-death journey by the self. Thus its continual attention to time, after the stage is initially set (a gesture toward Shakespeare's theme of moving time in *The Tempest,* to which "Masque" is obviously indebted), is altogether sound. The recurring attention to the great clock, cleverly associated with images of a coffin and death in its obtrusive "ebony" hue and in its sounds, is intensified by other themes and images of life's boundaries: the seven rooms, with color schemes indicative of life's dawn, zenith, and darkening close; Prospero's "journey" through those eerie chambers, in pursuit of the sinister masquer; the weird lighting, itself suggestive of artificial attempts at creating a light of life within surroundings just as unrealistically sealed off from "what's out there," to indulge for the nonce in recent colloquialism, or from what the uneasy dream figures believe may be lurking to expose their crazy revels as mere fantasy—and destructive fantasy at that. The "gigantic" size of the clock makes evident too the theme of time's pulsing in a vital, because natural, function throughout "Masque."

Despite its surfaces of melodrama and lurid spook-story supernaturalism, Poe's tale, in phrasing and parabolic method, reminds us of the King James Bible and the sober morals in its "stories." The solemnity of biblical tone is maintained through the dramatic qualities of "Masque"—those "It was" passages, for example, creating an illusion for the reader-audience akin to the distancing created by high tragedy upon the stage. There the action seems to transpire with agonizing slowness and relentlessness. Such ritardando tactics as the halting effect of the dash punctuation in the penultimate paragraph, or the "And" beginnings for most sentences in the last, allow readers to experience something of the painful emotions (moreso than physical excruciations) endured by the dramatis personae.

We watch the "Red Death's" moving, and time's passage—as it is depicted in Beardsley's graphics or in Faulkner's tortuous prose—seems temporarily suspended, or, at least, emphatically slowed: "the intruder, who at the moment was also near at hand, and now, with deliberate and stately step, made closer approach." Continuing, the masked figure

> passed within a yard of the prince's person; and, while the vast assembly, as if with one impulse, shrank, he made his way uninterruptedly, but with the same solemn and measured step through the purple to the green—through the green to the orange—through this again to the white—and even thence to the violet, ere a decided movement had been made to arrest him. (*M.* 2:676)

If this prose does not achieve slow motion as films do, then Poe is no artist. Theme and form coalesce exquisitely in this and other passages.[3]

When we turn from "Masque" to *The Shining,* we receive a jolt. However steeped in Poe its author may be, this novel is all too blatantly a stepchild, if not an abortive outgrowth, of Poe's aims and achievements. Like Poe, King begins with everyday reality, in this case the need for burnt-out college (English) professor Jack Torrance to maintain gainful employment and leisure to complete a play. Hoping to secure both during a winter's stint as caretaker for the "Overlook," a Colorado tourist hotel, he brings his wife and son with him, and, in effect, he attempts to shut out the normal world from their lives. After the manner of Poe's Prospero, Torrance creates increasing psychic torment for his family and himself, destructively spiraling into physical cruelty as well—with sadistic beatings, maimings, stabbings, and attempted murder, no less—before Halloran, a former cook at the hotel (whose "shining" or psychic empathy bonds him with little Danny, Torrance's son), returns, suffers at Torrance's hands, but finally breaks the spell that threatens them all.

*The Shining* emphatically reveals King's uncertain intentions. Is he writing a Gothic, has he created a sophisticated psychic drama, or does he attempt too much? With its theme of escape from reality (and retreating ever farther into psychological disorder, wherein the epigraph from "Masque" highlights the dreamy, non-rational undercurrents of his grim story), mingled heavy-handedly with melodramatic high jinks, King's novel betrays cross-purposes with tenuous connections. Poe's language in "Masque" is consistently dignified, but King's often unjustifiably veers into the vulgate with little reason other than that in this "modern" novel such language should be there. After all, "fuck" and its compounds do not constitute the final degree of modernity in American fiction, nor do King's recurring italics function as much other than signals of melodrama. His aim toward yoking of psychological and supernatural forces with the actual character of the murderous, has-been professor to recreate a "Red Death" protagonist, falls flat. Poe, we remember, centered (albeit covertly) upon sensations of an inward, emotional variety. King's hand falters, resulting in a "Red-Death"

character who is neither fish nor flesh. Instead of existing within a Poesque region of sensation, King's closing chapters assault us with the sensation*al*. His drawing upon "Masque," in situation or by means of quotation—as Torrance parties with his evil masquers (who are fantasy creations of his own warped psyche), then homicidally pursues his wife and son through the deserted hotel—is a poor attempt to rework Poe's substance. Furthermore, the animal-shaped shrubbery that comes to life lends too much of the ludicrous to this already strained novel. Considering the strong tendency toward parody among American writers, we might wish to defend King's handling of the Poesque as exemplifying this tendency.[4] If parody is deliberate in *The Shining*, however, it is much too clumsily bodied forth to elicit mirth.

In the main, *The Shining* is a pretty dreary takeoff from "Masque." This very quality, however, aligns King's conception of the Poesque with that of many another recent writer. In other words, present a weird setting, add a dash of psychic trauma (maybe intensify this upset by means of supernaturalism), spike all these ingredients with passing respects to sex, crime, pleasure-pain, and drunkenness. *The Shining* is an undertaking of such a feat, and in turn it implies the nature of King's conception of Poe the artist, as well as of Poe the legendary figure: both in despite of the epigraph from "Masque."

Moving now to address the attitudes and techniques of John Dickson Carr, we must be aware of his long years' awareness of and affection for the fiction, and especially the sensation fiction, of the last century. Doyle, Dickens, Collins, as well as Poe, reappear in Carr's own fiction and critical writings. Along the way to *Corpse in the Waxworks* we may profitably pause over some thoughts of Dorothy L. Sayers, authority in areas of horror and detective fiction and on Poe's centrality within their traditions:

> Mr. Carr can lead us away from the small, artificial, brightly lit stage of the ordinary detective plot into the menace of outer darkness. He can create illusion or delight with rollicking absurdity. He can invest a passage from a lost work of Edgar Allen [sic] Poe and make it sound like the real thing. In short, he can write...in the sense that every sentence gives a thrill of positive pleasure.

This comment epitomizes Carr's practice in *Corpse in the Waxworks*, although it actually appears in a 1934 London *Times* review of his first novel, *It Walks by Night* (1930). More important, the bracketing of Carr with Poe highlights the "menace of outer darkness" and the subtle buildup of atmosphere. Carr's continuing predilection for Poesque elements, as well

as for the personality of Poe himself, crops up in *The Mad Hatter Mystery* (1933), which focuses upon a newly discovered manuscript of another Dupin tale; in that fine story, "The Gentleman from Paris" (1950), featuring Poe as central character; and in *The Dark of the Moon* (1967), clearly derivative from that ever-popular ratiocinative tale, "The Gold-Bug." These titles are random samples of works by Carr that bear Poe's stamp.

With these externals in mind, we may now perhaps discern the importance in the leading epigraph to *Corpse in the Waxworks* of yet another passage from Poe's "Masque"

> Be sure they were grotesque. There were much glare and piquancy and phantasm...There were arabesque figures with unsuited limbs and appointments. There were delirious fancies such as the madman fashions. There were much of the beautiful, much of the wanton, much of the *bizarre*, something of the terrible, and not a little of that which might have excited disgust. To and fro in the seven chambers there stalked, in fact, a multitude of dreams. (*M.* 2:673)

This overview of Prince Prospero's surroundings and followers emphasizes the emotional-psychological underpinnings of Poe's appropriately named tale. The elements of dream and fantasy put forth by Poe reappear, modified to be sure, among salient features in Carr's novel, as do several other, more sensational constituents that Poe, more ably than King, incorporated into the stuff of his fiction. Possibly, and probably, "The Mystery of Marie Roget" and "The Cask of Amontillado" also contributed texture and character to Carr's book.

*Corpse in the Waxworks* is easy to outline in synopsis. Narrator as well as friend to Detective Bencolin, the young American, Jeff Marle, assists in investigating the murder of beautiful, wealthy Claudine Martel. She was found stabbed and left draped across the arms of a satyr statue in the waxworks of Monsieur Augustin. We are led through a series of hints concerning the murderer's identity, being misled by ingenious diversions as to whodunnit; introduced to Étienne Galant, aging rakehell of frightening mien and savage temper; taken to the home of the elderly, artistocratic, proud parents of the murdered Claudine; directed on into a suspense-filled, violent chase through the mysterious, terrifying Club of Masks and the Musée Augustin, where the wicked Galant ultimately falls dead from stab wounds; and brought to a conclusion in which the revelation of the genuine, doubtless unanticipated, murderer comes out at last.

Carr capitalizes upon the Poesque practice of involving dream structures to mute overt sensationalism. *Corpse in the Waxworks* depends heavily

upon maintenance of an appearance-reality oscillation—which serves to hold our interest in the detection—rather than fumbling with darker corridors of the psyche as King does. The nature of the waxworks and its foreboding statuary, the evening amidst weird, shadowy urban surroundings, the club with its mysterious keys, costumes, and, more important, characters, whose personalities seem constantly to shift, the reasons for the murders: all partake of near intangibility, although none save the last is actually abstract. Here, unlike King's persuasion in *The Shining,* we are never allowed to forget that we are reading a detective story, and the unnerving unrealities we encounter intensify the concept of mystery commonly associated with crime and detective fiction.

Instead of parading before us a crippled, deformed latter-day descendant of "Masque," Carr subtly incorporates several of the better qualities of that tale into *Corpse in the Waxworks,* thereby gracefully acknowledging his debt to and image of Edgar Allan Poe. If syntax and scene repeat in "Masque," the closing sections of Carr's novel recall the opening in a nightclub scenario redolent of Prospero's fantastic ballroom. Hints of illusion, nay of madness, that may lead into supernaturalism, point up how attentively the twentieth-century writer of detective fiction had mastered his Poe. Also, Galant's death from stabbing, at the close of Ch. 16, after a pursuit too reminiscent of Prospero's mad scramble toward the "Red Death" for us to overlook, attests Carr's vigilance. Like Prospero, Galant has "created" most of the fantasy in *Corpse in the Waxworks,* fantasy that enchants *and* terrifies those involved in the centers of its activity, as well as gripping the reader. Like Prospero, too, Galant's death involves a dagger. Galant's own grotesque countenance, his intent pursuits of those he victimizes, his ultimate responsibility for the girls' deaths, mark an additional ancestry for him in Poe's mummer.

Overall, Carr modifies Poe's haunting masquer by splitting that figure five ways as he models his own personae in *Corpse in the Waxworks:* Jeff, Marie, Bencolin, Galant, and Colonel Martel partake of the ambiguous "Red Death's" characteristics. Most notably, the blood-spattered Jeff—Galant's henchmen hot on his trail through the Club of Masks—like Poe's mummer, stalks his culprit through those strange surroundings. As in "Masque," half-lights and shadows furnish an appropriate backdrop to the quest after answers and clarity in *Corpse in the Waxworks.* Jeff's entrance into the club is fraught with Poesque descriptions, with phraseology and visual effects akin to those in the epigraph from "Masque." Just so, Marie Augustin's red gown and her role as Jeff's guide suggest inversions of Poe's strategy; she serves as mummer to his Prospero, although the implication and outcome differ considerably from the grim tragedy that draws "Masque" to a close.

Furthermore, her name recalls that of Poe's Marie Roget and of his C. Auguste Dupin. As with Marie Roget-Mary Rogers, there are hints of illicit sex and of crime hovering about Carr's enchantress.

Additional debts to Poe are not difficult to discover on the pages of *Corpse in the Waxworks.* Carr's "gardens of the Faubourg Saint-Germain" parallels Poe's use of that locale in "Murders." The chiming clock, the bizarre game of dominoes (suggestive of the games played by Prospero's phantasms), and the "ghosts" (of his past) so essential a part of Colonel Martel's life, recall similar trappings in "Masque." The ironic gambit concerning Masonic lore as regards Bencolin and Robiquet—over a coffin, no less—combines with the figure of Colonel Martel, the cloaked (thus disguised) assassin, calmly and relentlessly trailing his victims through dimly illuminated underground windings, whose confession is carefully reconstructed, to remind us of "Cask." Given Carr's demonstrable familiarity with Poe's work, such findings as these ought not to be dismissed as the incautious offerings of a Poe enthusiast.[5]

We must conclude, I believe, that Carr's vision embraced the Poesque conception of instability within the human self, a conception that frequently centered upon crime, violence, and madness, or near madness. Carr was quick to perceive how those shadowy regions of the mind could enhance a good tale of mystery and detection, as *Corpse in the Waxworks* reveals. Never overweeningly proud, John Dickson Carr modestly trod the paths of a literature much more "popular" than what exists (at least below surface) in Poe's greatest tales. The theme of "Masque"—how fine are the lines separating appearances from underlying, and vastly more consequential realities—Carr unpretentiously adapted to his own purposes within *Corpse in the Waxworks.* Unlike Stephen King, Carr does not over-reach his mark. Thus he succeeds where King falls short. A passage from Ch. 2 of *Corpse in the Waxworks* implies much about the methods in that book: "The man must be dead and buriable who does not respond to a healthy curiosity about things morbid." With such a thought in mind, Carr drew upon, but he did not adapt slavishly nor did he outrageously sensationalize, Edgar Allan Poe, creator of "Masque" and other tales, as demonstrated above. Both King and Carr, in the examples examined here, are valuable barometers to the image of Poe the literary artist and to what that image portends for writers of mystery and detective fiction in the twentieth century.

## NOTES

[1] I thank Craig Werner, of the University of Wisconsin, for his help in speeding along my work as he generously has. The misinformation on "Murders" appears in

E. T. Guymon, Jr., "Why Do We Read This Stuff?"—*The Mystery Story*, ed. John Ball (Del Mar, CA, 1976), p. 363.

[2] Evidence for Poe's influence on these two writers exists in King's "The Fright Report," *Oui*, 7(January 1978), pp. 76-78, 107-108; and in his foreward to a collection of his stories, *Night Shift* (New York, 1978), p. xvii. The first story, "Jerusalem's Lot," suggests a product from Poe's own pen. The Poe-Carr relationship is discussed by Robert Lewis Taylor, "Profiles: Two Authors in an Attic," *New Yorker*, 8 September 1951, pp. 42, 48; *idem.*, 15 September 1951, p. 38; J. R. Christopher, "Poe and the Tradition of the Detective Story," *The Mystery Writer's Art*, ed. Francis M. Nevins, Jr. (Bowling Green, O, 1970), pp. 24-27. In a letter to me, 15 August 1978, the late Larry French, a Carr expert *non pareil*, emphasized Poe's impact upon Carr. French more thoroughly outlined this relationship in *Culprit Confesses*, 9(1978), 7-8; and "The Baker Street-Carrian Connection," *BSJ*, 29(March 1979), pp. 6-10. I chart resemblances between Poe, on the one hand, and King and Carr, on the other, in "Best-Selling Horror," *Gothic*, 1(1979), 32-34.

[3] Poe made a signal revision in altering his original title, "The Mask of the Red Death—A Fantasy," to "The Masque of the Red Death," thereby placing the burden of interpreting ambiguities upon readers.

[4] Leslie Fiedler comments upon American writers' propensities toward parody and the blurring of conscious and unconscious parody in "The Dream of the New," *American Dreams, American Nightmares*, ed. David Madden (Carbondale and Edwardsville, 1970), pp. 24-25.

[5] James E. Rocks, "Conflict and Motive in 'The Cask of Amontillado'," *PoeS*, 5(1972), 50-51.

# THE INFAMY AND THE ECSTASY: CRIME, ART, AND METAPHYSICS IN EDGAR ALLAN POE'S "WILLIAM WILSON" AND JORGE LUIS BORGES'S "DEUTSCHES REQUIEM"

*MAURICE J. BENNETT*

*"I'll join with black despair against my soul*
*And to myself become an enemy."*
*—Richard III*

Many critics observe in passing that the Argentine writer Jorge Luis Borges is perhaps the most eminent perpetuator of Poe's pioneering efforts in the detective story and the short tale that turns dramatic narrative into philosophical speculation.[1] Their observations might sufficiently justify the present study, did not Borges specifically cite Poe as one of the authors to whom he is most indebted.[2] Similar temperaments and philosophical interests have led the two "Americans" to identical literary forms, and one can frequently observe in the thematic preoccupations and structural composition of Borges's work distinct echoes of his North American predecessor. He often takes a theme or a complete story and rewrites it in such terms as to create both a new tale and a striking illumination of his source. Borges cites "William Wilson" as one of the stories he innovates upon in what he considers to be his paradigmatic tale, "The Approach to al-Mu'tasim," but it is "Deutsches Requiem" that directly confronts the Poe story and extrapolates from it an equally compelling fiction.[3]

Borges states that "each writer *creates* his precursors" (*OI:*109),[4] and he immediately establishes a relationship to Poe in the opening sentence of "Deutsches Requiem." The protagonist's introductory "My name is Otto Dietrich zur Linde" is an unmistakable echo of "My name is Arthur Gordon Pym," the opening line of the Poe novel to which Borges repeatedly turns as an example of his taste in fiction.[5] That he is consciously alluding to Poe here is suggested by his choice in the Spanish original of the uncommon and formal *"Mi nombre es"* ("My name is") over the colloquial and more usual *"Me llamo"* ("I call myself") that might be expected in this confessional narrative.[6] The line's relationship to "Let me call myself, for the present, William Wilson" is more oblique and already points to an interpretation. A direct allusion to the beginning of *Pym*, attached to a plot borrowed from "Wilson," essentially conflates the two Poe stories. The psychologizing of one is juxtaposed with the symbolic topography of the other, providing Wilson's seemingly motivationless behavior with a context that begins to

expand its significance beyond an apparent focus on mere eccentricity.

This broadening of the implications of "Wilson" constitutes a major aspect of the relationship between Poe's story and Borges's revision. In their broadest outline, the plots of the two tales are nearly identical, but analogous events consistently diverge toward psychological analysis in one and metaphysical emphases in the other. In part, such divergences reflect the historical moments that produced the two stories. Poe's focus on the subjective repeats a preoccupation with personal experience that was central to Romanticism. As Lucien Goldmann notes in his essay on Malraux, however, the problem of the mid-twentieth century is precisely the value (or possibility) of such experience in the face of overwhelming historical and technological change.[7] Borges's response to the general cultural dilemma has been to turn to doctrines that posit an atemporal reality inhabited by a meta-self beyond the vagaries of history. "To deny temporal succession, to deny the ego," he writes, "...are apparent desperations and secret assuagements" (*OI:* 186-187)—an attempt to convince ourselves that "no opprobrium, no calamity, no dictator will be able to impoverish us."[8]

The two stories not only begin with similar rhetorical flourishes, but they make the same narrative gestures. The suppressed identity indicated by Wilson's resort to a pseudonym is repeated by Borges through a footnote that reveals Otto's omission of the prominent Jewish theologian, Johannes Forkel, from the list of his German ancestors. But where Wilson's gesture appears as a narrative stratagem or genuflection to conventional morality ("The fair page now lying before me need not be sullied by my real appellation," he writes), Otto's omission is an act of symbolic self-violence that will be repeated and magnified in the central event of his tale.

Both characters also present their experience from the moral perspective of conventional humanity. Wilson projects himself as the object of "scorn," "horror," and "detestation," having led a life of "unparalleled infamy," "unspeakable misery," and "unpardonable crime" (*H.* 3:299).[9] His claim to have surpassed Elah-Gabalus in viciousness suggests that his crimes resembled the sensual extravagances for which the Roman emperor is notorious. As the former sub-director of the Nazi concentration camp at Tarnowitz, Poland, however, Otto's criminality is presented less as the product of personal excess than as the result of broad political, ideological, and historical extravagances. He presents the problematic case of the "martyr" whose outlaw status derives primarily from the historical defeat of his sect rather than from an innate moral depravity. He, too, assumes the vocabulary of his judges, admitting that he has been a "torturer and murderer" (*L.*:141). But where Wilson at least mouths the rhetoric of repentance, exclaiming at the

"dense, dismal, and limitless" cloud that hangs between his "hopes and heaven" (*H*. 3:299), the essential project of Otto's narrative is the remorseless assumption of the terms of opprobrium and their transformation into the badges of affirmation.

The difference in Wilson's and Otto's reaction to what they both feel is the justified hostility of their fellow men derives from the divergent motivations of their confessions. Wilson's preoccupations are basically affective: faced with his imminent death, he desires the human connection, the "sympathy," from which his career in infamy has excluded him. Otto, however, is more philosophically disposed—he merely wishes to be understood in terms of the larger forces for which he has labored: "Those who care to listen to me will understand the history of Germany and the future history of the world.... Tomorrow I will die, but I am a symbol of future generations" (*L:*142). He thus moves immediately from the inevitable futility of personal defiance to the justification available on the suprapersonal plane of Hegelian "history."

The distinction between Wilson's personalism and Otto's more abstract identity is highlighted in the sense of individual singularity they both feel. For instance, Wilson writes that "although temptation may have erewhile existed as great, man was never *thus,* at least, tempted before—certainly, never *thus* fell" (*H*. 3:300), and Otto asserts that although he is a symbol of the future, at present "cases" like his are "exceptional and astonishing" (*L:*142). But the German does not wear his singularity with the American's bravado; instead, he attempts to eschew all individuality. Comparing the Nazi movement to the early stages of Christianity and Islam, he claims that a "new kind of man was needed" and records his attempt "to reason that we had to suppress our individuality for the lofty purpose which brought us together" (*L:*143).

It is the nature of the two characters' criminality, however, that most profoundly indicates the radically personalized focus of the Poe story and Borges's meta-personal interests. Not only does Wilson cheat at cards, but he is driven to his final extremity when his double interferes with his plans to seduce the beautiful young wife of the Duke Di Broglio. His dishonorableness and his sensuality depend on the official morality of middle-class Victorian respectability for their shock value; today, they appear rather venial when compared with the nature and scale of Otto's atrocities. In any case, Wilson's failures are personal and eccentric, and there is no attempt to encourage, or even to allow, the reader to identify with them or to view them as in any way familiar.

Otto's aberration, however, symbolizes a broad cultural debacle. On a general level, Borges cites the simplicity of Poe's notions of horror as deriv-

ing from the comparative simplicity of the nineteenth century: "Our century is more unfortunate than the nineteenth," he claims, "to that sad privilege it is owed that the hells subsequently worked out (by Henry James, by Kafka) might be more complex and more intimate than Poe's."[10] More specifically, he notes that "Notoriously, the gods have denied the Germans spontaneous beauty," that they "appear incapable of working without some hallucinatory apprenticeship," and that where "The men of other lands can be absent-mindedly atrocious, eventually heroic; Germans demand seminaries of abnegation, ethics of infamy."[11] And in a meditation on the Allied liberation of Paris, he observes:

> for Europeans and Americans, one order—and only one—is possible; it used to be called Rome and now is called Western Culture. To be a Nazi (to play the game of energetic barbarism, to play at being a Viking, a Tartar, a sixteenth-century conquistador, a Gaucho, a redskin) is, after all, a mental and moral impossibility. Nazism suffers from unreality, like Erigena's hells. It is uninhabitable; men can only die for it, lie for it, kill and wound for it. No one in the intimate depths of his being, can wish it to triumph. I shall hazard a conjecture: *Hitler wants to be defeated.* Hitler is collaborating blindly with the inevitable armies that will annihilate him, as the metal vultures and the dragon (which must not have been unaware that they were monsters) collaborated, mysteriously, with Hercules. (*OI*: 135-136)

Borges's conceptions of the twentieth century, of Germans, and of the Nazi enterprise thus combine to provide the contours for the portrait of his protagonist. Otto is a self-conscious "monster," and his reference to himself as "the abominable" moves him beyond Wilson's personal sensuality toward a ritual impurity whose very nature valorizes the virtue from which he is excluded. His apostasy from "Western Culture" assumes a religious dimension, and his heresy becomes an inverted affirmation.

Where Wilson's behavior never rises above the details of his physical and social existence and lacks any consciously held informing principle, Otto's perversity constitutes a program for salvation. The depth of his "religious" ardor is indicated by a kind of spiritual strenuousness. The amputation of his leg as the result of a wound received in the anti-Jewish riots in Tilsit denies him the direct and palpable exhilarations of action, but his enforced civilianism clarifies for him the spiritual nature of his vocation: "To die for a religion is easier than to live it absolutely; to battle in Ephesus against the wild beasts is not so trying (thousands of obscure martyrs did it) as to be Paul, servant of Jesus; one act is less than a man's entire life. War and glory are *facilities;* more arduous than the undertaking of Napoleon was that of Raskolnikov" (*L:* 143-144).

Both tales, then, dramatize the psychomachy of particular kinds of criminal personality, and in each the central event is a symbolic suicide. They generate alter-egos that would connect the protagonists to conventional morality and community. Wilson describes his antagonist as the suggestion of "dim visions of my earliest infancy—wild, confused and thronging memories of a time when memory herself was yet unborn" (*H.* 3:311). He proceeds from the period anterior to the differentiation of consciousness into the reasoning and imaginative faculties, before the separation of the moral sense from desire. Wilson's commitment to imagination and crime forces him to define his double's moral advice as a "rebellion," and, although he admits that heeding this advice would have made him a happier man, it would also have made him less singular and removed both the need and the occasion for the present tale.

For Otto, Nazism is "an act of morality" that attaches a holiness to evil. It is the twentieth century's attempt to purge itself of the undesirable sentimentalism and personalism bequeathed to it by the nineteenth. Where the naturalistic environment of the battlefield quickly strips away the veneer of humanist culture, "such is not the case in a wretched cell"—in the close quarters of the private self—"where insidious deceitful mercy tempts us with ancient tenderness" (*L.*:144). Nietzsche is the apostle appealed to here, for whose Zarathustra "mercy is the greatest of sins" (*L.*:144). But just as Wilson is haunted by the representative of communal order, an externalized conscience, so Otto has his temptation to "ancient tenderness," the poet David Jerusalem of Breslau, an inmate of his camp. Jerusalem is the singer of joy and love, and Otto confesses the indelible impression made on him by the man's two great works, the poem *Tse Yang, Painter of Tigers* and the soliloquy *Rosencrantz Speaks with the Angel;* he knows them by heart.

Borges footnotes that Jerusalem is not mentioned in the critical study by Albert Soergel to which Otto refers, in any history of German literature, or even in the camp's records. And Otto explicitly states: "In my eyes he was not a man, not even a Jew; he had been transformed into a detested zone of my soul. I agonized with him, I died with him and somehow I was lost with him; therefore, I was implacable" (*L.*: 145). His violence against Jerusalem culminates the violence against himself that first appeared in his suppression of his Jewish identity or in his admission that his early years in the party were difficult because, "although I do not lack courage, I am repelled by violence" (*L.*: 142-143). Permitting neither Jerusalem's "glory" nor his own "compassion" to soften him, Otto drives the poet to suicide and, thus, effectively eliminates the "ancient tenderness" proscribed by his cult of violence.

Self-murder is thus the apparently inevitable climax to careers of almost hysterical perversity in these tales. In particular, Wilson's murder of his conscience is the event toward which his narrative inexorably moves. Its occurrence returns the tale to its origin: Wilson's alienation. Thus, the alter-ego's dying words, *"henceforward art thou also dead—dead to the World, to Heaven and to Hope!"* (*H.* 3:325), echo those with which the story began: "to the earth art thou forever dead? to its honors, to its flowers, to its golden aspirations?" (*H.* 3:299). This narrative circularity provides the structural analog to the Romantic solipsism to which Wilson is condemned.

Otto's murder of Jerusalem, however, is but the definitive gesture in a series of outrages whose goal is essentially spiritual; it is part of a linear, or vertical, movement toward transcendence. Jerusalem's death liberates Otto into a sense of fullness that is the actual justification for his narrative; it is a vehicle for the attainment of religious ecstasy. By describing Otto's spiritual elevation as a "plenitude," Borges places it within a tradition of the mystical attainment of divine awareness through suffering. "I thought I was emptying the cup of anger," Otto writes, "but in the dregs I encountered an unexpected flavor, the mysterious and almost terrible flavor of happiness" (*L:* 146). He has attempted the inverse affirmation of happiness, beneficence, and order through a radical pursuit of horror, evil, chaos, so that he can write at the end with a kind of exultation: "If victory and injustice and happiness are not for Germany, let them be for other nations. Let Heaven exist, even though our dwelling place is Hell" (*L:*147). Infamy affirms sanctity; hell not only implies but demands heaven.

"William Wilson" and "Deutsches Requiem" end with the vivid image of their narrators staring into mirrors. In "Wilson," the gesture condenses the essential narcissism represented by the protagonist's fascination with his *personal* experience; it is analogous to the encompassing narrative, which is itself but a larger mirror in which Wilson reflects himself. Despite the moral outrage customarily directed at the Nazis, however, Borges's image conveys a tranquility absent in Poe. The explicit reference to Christianity and to Islam, the biblical allusions and prose rhythms, remind the reader that Otto's dilemma, however perversely mishandled, is not only human, but disturbingly similar to the enthusiasms that have produced our more received and cherished dogmas. Emile Cioran, observing the homology between the mystic, the saint, and the heretic, writes of the inevitable consequence of their intrusion into history:

> Idolaters by instinct, we convert the objects of our dreams and our interests into the Unconditional. History is nothing but a procession of

> false Absolutes...We kill only in the name of a god or of his counterfeits...The ages of fervor abound in bloody exploits: Saint Teresa could only be the contemporary of the auto-da-fé, a Luther of the repression of the Peasants' Revolt. In every mystic outburst, the moans of victims parallel the moans of ecstasy....Scaffolds, dungeons, jails flourish only in a shadow of a faith—of that need to believe which has infested the mind forever.[12]

It is apparent that Otto has converted "History" into the operant deity in his tale, and it is this basic identity between his spiritual aspirations and historical precedent—his fundamental humanity—that seduces the reader into sharing his sense of losing the personal self in a cosmic enterprise in which all plenitude resides. The tale ends on a note of beatitude: "I look at myself in the mirror to discover who I am, to discover how I will act in a few hours, when I am face to face with death. My flesh may be afraid; I am not" (*L*:147).

Wilson's and Otto's careers may be explained as an attraction to crime as a kind of self-torture; their tales record the transformation of homicide into suicide, which, in turn, ultimately becomes a self-mortification that leads to transcendence. For both Poe and Borges are interested in crime as an aspect of the aesthetic metaphysic that underlies their work. Poe, for instance, claimed that "beauty" was the sole attribute through which man could apprehend God—and only poets, with "hearts of maddening fervor" and possessing "that divine sixth sense," approach divinity (*H.* 11:255-256). In his major aesthetic statement, "The Poetic Principle," he added that the poet, "Inspired by an ecstatic prescience of the glories beyond the grave," became frustrated to madness by his inability to grasp immediately the Beauty of which art gave "but brief and indeterminate glimpses" (*H.* 14:273-274). The permanent attainment of beauty was possible only by escaping mortality, and such tales as "The Conversation of Eiros and Charmion" and "The Colloquy of Monos and Una" attempt to portray aesthetic paradises inhabited by the disembodied spirits of the blessed—the realm Poe called "Aidenn." Thus, "what we call death" is the precondition for transcendence, and crime provokes reprisals that may involve that "painful metamorphosis."[13] Evil, and madness as a kind of psychological outlawry, impel Poe's imaginative characters towards a desired consummation; they are the behavioral and mental analogs of the indirection he makes requisite for the vision of truth.[14]

Borges himself repeatedly invokes those sects and religions that incorporate a radical pursuit of evil and abomination as a means of spiritual purification. "The Theologians" directly addresses this kind of search for ecstasy in terms of the heresies of historical Christianity, but his conception

of the poet's necessary exhaustion of the possibilities of being—including crime and alienation—is central to his artistic effort.[15] Any given character's criminality, then, becomes a means of separating him from a contingent, quotidian existence and moves him closer to its opposite: metaphysical reality. Thus, when Barton Levi St. Armand observes that Borges is the "heir" of Poe's "occult metaphysics," he points to both writers' interest in those beliefs that view evil as a cosmic principle of equal or superior efficacy to virtue as an instrument for man's triumph over disorder, despair, and death.[16]

The aesthetic aspect of the will to crime derives from Wilson's and Otto's profoundly imaginative natures. Not only do they specifically emphasize their writing of their tales, but, in some sense, they actually adumbrate their authors' conception of the artist-personality. The most noted consequence of Poe's principle of perverseness, for instance, is irrational, self-destructive behavior adequately illustrated by Wilson's conduct. But another result is a linquistic obliquity that is the basis of all literary language—of metaphor—and that describes Poe's own techniques, as he cites the "earnest desire to tantalize a listener by circumlocution" and the exchange of clarity and precision for "certain involutions and parentheses" (*H.* 6:148). Wilson claims to have come from "a race whose imaginative and easily excitable temperament has at all times rendered them remarkable" (*H.* 3:300), and when he refers to his "passionate energy of mind," he echoes Poe's attribution of "hearts of maddening fervor" to lovers of the Beautiful. His gambling at cards points to Poe's explicit use of card-playing in "The Murders in the Rue Morgue" as a metaphor to describe the creative-critical faculties of the intuitive artist. And the murder of his admonishing conscience is the dramatic enactment of Poe's exorcism of the "heresy" of the didactic in "The Poetic Principle"—his exclusion of moral consideration from among the central aims of poetry.

The passive, tender, imaginative side of Otto's sensibility is represented by his attraction to music, metaphysics, and drama—symbolized by the "Germanic" names of Brahms, Schopenhauer, and Shakespeare. "He who pauses in wonder, moved with tenderness and gratitude, before any facet of the work of these auspicious creators, let him know that I also paused there, I, the abominable" (*L.*:142), he writes. His literary propensities have surfaced in a polemical article against Spengler, and it should be noticed that his conception of Nazism as a creative movement and his participation in it essentially confound him with those other "German" creators he regards with such piety.

Otto is particularly haunted by David Jerusalem's soliloquy, *Rosen-*

*crantz Speaks with the Angel,* "in which a sixteenth-century London money-lender vainly tries on his deathbed to vindicate his crimes, without suspecting that the secret justification of his life is that of having inspired in one of his clients (whom he has seen but once and does not remember) the character of Shylock" (*L*:144). This brief passage may be regarded as the tale's aesthetic center. Otto, himself a Jew and a criminal, also attempts a self-vindication on the eve of his death, equally ignorant that his own value lies not in his historically discredited reasonings, but in his becoming a literary subject. Borges thus calls attention to the parasitic nature of the literary process (the explicit borrowing from Shakespeare) and the essential amorality of a procedure that often finds its choicest inspiration among outcasts. The drama of a sixteenth-century merchant and the testament of a twentieth-century bureaucrat are essentially the same story refracted through the distorting medium of history. In the background is also the confession of a nineteenth-century sensualist, though, and Shakespeare, Poe, and Borges are conflated into a single metapersonal figure—the artist.[17]

The documents composed by Wilson and Otto are compensations for the exile imposed on the artist by his criminal status. The contact with humanity that has been willfully ruptured by the protagonists themselves is reestablished by apologia that appeal for forgiveness or understanding, both of which are forms of sympathy. The narratives are penned *de profundis* at the symbolic moment of the protagonists' most extreme moral and existential isolation. They are composed literally at the moment immediately preceding death, so that its imminence becomes both their occasion and their justification. The literary moment is that in which the character-as-author confronts physical extinction; the work originates in crime but takes shape at the intersection of his perverse participation in human existence and his final, definitive exile. As authors, these characters die into their works; their "mortal" existence ends, but they are enshrined in the texts and will exist henceforth as literature.[18]

These tales thus reflect a literary metaphysic implicit in Poe and more explicitly addressed in Borges. Poe's atomic theory of the cosmos as the dispersed particles of an original essence, and his aesthetic definition of the universe as a divine "plot," make each fragment a character in a supreme fiction created by the death of God. In so far as Wilson's narrative results from his self-murder, it becomes a human reenactment of this original divine gesture of creation. In Borges, the voracious subsuming of the objective world by fictive constructs is a persistent theme: Shakespeare exists only in his work; like God and Valéry, he is implicit in his creation but nothing in himself. Borges himself is gradually replaced by the literary figure created by

his *oeuvre,* while the actual earth recedes before the imaginary universe of Tlön. And, finally, Borges describes a man who "peoples a space with images" of the world's myriad objects only to discover just before his death that "the patient labyrinth of lines traces the image of his own face."[19] Thus, the death of the biological Otto is the necessary precondition and the inevitable consequence of his literary activity.

In a meditation on Edward Fitzgerald, Borges claims that "every cultivated man is a theologian," and elsewhere he writes of metaphysics as "the only justification and finality of any theme," while admitting his own "incredulous and persistent passion for theological difficulties" (*OI:*76, xiv).[20] He thus provides an explicit thrust for his fiction that is absent in Poe. "William Wilson" merely presents a psychological process that leads to the loss of a contingent, historical identity, but which stops short of transcendence, leaving the protagonist in anguished review of the past and anxious anticipation of death. "Deutsches Requiem," however, is the immediate vehicle through which Otto attains that self which can confront death with equanimity. His achieved sense of a partnership with "History" removes him from temporal considerations and identifies him with the other literary figures around which his tale revolves and, ultimately, with God.

Poe's *Eureka,* however, embodies a theological passion similar to Borges' own, and it provides a metaphysic that, discretely and cautiously read into the earlier work, illuminates what otherwise appears as gratuitously aberrant. For example, where Wilson merely points to the hypertrophy of his will as the inevitable phenomenon of his moral and intellectual existence, the inexplicable growth of "evil propensities" which no agents of the moral order—least of all his "weak-minded" and similarly "afflicted" parents—could check, Otto finds a philosophical and vindication for his behavior in Schopenhauer:

> In the first volume of *Parerga and Paralipomena* I read again that everything which can happen to a man, from the instant of his birth until his death, has been preordained by him. Thus, every negligence is deliberate, every chance encounter an appointment, every humiliation a penitence, every failure a mysterious victory, every death a suicide. There is no more skillful consolation than the idea that we have chosen our own misfortunes; this individual teleology reveals a secret order and prodigiously confounds us with divinity. (*L:*143)

His own persecution, the defeat of Germany, and his murder of Jerusalem are thus but aspects of a cosmic drama of which he is both protagonist and author.

Wilson abandons such rationalizing to the reader, pleading for him to

"seek out for me, in the details I am about to give, some little oasis of *fatality* amid a wilderness of error" (*H.* 3:300). In the peroration that closes *Eureka,* though, Poe explains the import of his theory concerning the apocalyptic reunion of all matter with God in terms nearly identical to those Otto retrieves from Schopenhauer:

> In this view, and in this view alone, we comprehend the riddles of Divine Justice—of Inexorable Fate. In this view alone the existence of Evil becomes intelligible; but in this view it becomes more—it becomes endurable. Our souls no longer rebel at a *Sorrow* which we ourselves have imposed upon ourselves, in furtherance of our own purposes—with a view—if even with a futile view—to the extension of our own *Joy.* (*H.* 16: 313)

The metaphysic underlying these two stories, then, on some level, assumes man's complicity in his own fate; the soul attains a sense of universal adequacy that, in its final denial of otherness, obliterates the dichotomy between subject and object that has haunted modern consciousness.

Poe's conception of the universe as divine literature—as plot—finds an analog in Borges's preferred metaphor for the cosmos, the labyrinth, which he views as an existential consolation: it suggests a "hidden cosmos," in which there is a "center, a plan, [and] everything is foreseen."[21] Such metaphors demand that man be launched on a ceaseless quest for meaning—to identify the plot, decipher the text, discover the center of the cosmos. It is a challenge that Wilson presents directly to the reader when he invites him to discover the "fatal" principle that informs his behavior and, thus, organizes his narrative. Otto attempts to answer this challenge himself with his metaphysical speculations, but with both characters explanation, coherence, meaning is the goal.

Literature thus becomes an embodiment of the identifyingly human acts of construction and exegesis. Man, however, undertakes these tasks only under the inspiration of crime and alienation, with which, on one level, they are synonymous. Poe writes that true intellectual and moral greatness would be confused inevitably with their opposites: madness and depravity. Thus, in order to uncover real genius, one should ignore canonical figures and, instead, "search carefully the slight records of wretches who died in prison, in Bedlam, or upon the gallows" (*H.* 14:166). Similarly, Borges approvingly quotes Shakespeare's observation that "sweet are the uses of adversity," although adding: "all writing comes from unhappiness."[22] With these writers, infamy, madness, and crime (especially the symbolic suicides recounted in the present tales) are the moral, psychological, and gestural equivalents of

the conceptual paradox and verbal oxymoron that are essential to their artistic method.[23] Just as paradox confounds ordinary logic and oxymoron offends habitual linguistic expectations in order to achieve extraordinary perception, so crime dislocates the artist from conventional existence and sets him upon that paradigmatically human search whose goal is order—whether personal, as with Wilson's psychological case history, or cosmic, as with Otto's treatise. "The tools of my art are humiliation and anguish," confesses the unknown poet of a Borges poem.[24] Crime deflects the aesthetic sensibility into that suffering which is the inspiration, methodology, and price of artistic creation.

Ultimately, both the similarities and the differences between the Poe and Borges stories are the result of a shared project: they can be read as dramatizations of separate stages of a single movement of consciousness—the Romantic quest for transcendence. Harold Bloom describes these stages as the "Promethean" and the "Real Man" or "Imagination" stages, where the one represents the initial rejection of conventional modes of being and the other describes the imaginative freedom that the artist seeks.[25] The first stage necessarily involves the destruction of the purely social self, the rejection of ties with ordinary human community, but its inevitable danger is the failure to escape the restrictive focus on the now isolated self that the movement entails. It is haunted by the spectre of solipsism. The real goal, however, is the disconnection not only from convention but also from the natural, historical self that produced the original rupture and the attainment of an enlarged, intensified consciousness that produces a self commensurate with the universe, not merely alienated from it. From "A sordid solitary thing" who feels himself "his own low self the whole," the Romantic artist shared Coleridge's desire to become one with "Supreme Reality,"

> When he by a sacred sympathy might make
> The whole one self! self, that no alien knows!
> Self, far diffused as Fancy's wing can travel!
> Self, spreading still! Oblivious of its own,
> Yet all of all possessing![26]

"William Wilson" presents the first stage in this process, as Poe emphasizes the inextricable combination of imagination and libido in his protagonist's career. His rebellion produces an alter-ego that, complete with the symbolic, up-raised, admonishing finger, can only represent the social connection that Wilson must deny. Wilson fails to complete the progress toward transcendence, however, and is ensnared by the sterile, asphyxiating solipsism that the Romantics feared. At the last, his rebellion has only led to a

desire to recover the human community he has lost: "I long, in passing through the dim valley," he writes, "for the sympathy—I had nearly said for the pity—of my fellow men" (*H.* 3:299-300).

Otto, however, achieves the necessary second stage; having disconnected himself from convention, he also escapes mere sensuality. Where the double that Wilson generates, and destroys as the primary obstacle to imaginative freedom, represents the ethics of human community, Otto's double is the very sensual, imaginative, isolated creature that Wilson himself becomes. The opprobrium and obloquy that Wilson earns are shared by David Jerusalem, who has himself been "persecuted, denied, vituperated" (*L.*:144). More importantly, as the poet of "joy," Jerusalem is a kind of Whitmanesque caresser of sensuous detail who is attracted to "each thing, with a scrupulous and exact love."[27] Thus, Otto's murder of Jerusalem as a symbolic elimination of a "detested zone" of his soul is more complex than a mere Nazi rejection of humanist values. It liberates him from any connection to nature, to "things," and allows the attainment of ecstasy in the word's root sense of *ec-stasis*—an escape from the self unavailable to Wilson.[28] Otto thereby completes the process that Wilson inaugurates by rejecting Wilson's sensuality and its attendant solipsism. Between them, the two characters offer a unified portrait of the Romantic sensibility in pursuit of a transforming reality, the "plenitude" and peace that Otto experiences during his final hours. Thus, when Borges claims to have rewritten "Wilson's" essentially "ethical" emphasis, he is pointing to the incompleteness of the psychic and spiritual drama that Poe has undertaken to write. "Deutsches Requiem" is a specific response to that inadequacy, and Borges becomes the *reader* to whom Wilson has successfully appealed for an *interpretation* of his tale.

The intimate relationship between writing, reading, and rewriting is one of Borges's major subjects and a fundamental aspect of his style.[29] Characteristically, his work reveals literature in the dialectical process of criticism and revision. By taking Poe's psychological tale as the basis for his own heretical parody of the tradition launched by Augustine, he provides an indirect commentary on the nature and implications of his source. Otto's theodicy both reveals the limitations of Wilson's psychological and ethical conception of his dilemma and indicates the essential *direction* of his actions—something of which Wilson himself remains ignorant. "Deutsches Requiem" thus undertakes the critical task of salvaging the covert metaphysical implications of the Poe original. "Fate takes pleasure in repetitions, variants, symmetries," Borges claims, in which terms Otto becomes Wilson interpreted in the twentieth century, and Wilson a nineteenth-century Otto. They provide but another instance of those "tautologies" he identifies as the

"business" of his life. Thus, if Poe writes that "The human mind seems to perform, by some invariable laws, a sort of cycle, like those of the heavenly bodies" (*H.* 8: 266), it is fitting that Borges should echo across years, continents, cultures: "Perhaps universal history is the history of the diverse intonation of a few metaphors" (*OI*:9).[30]

## NOTES

[1] No extended study of Borges can avoid the spectre of Poe, so that his name appears repeatedly in critical studies of the Argentine's work. But for specific notations of identities in form and content between their work, see Gérard Genette, "La Littérature selon Borges," *Jorge Luis Borges, L'Herne* (Paris, 1964), p. 324; Robert E. Scholes and Eric S. Rabkin, *Science Fiction: History, Science, Vision* (New York, 1979), p. 8; and Barton Levi St. Armand, "'Seemingly Intuitive Leaps': Belief and Unbelief in *Eureka*," *Poe as Literary Cosmologer: Studies in Eureka: A Symposium*, ed. Richard P. Benton (Hartford, 1975), p. 14 n. 13.

[2] Borges's most extensive tributes to Poe are contained in *"El arte narrativo y la magia" Discusión* (Buenos Aires, 1957), pp. 86-91; and in "Edgar Allan Poe," *La nación*, [Buenos Aires], 2 October 1949, Section 2, p. 1. A few of the briefer notations of his awareness of, debt to, and appreciation of Poe occur in *The Aleph and Other Stories, 1933-1969*, trans. Norman di Giovanni (New York, 1970), pp. 237, 273; *The Book of Sand*, trans. Norman Thomas di Giovanni (New York, 1977), pp. 7-8; *Other Inquisitions, 1937-1952*, trans. Ruth L. C. Simms (New York, 1964), p. 86; and, with Adolfo Bioy-Casares, *Six Problems for Don Isidro Parodi*, trans. Norman Thomas di Giovanni (New York, 1980), p. 12.

[3] *The Aleph*, p. 266.

[4] Reference to Borges's works frequently cited here will be included in the text by abbreviation and page number: *Labyrinths: Selected Stories and Other Writings*, ed. Donald Yates and Frank Irby (New York, 1962), cited as *L*, and *Other Inquisitions* cited as *OI*.

[5] One half of Borges's essay on the nature of narrative is devoted to the Poe novel (*Discusión*, pp. 86-91), and his interest in the symbolic nature of the tale's opening line is indicated in a discussion of Poe's contribution to the detective story in *Borges Oral* (Buenos Aires, 1979), pp. 69, 77.

[6] Ronald Christ interestingly observes Borges's tendency to compose in several languages simultaneously. Particularly relevant here is his habit of searching out Latinisms that he then uses in their *English* rather than their root sense. Borges's prose frequently gives the impression of being a spare English translation of some Spanish original. See Christ's "A Modest Proposal for the Criticism of Borges" *The Cardinal Points of Borges*, ed. Lowell Dunham and Ivar Ivask (Norman, 1971), pp. 11-12.

[7] Lucien Goldmann, *Towards a Sociology of the Novel*, trans. Alan Sheridan (London, 1975), pp. 29-30, 64, 79.

[8] Borges concludes "El tiempo circular" with the observation that "In times of growth, the conjecture that man's existence is a constant quantity, invariable, can sadden or irritate; in times of decline (like these), it is the promise that no opprobrium, no calamity, no dictator will be able to impoverish us" (*"En tiempos de auge la conjetura de que la existencia del hombre es un cantidad constante, invariable, puede entristecer o irritar; en tiempos que declinan [como éstos], es la promesa de que ningún oprobrio, ninguna calamidad, ningún dictador podrá empobrecernos"*), *Historia de la eternidad*, my trans. (Buenos Aires, 1971), p. 103. See also, *OI*:19, 166, 175.

[9] All citations of Poe's work will be included in the text by volume and page number from *H*.

[10] *La nación*, 2 Oct. 1949, Section 2, p. 1.

[11] From a review of Gilbert Waterhouse's *A Short History of German Literature*: *"Los alemanes parecen incapaces de obrar sin algún aprendizaje alucinatorio... Notoriamente, los dioses han negado a los alemanes la belleza espontánea.* [...] *Los hombres de otras tierras pueden ser distráidamente atroces, eventualmente heróicos; los alemanes requieren seminarios de abnegación, éticas de la infamia."—Discusión*, my trans., pp. 170-171.

[12] Emile M. Cioran, "Directions for Decomposition," *A Short History of Decay*, trans. Richard Howard (New York, 1975), pp. 3-4.

[13] See Poe's letter to James R. Lowell of 2 July 1844—*O*.1:57.

[14] Poe's central metaphor for the proper interrogation of reality is a star beheld indirectly; for this recurrent image, see *H*. 4:166; 7:xxxix; 14:189-190; 16:164. For an excellent discussion of Poe's aesthetic of the oblique and the arabesque, see David Ketterer, *New Worlds for Old: The Apocalyptic Imagination, Science Fiction, and American Literature* (Garden City, 1974), pp. 55, 57-58.

[15] See, in particular, the sketches "Everything and Nothing" and "The Maker," *A Personal Anthology*, ed. Anthony Kerrigan (New York, 1967).

[16] *Poe as Literary Cosmologer*, p. 14 n. 13. In the same volume, Perry F. Hoberg discovers in the mystical heresy of Sabbatianism "A more fully articulated" conception of this idea of "the holiness of sin." Borges's attraction to Gnosticism is well known, which sect, in some of its versions, believed that man could void himself of sin only by committing it. Both heresies are applicable to the ethical and moral dramas that Poe and Borges address in their fiction. See pp. 34-36.

[17] Borges's sketches "Everything and Nothing" and "The Maker," as well as his story, "The Immortal," address this idea. See, also, Gérard Genette, "L'utopie littéraire," *Figures* (Paris, 1966), 1: 124-126, 127, 131.

[18] In the *Nación* article, Borges writes: "It would also be just to say that Poe sacrificed his life to his work, his human destiny to immortality" (*"También cabriá decir que Poe sacrificó la vida a la obra, el destino mortal al destino pósthumo"*), my trans. This is precisely the drama enacted by Wilson and imitated by Otto. For contemporary expressions of this idea, see Roland Barthes, "The Death of the

Author," *Image-Music-Text*, trans. Stephen Heath (Glasgow, 1977), pp. 142-148, and Michel Foucault, "What is an Author," *Language, Counter-Memory, Practice: Selected Essays and Interviews*, ed. and trans. Donald F. Bouchard and Sherry Simon (Ithaca, NY, 1977), pp. 116-118.

[19] *A Personal Anthology*, p. 203. See, also, "Tlön, Uqbar, Orbis Tertius" and "Borges and *I*," *L:* 3-18; 246-247; "From Someone to No One," *A Personal Anthology*, pp. 118-121; and "Valry as Symbol," *OI:* 73-74.

[20] In the "prólogo" to *Discusión*, Borges writes of his "afición incrédula y persistente por las dificultades teológicas"—my trans., p. 9.

[21] "The labyrinth is a hidden cosmos although the world is nothing more, perhaps, than chaos, illusion. In the labyrinth, there is a center, a plan, everything is forseen" (*"Le labyrinthe est un cosmos caché tandis que le monde n'est peut-être que le chaos, que l'illusoire. Dans le labyrinthe, il y a un centre, un plan, tout y est prévu"*)—from an interview with Jean Montalbetti in a Borges issue of *Magazine Littéraire*, 148 (1979), 22.

[22] Richard Burgin, *Conversations with Jorge Luis Borges* (New York, 1968), p. 140, and *La nación*, loc. cit.

[23] For Borges, see, for instance, Jaime Alazraki, "Oxymoronic Structure in Borges' Essays," and Ronald Christ, "A Modest Proposal for the Criticism of Borges," *The Cardinal Points of Borges*, pp. 7-15, 47-52; Christ's *The Narrow Act: Borges' Art of Allusion* (New York, 1969), pp. 15, 60-70; William Gass, "Imaginary Borges and His Books," *Fiction and the Figures of Life* (New York, 1970), pp. 120-133; and Lloyd King, "Antagonism, Irony, and Death in Two Stories by Jorge Luis Borges," *CLAJ*, 23 (1980), 399-408. For Poe, see Robert Daniel, "Poe's Detective God," *Furioso*, 6 (1951), 46, 47; James M. Cox, "Edgar Poe: Style as Pose," *VQR*, 44 (1968), 67-89; Alan Golding, "Reductive and Expansive Language: Semantic Strategies in *Eureka*," *PoeS*, 11(1978), 1-5; Roman Kakobson, "Linguistics and Poetics," *The Structuralists: From Marx to Levi-Strauss*, ed. Richard T. and Fernande M. De George (Garden City, 1972), pp. 102, 107; and Joseph J. Moldenhauer, "Murder as a Fine Art: Basic Connections Between Poe's Aesthetics, Psychology, and Moral Vision," *PMLA*, 83 (1968), 288, 295.

[24] "The Poet Tells of His Fame," *Selected Poems*, 1923-1967, ed. Norman Thomas di Giovanni (New York, 1972), p. 239.

[25] "The Internalization of the Quest-Romance," *Romanticism and Consciousness: Essays in Criticism*, ed. Harold Bloom (New York, 1970), pp. 10-18.

[26] *The Complete Poems of Samuel Taylor Coleridge*, ed. Morchard Bishop (London, 1954), p. 69. The poem: "Religious Musings," ll. 149-157.

[27] Borges takes pains to distinguish Jerusalem from Whitman, but this may be considered as but another of his many subtle uses of allusion. He not only repeatedly acknowledges his own admiration for and early imitation of Whitman, but his meditations on the American poet refer to him in precisely the same terms as he uses to describe Jerusalem, especially as the poet of joy (*OI*:68, 73), tenderness (*OI*:68), and the rich gift of a fluid, contingent reality (*Discusión:* 54). Thus, the negative reference evokes the very poet-figure that Borges wants associated with Otto's double.

[28] I am indebted for this distinction to John Sturrock's discussion of *Six Problems for Don Isidro Parodi* in his *Paper Tigers; The Ideal Fictions of Jorge Luis Borges* (Oxford, 1977), pp. 36-39.

[29] See Genette's excellent summary of this aspect of Borges' work in "L'utopie littéraire," in *Figures*.

[30] *A Personal Anthology*, p. 15.

# "IN THE PERILOUS REALM": THE FANTASTIC GEOGRAPHIES OF TOLKIEN AND POE

*CAROL MARSHALL PEIRCE*

In his critical study of fantasy and fairy tale, "On Fairy-stories," J. R. R. Tolkien identifies most such stories as "about the *adventures* of men in the Perilous Realm or upon its shadowy marches." He also writes: "To the elvish craft, Enchantment, Fantasy aspires, and when it is successful of all forms of human art most nearly approaches." At another point he adds that fantasy must combine Imagination with unreality, have "a quality of strangeness and wonder in the Expression"—an "arresting strangeness"—and possess an "inner consistency." It demands, says Tolkien, "a special skill, a kind of elvish craft." "Few," he adds, "attempt such difficult tasks."[1]

One of those few who did attempt the craft was Edgar Allan Poe. In his poetry and tales one not only enters the Perilous Realm, one feels the very air that blows from that far countree. Indeed, in "Journey to the End of the Night," a chapter in his book, *The Power of Darkness,* Harry Levin speaks of Poe's "unique absorption in atmosphere" and concludes, "If he was at home anywhere, perhaps it was in his 'Dreamland'."[2] Like Tolkien, Poe had the "enchanter's power" (to use Tolkien's words) to "put a deadly green upon a man's face and produce a horror," to "make the rare and terrible blue moon to shine," and to "cause woods to spring with silver leaves and rams to wear fleeces of gold."[3]

Of course, Poe and Tolkien differ in many major ways. Although each wrote poetry, and criticism, Poe is best known for his short stories and mood essays or "mindscapes," undertaking only two longer works, the unfinished *Pym* and the philosophic probe of the universe, *Eureka.* Tolkien, on the other hand, did write a few short tales but concentrated his major publication on *The Hobbit* and the long three-volume *Lord of the Rings.* Meanwhile, he bore in his heart of hearts *The Silmarillion,* the constantly rewritten, never totally consolidated epic of the earliest ages of Middle-earth. *The Silmarillion* materials also encompassed his studies of language and related to them, for it was from the creation of the Eldarin languages that Tolkien turned to write the *Ring* trilogy. Here, too, is another difference from Poe (but, paradoxically, in some ways a likeness too), for whereas languages (the reconstruction of certain ancient languages and the creation of new ones) enthralled Tolkien most, Poe loved ratiocination, as he called his involvement with reasoning out mysteries—he was equally intrigued with solving real ones and with creating new ones himself for others to solve. Just as Tolkien invented languages, so Poe invented the modern detective story.

Poe's characters, too, differ from Tolkien's. Although in both men's works the characters are generally other-worldly, not of this time or place, Poe's greatest creations—his Ligeias, his Berenices, his Roderick Ushers, and even his omnipresent narrators—are often in their depths psychological studies in passionate abnormality or even madness. Tolkien's, however, are mythic in their deepest being and seem to emerge from fairy lore and legend: " ' And now the songs have come down among us out of strange places, and walk visible under the Sun,' " says Théoden.[4]

Finally, in their culminating visions—in their mythic and mystic journeys—they ride toward different ends. For Poe (except in his detective fiction which does not pertain here) forever moves out of light into darkness, despair, and tragedy: there exists always the hope of beauty but the threat of oblivion. Tolkien, facing a world of darkness and of terror, a Götterdämmerung, strives on toward light and toward the *Eucatastrophe,* as he calls it, the fairy-story opposite. In "On Fairy-stories," he writes:

> In its fairy-tale—or other world—setting, it [the *Eucatastrophe*] is a sudden and miraculous grace: never to be counted on to recur. It does not deny the existence of *dyscatastrophe,* of sorrow and failure...it denies (in the face of much evidence, if you will) universal final defeat...giving a fleeting glimpse of Joy, Joy beyond the walls of the world, poignant as grief.[5]

Though some of the realms Poe and Tolkien inhabit are not the same, however, others reveal a profound affinity. Both authors are mythmakers who open windows on the world of the creative imagination. Fascinatingly, some of the windows reveal the same landscape of fantasy. Surely there are archetypal worlds, as well as archetypal gods, that still call us home. Some of these primordial lands, then, exist in the geographies of both Tolkien and Poe, especially the dark world of horror and the bright world of Faërie.

To begin, each author sets his characters a-questing, riding down the Road of Trials on the journey inward to illumination.[6] Like Frodo and Gandolf and Aragorn in Tolkien's *Lord of the Rings,* Poe's hero persona sets out in "Eldorado":

> Gaily bedight,
> A gallant knight,
> In sunshine and in shadow,
> Had journeyed long,
> Singing a song,
> In search of Eldorado.

And just as in Tolkien's definition in "On Fairy-stories" and in the plot of *The Lord of the Rings,* he sojourns long and penetrates deep into its shadows and perils:

> "Shadow," said he
> "Where can it be—
> This land of Eldorado?"
>
> "Over the Mountains
> Of the Moon,
> Down the Valley of the Shadow,
> Ride, boldly ride,"
> The shade replied,—
> "If you seek for Eldorado!"[7]

The world that most of Poe's knight-errants reach, however, like the world of his poems, "Dream-land" and "Ulalume," seems in its fantastic natural features and its horror most to resemble Tolkien's Mordor and the lands lying near it. Both are terrible worlds ruled by princes of Darkness and inhabited by Orcs in Tolkien and Ghouls in Poe. Tolkien writes: "Sauron the Great, the Dark Lord....has indeed arisen again and left his hold in Mirkwood and returned to his ancient fastness in the Dark Tower of Mordor ....like a shadow on the borders of old stories."[8] Frodo and Sam must travel a long and deadly road into Sauron's kingdom in their quest to destroy the ring of power in the fires of Mount Doom. Poe, too, has his own dark king described in the poem, "Dream-land":

> By a route obscure and lonely,
> Haunted by ill angels only,
> Where an Eidolon, named Night,
> On a black throne reigns upright,
> I have reached these lands but newly...

He writes of his realm, "...a wild weird clime that lieth, sublime,/Out of Space—out of Time."[9] Tolkien, similarly, lists, as one of man's archetypal desires, this very ability "to survey the depths of space and time."[10]

Again, Poe's journeyer in "Dream-land" must go through "Bottomless vales and boundless floods,/And chasms, and caves, and Titan woods."[11] So too, the quest of Tolkien's Fellowship leads to the crest of a great flood just outside the Elven valley of Rivendell: "At that moment there came a roaring and a rushing: a noise of loud waters rolling many stones. Dimly Frodo saw the river below him rise, and down along its course there came a plumed cavalry of waves."[12] It leads, also, to the fight of Gandalf with the Balrog at

the Bridge of Kazad-Dûm. Defeated by the wintry mountains, the company enters the caverns of Moria beneath them. Pursued by "the certainty of evil ahead and of evil following," the *doom, doom* of the orcic drum, "Suddenly Frodo saw before him a black chasm. At the end of the hall the floor vanished and fell to an unknown depth."[13] Later, as they approach the Elven city of green towers, Caras Galadon of Lothlórien, they look back at the "Titan woods" behind them: " 'There lies the fastness of Southern Mirkwood,' " said Haldir. " 'It is clad in a forest of dark fir, where the trees strive one against another and their branches rot and wither.' "[14] One feels one has almost here in Tolkien explored Poe's vales and floods and caves and woods, especially when one finds in "Silence—A Fable," this description:

> "...there is a boundary to their realm—the boundary of the dark, horrible, lofty forest. There...the low underwood is agitated continually....And the tall primeval trees rock eternally hither and thither with a crashing and mighty sound."
>
> . . . .
>
> "The waters of the river have a saffron and sickly hue; and they flow not onward to the sea, but palpitate forever and forever beneath the red eye of the sun with a tumultuous and convulsive motion....in that solitude."[15]

This last could almost be a sentence from Tolkien's description of the riveting eye of Sauron, gazing down on Middle-earth: "The Eye was rimmed with fire, but was itself glazed, yellow as a cat's, watchful and intent, and the black slit of its pupil opened on a pit, a window into nothing."[16]

Indeed, with every step, Tolkien's Fellowship is approaching Mordor. As Frodo and Sam leave the company and press closer alone, they must pass the Dead Marshes:

> "Who are they? What are they?" asked Sam shuddering, turning to Frodo, who was now behind him.
>
> "I don't know," said Frodo in a dreamlike voice. "But I have seen them too. In the pools when the candles were lit. They lie in all the pools, pale faces, deep deep under the dark water. I saw them: grim faces and evil, and noble faces and sad. Many faces proud and fair, and weeds in their silver hair. But all foul, all rotting, all dead. A fell light is in them." Frodo hid his eyes in his hands. "I know not who they are; but I thought I saw there Men and Elves, and Orcs beside them."[17]

Poe, still wandering in "Dream-land," sees something like the same horror:

By the grey woods,—by the swamp
Where the toad and the newt encamp,—
By the dismal tarns and pools
    Where dwell the Ghouls,—

. . . .

There the traveller meets aghast,
Sheeted Memories of the Past—
Shrouded forms that start and sigh
As they pass the wanderer by—
White-robed forms of friends long given,
In agony, to the Earth—and Heaven.[18]

Such is the character of Poe's "Dream-land" and of the marches of Tolkien's Mordor.

In an even more mysterious poem, "Ulalume," "down by the dank tarn of Auber, /In the ghoul-haunted woodland of Weir," Poe, in progress of a last terrible journey, in depths of agony, sees a star, a star that seems to "point us the path to the skies." His soul warns him, but he does not heed: "Let us bathe in this crystalline light! Its Sibyllic splendor is beaming With Hope and in Beauty to-night." But the star ("Ah, what demon hath tempted me here?") misleads him and he comes in the end to the grave of his lost love, Ulalume:

These were days when my heart was volcanic
    As the scoriac rivers that roll—
    As the lavas that restlessly roll
Their sulphurous currents down Yaanek,
    In the ultimate climes of the Pole.[19]

So in *The Lord of the Rings* Sam, with Frodo, striving along the final road to the volcanic mountain, looks up:

> There, peeping among the cloud-wrack above the dark tor high up in the mountains, Sam saw a white star twinkle for a while. The beauty of it smote his heart, as he looked up out of the forsaken land, and hope returned to him. For like a shaft, clear and cold, the thought pierced him that in the end the Shadow was only a small and passing thing: there was light and high beauty forever beyond its reach.[20]

Sam takes new heart, and the star, unlike that in Poe, has not deceived him. He and Frodo come in the end to witness and participate in the destruction of evil for their time.

Another fascinating parallel lies in Tolkien's description of the last moments of Mount Doom and the Dark Tower, Sauron's inner citadel of power, with Poe's description of "The City in the Sea." Tolkien writes:

> A brief vision he had of swirling cloud, and in the midst of it towers and battlements, tall as hills, founded upon a mighty mountain-throne above immeasurable pits; great courts and dungeons, eyeless prisons sheer as cliffs, and gaping gates of steel and adamant: and then all passed. Towers fell and mountains slid; walls crumbled and melted, crashing down; vast spires of smoke and spouting steams went billowing up, up, until they toppled like an overwhelming wave, and its wild crest curled and came foaming down upon the land.[21]

The flood is a metaphor here and a symbolic repetition of the "devouring wave" that "rolled over the land" and toppled Númenor, "Land of the West," in Tolkien's *Silmarillion.*[22] This mythic theme, like the medieval Celtic stories of drowned cities, like the ancient story of Atlantis,[23] also forms the thematic basis for Poe's poem, "The City in the Sea":

> Lo! Death has reared himself a throne
> In a strange city lying alone
> Far down within the dim West,
>
> . . . .
>
> No rays from the holy heaven come down
> On the long night-time of that town;
> But light from out the lurid sea
> Streams up the turrets silently—
> Gleams up the pinnacles far and free
> Up domes—up spires—up kingly halls—
> Up fanes—up Babylon-like walls—
>
> . . . .
>
> Resignedly beneath the sky
> The melancholy waters lie.
> So blend the turrets and shadows there
> That all seem pendulous in air,
> While from a proud tower in the town
> Death looks gigantically down.[24]

Thus Poe and Tolkien cross some of the same shadowy lands of Dark-

ness and see some of the same green iridescence of Death. But they share happier and more poignant moments and visions too, as they pause in their quests to linger awhile in Faërie, breathe its sweet airs, and rest in its riddle of beauty and loss. They both linger in the silver woods and sleep beneath the blue moon. In fact the most striking correspondences of all occur in their ideas of Fairyland.

Poe describes that evanescent world especially in his poems, "Fairy-land" and "The Valley of Unrest," and in his stories, "Eleonora" and "The Island of the Fay." "Fairy-land," an early poem, is filled with marvelous moonlight:

Huge moons there wax and wane—

. . . .

Forever changing places—
And they put out the star-light
With the breath from their pale faces.[25]

The moon bathes in its light strange woods and spirits on the wing—and "every drowsy thing." Butterflies rise forever toward it, as well, bringing back its light on their wings. This is a simpler work than some of his others on the fairy world, and one thinks instinctively of Tolkien's earlier children's story, *The Hobbit.* There "hundreds of butterflies" flutter high in the wood-elves' trees.[26] And there one visits Elrond's Last Homely House in the fair "secret valley of Rivendell," where the air is always warm, the water running, and the evening filled with the scent of flowers and pine-trees, making one "drowsy": " 'Hmmm! it smells like elves!' thought Bilbo, and he looked up at the stars. They were burning bright and blue. Just then there came a burst of song like laughter in the trees."[27] Here, too, Elrond discovers the moon-letters on Bilbo's map: "They can only be seen when the moon shines behind them...."[28] Of such "filmy," "mooney" correspondences are these fairylands created. In *The Lord of the Rings,* however, Tolkien sees an end coming to his Elven race. With the fourth age—of men—the Elf people will gradually fade from the earth and all their lands be left mourning. So, it is, too, in Poe's poem, "The Valley of Unrest," which seems like nothing so much as the Vale of Rivendell after the Elves' departure to the West:

*Once* it smiled a silent dell
Where the people did not dwell;
They had gone unto the wars,
Trusting to the mild-eyed stars,
Nightly, from their azure towers,
To keep watch above the flowers.

Now, eternal dews fall from the "fragrant tops" of ever-stirring trees, "over the violets," "over the lilies" that there still wave.[29] " 'And many fair things,' " said Tolkien's Elrond, " ' will fade and be forgotten.' "[30]

Most beautiful of all the realms of Tolkien is Lothlórien "fair and perilous," and it has its parallels too in Poe: "Frodo stood awhile still lost in wonder. It seemed to him that he had stepped through a high window that looked on a vanished world. A light was upon it for which his language had no name." Aragorn explained it simply: " 'Here is the heart of Elvendom on earth,' he said, 'and here my heart dwells ever, unless there be a light beyond the dark roads that we still must tread, you and I.' "[31] Lothlórien too must slowly vanish and its elf queen, Galadriel, diminish and pass: " 'Lothlórien will fade, and the tides of Time will sweep it away. We must depart into the West, or dwindle to a rustic folk of dell and cave, slowly to forget and to be forgotten.' "[32]

This conception of Lothlórien compares on many levels with that of Poe in his stories, "Eleonora" and "The Island of the Fay." Their geographies, and not only their geographies, are remarkably similar to Tolkien's. To begin with, even their place-names relate. Early in "Eleonora" Poe explains, "We had always dwelled together...in the Valley of the Many-Colored Grass."[33] Tolkien writes that Lothlórien is only a shorter version of the old Elven name, Laurelindórenan—"Land of the Valley of Singing Gold, that was it, once upon a time."[34] Tolkien tells us further that the Fellowship of travellers, arriving, pass the source of the swift river, the Silverlode, which rushes over "shining pebbles" as it branches into many small streams, "leaping down to the trough of the valley, and then running on and away into the lower lands, until it [is] lost in a golden haze." Of the woods and its leaves he writes: "Not till the spring comes and the new green opens do they fall, and then the boughs are laden with yellow flowers; and the floor of the woods is golden, and golden is the roof, and its pillars are of silver, for the bark of the trees is smooth and gray."[35] Finally in the very center, "the heart of the ancient realm":

> ...Frodo looked up and caught his breath. They were standing in an open space. To the left stood a great mound, covered with a sward of grass as green as Spring-time in the Elder days. Upon it, as a double crown, grew two circles of trees: the outer had bark of snowy white, and were leafless but beautiful in their shapely nakedness; the inner were mallorn-trees of great height, still arrayed in pale gold....At the feet of the trees, and all about the green hillsides the grass was studded with small golden flowers shaped like stars. Among them, nodding on slender stalks, were other flowers, white and palest green: they glimmered as a mist amid the rich hue of the grass. Over all the sky was blue, and the sun of afternoon

glowed upon the hill and cast long green shadows beneath the trees.[36]

In "Eleonora," likewise, Poe writes of the Valley of the Many-Colored Grass:

> From the dim regions beyond the mountains at the upper end of our encircled domain, there crept out a narrow and deep river, brighter than all save the eyes of Eleonora; and, winding stealthily about in mazy courses, it passed away, at length, through a shadowy gorge, among hills still dimmer than those whence it had issued....No murmur arose from its bed, and so gently it wandered along that the pearly pebbles upon which we loved to gaze, far down within its bosom, stirred not at all, but lay in a motionless content, each in its own old station, shining on gloriously forever.
>
> The margin of the river, and of the many dazzling rivulets that glided, through devious ways, into its channel, as well as the spaces that extended from the margins away down into the depths of the streams until they reached the bed of pebbles at the bottom,—these spots, not less than the whole surface of the valley, from the river to the mountains that girdled it in, were carpeted all by a soft green grass, thick, short, perfectly even, and vanilla-perfumed, but so besprinkled throughout with the yellow buttercup, the white daisy, the purple violet, and the ruby-red asphodel, that its exceeding beauty spoke to our hearts...
>
> And, here and there, in groves about this grass, like wildernesses of dreams, sprang up fantastic trees, whose tall slender stems stood not upright, but slanted gracefully toward the light that peered at noon-day into the centre of the valley. Their bark was speckled with the vivid alternate splendor of ebony and silver, and was smoother than all the cheeks of Eleonora.[37]

Much the same scene is set in "The Island of the Fay." Through mountain locked in Mountain "I", the searcher (unlike the narrator of "Eleonora" who lived in the valley and saw it fade away), comes to find a river, with the green forest surrounding it and in the center a small circular island. The western side glows with sunlight and flowers and grass interspersed with asphodel. The trees are tall and slender, and butterflies move in their "gentle sweepings" of joy. The east, though, is dark, shrouded in shade, cypress, and death.

> "If ever island were enchanted," said I to myself, "this is it. This is the haunt of the few gentle Fays who remain from the wreck of the race. Are these green tombs theirs?— or do they yield up their sweet lives as mankind yield up their own? In dying, do they not rather waste away mournfully; rendering unto God little by little their existence, as these

> trees render up shadow after shadow, exhausting their substance unto dissolution?"

It then appears to him that he sees one of the Fays in a "singularly fragile canoe" circling the island. Each time she circles she grows fainter and fainter until at last he loses her fragile sight in the darkness.[38]

So, too, as Frodo and the Company leave Lothlorien, Galadriel appears a last time in a Swan-ship: "She seemed no longer perilous or terrible, nor filled with hidden power. Already she seemed to him, as by men of later days Elves still at times are seen: present and yet remote, a living vision of that which has already been left far behind by the flowing streams of Time."[39]

Finally, to conclude and also to touch on two last particularly illuminating parallels, it should be noted that Tolkien sees fantasy and fairy-stories as having "three faces." These include the "Magical" that they turn "towards Nature," "the Mystical towards the Supernatural," and "the Mirror of scorn and pity towards Man."[40] Both writers have looked on all three faces, and the correspondences again are fascinating in their varied nuances.

The Magical face that Faërie turns to Nature appears in central passages of both writers. Poe, for example, in "To Helen," is drawn back to imagine beauty so haunting that "On desperate seas long wont to roam, Thy hyacinth hair, thy classic face, Thy Naiad airs have brought me home...."[41] In *The Lord of the Rings* Tolkien describes the music of Elven voices: "Almost it seemed that the words took shape, and visions of far lands and bright things that he had never yet imagined opened out before him; and the firelit hall became like a golden mist above seas of foam that sighed upon the margins of the world."[42] Not only do these writers discover seas in their visions of Nature but seas described with adjectives that evoke the very magic of Fairyland. As Keats put it earlier:

> The voice I hear this passing night was heard
> In ancient days by emperor and clown:
> Perhaps...
> The same that oft-times hath
> Charm'd magic casements, opening on the foam
> Of perilous seas, in fairy lands forlorn.[43]

Second, the face of the mystical toward the supernatural can be seen in two powerful images that seem each to reveal in its own epiphany the different vision but mystic likeness of Tolkien and Poe. Toward the final battle for Middle-earth, Gandalf, the Grey Wizard, seemingly destroyed by the Balrog at the Bridge of Kazed-Dûm, after passing in travail through fire,

earth, water, and air, returns to the green earth to lead the Quest again. But now he has become the "White Rider." Aragorn, who, like Arthur, again shall be king, rises to meet him:

> The others gazed at them in silence as they stood there facing one another. The grey figure of the Man, Aragorn son of Arathorn, was tall, and stern as stone, his hand upon the hilt of his sword; he looked as if some king out of the mists of the sea had stepped upon the shores of lesser men. Before him stooped the old figure, white, shining now as if with some light kindled within, bent, laden with years, but holding a power beyond the strength of kings.[44]

> A gleam of sun through fleeting clouds fell on his hands, which lay now upturned on his lap: they seemed to be filled with light as a cup is with water. At last he looked up and gazed straight at the sun.[45]

Merlin? One of the mythic Northern Gods? Gandalf has returned from beyond this world, an angel figure who would save Man, Tolkien suggests.

In comparison, one thinks immediately of Poe's symbolic figure at the end of *Pym*. At the farthest point Poe's voyager had journeyed toward the Southern Pole in darkness visible, "relieved only by the glare of the water thrown back from the white curtain before us," his boat still hurried "on to the southward under the influence of a powerful current":

> "And now we rushed into the embraces of the cataract, where a chasm threw itself open to receive us. But there arose in our pathway a shrouded human figure, very far larger in its proportions than any dweller among men. And the hue of the skin of the figure was of the perfect whiteness of the snow."[46]

Whiteness incarnate? Some primitive White God or Goddess? Here again is the face of the Mystical towards the Supernatural. And now here too in Poe—as seen again and again in Tolkien, from the ever changing vision Galadriel may grant to the powerful voice and spirit of Gandalf—is the very Mirror of scorn and pity that Faërie turns toward Man. Indeed, what strangely different yet what hauntingly similar conceptions exist in the works of Tolkien and Poe. For all these versions of fantasy have a profound affinity of archetypal heritage, of visions held deep in our unconscious, of other worlds existing on the shores of other seas.

## NOTES

[1] *The Tolkien Reader* (New York, 1966), pp. 9, 53, 47-49.

[2] Harry Levin, *The Power of Darkness: Hawthorne, Poe, Melville* (New York, 1958), pp. 102, 103.

[3] *Reader*, p. 22.

[4] *The Two Towers: being the second part of The Lord of the Rings*, 2nd ed. (Boston, 1966), p. 155.

[5] *Reader*, p. 68.

[6] Joseph Campbell, *The Hero with a Thousand Faces*, 2nd ed. [Bollingen Series XVII] (Princeton, 1968), pp. 97 ff.

[7] *M.* 1:463.

[8] *The Fellowship of the Ring: being the first part of The Lord of the Rings*, 2nd ed. (Boston, 1966), p. 60.

[9] *M.* 1:343-344.

[10] *Reader*, p. 13.

[11] *M.* 1:344.

[12] *Fellowship*, p. 227.

[13] *Fellowship*, pp. 325, 337-346, 343 (quotation).

[14] *Fellowship*, p. 366.

[15] *M.* 2:195.

[16] *Fellowship*, p. 379.

[17] *Two Towers*, p. 235.

[18] *M.* 1:344.

[19] *M.* 1:415-418.

[20] *The Return of the King: being the third part of The Lord of the Rings*, 2nd ed. (Boston, 1966), p. 199.

[21] *Return*, p. 224.

[22] *The Silmarillion*, ed. Christopher Tolkien (London, 1977), pp. 279-280.

[23] Ruth S. Noel, *The Mythology of Middle-earth* (London, 1977), pp. 48-49.

[24] *M.* 1:201-202.

[25] *M.* 1:140-141.

[26] *The Hobbit: or There and Back Again* (Boston, 1958), p. 159.

[27] *The Hobbit*, pp. 58-59. Cf. *Fellowship*, p. 238.

[28] *The Hobbit*, p. 64.

[29] *M.* 1:195-196.

[30] *Fellowship*, p. 282.

[31] *Fellowship*, pp. 365, 367.

[32] *Fellowship*, p. 380.

[33] *M.* 2:639.

[34] *Two Towers*, p. 70.

[35] *Fellowship*, p. 349.

[36] *Fellowship*, pp. 364-365.

[37] *M.* 2:639-640.

[38] *M.* 2:603-604.

[39] *Fellowship*, p. 389.

[40] *Reader*, p. 26.

[41] *M.* 1:166.

[42] *Fellowship*, p. 245.

[43] John Keats, *Complete Poems and Selected Letters*, ed. Clarence DeWitt Thorpe (New York, 1935), p. 351.

[44] *Two Towers*, p. 104.

[45] *Two Towers*, p. 103.

[46] Edgar Allan Poe, *The Complete Tales and Poems* (New York, 1938), pp. 881-882.

# RODERICK USHER IN OUR TIME: STYRON'S MASON FLAGG

*LINDA E. McDANIEL*

In his examination of twentieth-century evil and insanity in *Set This House on Fire,* William Styron develops his history of the "house of Flagg"[1] with details recalling Poe's treatment of moral and psychic disintegration in "The Fall of the House of Usher."[2] Styron's tone and plot often suggest Poe's masterpiece and link Mason Flagg to Roderick Usher. The "proprietor" of an ancient palace, Flagg exhibits eccentric tastes in music, art, and literature; and he has a singular involvement with a young woman who dies horribly on the same day Mason falls to his death. Whereas Poe presents a creative madman who makes death instead of life his study, Styron exposes a loony fraud who makes sex instead of love his obsession. Although discussions of the novel frequently point out its Gothic elements and rich variety of sources,[3] recognition of Styron's indebtedness to Poe provides another approach to Styron's analyses of twentieth-century madness.

Poe and Styron introduce first-person observers who journey alone after receiving a letter from a boyhood friend. In "Usher," Poe's narrator explains that he embarked from "a distant part of the country" after "a very singular summons" from his boyhood companion, Roderick Usher (p. 398). In *Set This House on Fire,* Styron's "rationalist" narrator, Peter Leverett, travels from Rome to the remote village of Sambuco after Mason writes a "breezy, but specific" letter inviting Leverett "for a visit" (pp. 19, 21).

Both narrators recount long journeys, made with horse (Poe) and with sportscar (Styron), and they detail the approaches to their destinations. After "passing alone, on horseback, through a singularly dreary tract of country," Poe's traveler comes "within view of the melancholy House of Usher." Feeling "a sense of insufferable gloom" and "an utter depression of the soul," he shudders and reins his horse "to the precipitous brink of a black and lurid tarn" (pp. 397-398). Peter Leverett narrates at length his trip and approach to the palace of Flagg. With a pint of bourbon in the glove compartment of his Austin, Leverett has also driven through a "singularly dreary tract of country": "For miles at a stretch I could see nothing at all on either side of me—no homes, no humans, no growing things....Then abruptly I was in cliff country, ascending the flanks of gaunt, wounded hills where nothing grew and no one lived" (p. 26). During his ride, Peter feels a sense of "desolation" and a "shadow" in his mind "of some dim but incomparable misery" (p. 37). Finally, when he comes "in sight of Sambuco's archaic gate," the battered car quivers and dies "as the magnificent sea [comes] into view a thousand feet below" (p. 56). Finding the town "unnaturally silent," Peter is "troubled once more, and despairing" before he walks

through the "mildewed archway" (p. 56). Additional Poe titles, namely, "Shadow—A Parable," "Silence—A Fable," and *The Narrative of Arthur Gordon Pym,* may contribute their share to these passages by Styron. "Usher," nonetheless, remained paramount as his imagination built upon Poe.

Examining the residence of the "proprietor,"[4] each narrator experiences an increased gloom. Entering a "Gothic archway," Usher's guest is met first by a servant in waiting who takes the horse, and then by a valet who acts as guide through the house. The narrator describes the "excessive antiquity" of the place, with its "vaulted and fretted ceiling," "encrimsoned" windows, "dark draperies," and "black oaken" floors. He then remarks, "An air of stern, deep, and irredeemable gloom hung over and pervaded all" (p. 401). Especially significant in Poe's story, of course, are the descriptions of the "crumbling condition of the individual stones" of the house and the zigzag fissure which extends from the roof to the waters below (p. 400).

In Styron's novel, instead of a servant in waiting, a foul-mouthed idiot peasant named Saverio encounters Leverett and announces: "I am taking care of your car" (p. 68); and the hotel manager guides and directs Peter through the place. Leverett feels "burdened under the blackest sort of gloom" (p. 63) even before entering the palace Mason rented. Built in the thirteenth century, the Palazzo d'Affitto, like the House of Usher, shows "excessive antiquity." Peter observes vaulted ceilings, massive doors, red drapes, and particularly remarks the tiles, which, unlike Usher's dreary floors, repeat a bright red and blue pattern. Instead of a fatal fissure, Mason's palace is marred by an exclusively twentieth-century defect that initially puzzles Peter: "as I accustomed my eyes to the place I could tell that something was wrong here." He realizes that the movie cameras and machines, crisscrossing the floor, have marked and gouged out "ugly channels" in the tiles (p. 97).

The masters of the houses also evince, in Poe's words, "an incoherence—an inconsistency" (p. 402). Although both hosts greet their guests warmly, the narrators register early misgivings about their friends. According to Poe's observer: "Usher arose from a sofa...and greeted me with a vivacious warmth which had much in it, I at first thought, of an overdone cordiality....A glance, however, at his countenance, convinced me of his perfect sincerity" (p. 401). A glance at his friend's face also impresses the guest with a terrible change in Usher: "Surely, man had never before so terribly altered, in so brief a period, as had Roderick Usher!" (p. 401). Furthermore, the narrator easily discerns in his friend "an excessive nervous agitation" (p. 402).

Despite a cordial greeting, Peter's host too shows signs of change and inconsistency. Mason greets "Petsey" with giggling and pumping of his

hand (p. 58); and Leverett later recalls how Mason could make a friend feel "warmed by his energy, his big grin, and by the note in his voice...of honest affection" (p. 132). Nevertheless, Peter soon discerns inconsistencies in Flagg's conduct: "He was grinning broadly but his jacket was drenched in sweat: he seemed eaten up by some furious inner agitation" (p. 185). In contrast to Usher, Flagg at first seems unaltered: "On the outside he had changed hardly at all," remarks Leverett (p. 63). A family friend, however, hints at another kind of change in Mason: "I mean—well, he's a weird boy. He's altogether different from the kid I remember down in Virginia" (p. 115). Leverett ultimately realizes that Flagg has gone "beyond recapture" (p. 184).

Musical, artistic, and literary pursuits of Usher and Flagg indicate the nature of their agitation and change. Especially partial to dirges, Usher selects music that attests his obsession with death and the afterlife. Because of a "morbid acuteness of the senses," he can tolerate only the sounds of stringed instruments. His impromptus and improvisations on his guitar impress his observer, particularly "a certain singular perversion and amplification of the wild air of the last waltz of Von Weber" (p. 405). At other times, Usher accompanies his music with "rhymed verbal improvisations," such as the symbolic lyric entitled "The Haunted Palace" (pp. 406-407).[5]

Mason's musical selections, on the other hand, support the statement that Flagg has " 'sex in the head like a tumor' " (p. 441). Although Usher creates and performs his own music, Flagg hires or arranges for someone else to improvise or perform. Mason does share Usher's interest in improvisational music, such as jazz or the impromptus of Billy Raymond. Inside Mason's apartment, the black entertainer improvises "naughty tunes" and accompanies his improvisations on the piano with "lascivious groans" (pp. 99-101). As an added attraction, Mason's artist, Cass Kinsolving, recites limericks and improvises degrading pantomimes. Leverett's first impressions of the music at Palazzo D'Affito demonstrate how much the "morbid condition" of Flagg's auditory nerve differs from Usher's: "a hell of a racket broke loose. From the regions upstairs...came the noise of a tinkling piano, feet thumping, a high falsetto voice singing above it all, then wave upon wave of hysterical laughter. Close by us, from a doorway at the level at which we were standing and so loud that each crashing bass note had the effect of the tread of elephants, a phonograph erupted the opening bars from the overture to *Don Giovanni*" (p. 97).

Besides passing the melancholy time with music, Poe's characters also paint and read together (p. 404). Although Usher's abstract paintings do not "lie within the compass of merely written words," the narrator describes one painting of the interior of a long white tunnel that conveys a ghastly sense of

space "below the surface of the earth" (pp. 405-406) and which foreshadows the burial vault into which the two friends later descend.[6]

Again, Usher's strange creations are his own; Flagg commissions his—by blackmailing an artist to paint " 'one filthy picture, to be skilfully executed' " (p. 421) in exchange for booze and medicine. Thus, working "in a shadowland frontier between reason and madness," Cass Kinsolving executes a graphically pornographic painting of a nude youth and a lovely young girl (p. 405). Like Usher, Flagg expresses interest in abstract art, and gushes over the " 'sense of *space*' " in Kinsolving's drawings. According to the artist himself, however, Mason is a fraud because " '[t]here wasn't no more space or humanity in those drawings than you could stuff up the back end of a flea' " (p. 386).

The hosts' libraries provide other indicators of their owners' nineteenth- and twentieth-century preoccupations. Usher's titles underscore his interests in the mysteries of heaven and hell, demonic possession, damnation and death.[7] In a lengthy paragraph, Poe catalogues Usher's collection of rare exotica—"such works as the Ververt et Chartreuse of Gresset, the Belphegor of Machiavelli, the Heaven and Hell of Swedenborg; the Subterranean Voyage of Nicholas Klimm by Holberg," to name a few. Usher's friend speculates on the "probable influence" on his host's psyche from reading, for instance, the *Vigiliae Mortuorum*...("Vigils for the dead according to the use of the church of Mainz"—pp. 408-409).

Styron spends pages listing the areas of Flagg's reading—from the origins of Rosicrucianism to books on natural history, from studies of primitive cultures to Ranulf de Glanvill's theories of law (pp. 147-148). In addition, Flagg's collection includes "such grizzled entries" of erotica as "*The Thousand Nights and a Night* (London, privately printed, 1921)" or the complete works of the " 'divine' " Marquis de Sade. Flagg himself demonstrates the "probable influence" of such studies. In his diatribe on "sex as the last frontier," Mason talks about "the total exploration of sex, as Sade envisioned it...which makes a library like this so important to the psyche, and so rewarding" (pp. 150-151).

His artistic and literary interests inform each master's relationship with a young woman,[8] whom the narrator glimpses only once before hearing of her death. Soon after his arrival, Poe's narrator sees Roderick's ailing sister, Madeline; she "passed slowly through a remote portion of the apartment, and, without having noticed my presence, disappeared...A sensation of stupor oppressed me, as my eyes followed her retreating steps" (p. 404). Only once and just as briefly does Peter see Francesca, a beautiful peasant girl hired by Flagg: "a door burst open a few feet away from me, exposing a glimpse of

an ascending stairway, and a girl...who came skidding out into the room as if upon glass." Peter barely has time to note the details of a torn bodice and "brown eyes round with hurt and terror" before "she pushed past me with a little groan of anguish...bare feet pattering in diminishing terrified flight down the hallway" (pp. 122-123).

The narrator's only subsequent picture of the woman depicts her in profound repose. After Usher and friend bear Madeline's coffin to the underground vault, the narrator regards her face: "The disease...had left, as usual in all maladies of a strictly cataleptical character, the mockery of a faint blush upon the bosom and the face, and that suspiciously lingering smile upon the lip which is so terrible in death" (p. 410). The descriptions of the beaten, ravished, and dying Francesca recall Madeline's picture: "Once [Francesca] moaned and her eyelids flickered, and a flush came to rouge the pallor of her cheeks. Then again she went pale, and sank back into her coma, barely breathing" (p. 465). Later: "faint color had returned to [Francesca's] cheeks... and her eyes were closed as if in death, lids chalky white, and she uttered no sound" (pp. 467-468). As Usher fears of Madeline, a character in the novel reports of Francesca: " 'she is still alive—but the horror!' " (p. 456).

Francesca, however, does not rise from her catatonic unconsciousness[9] to return in any form to her tormentor's room. Instead, Cass Kinsolving assumes the role of nemesis, on behalf of Francesca (and himself); and Mason dies at the hands of the artist—whose actions parallel those of Ethelred, the hero of "The Mad Trist." In Poe's story, passages read from the romance by the narrator accompany and correspond to sounds and events preceding Usher's death. Like Ethelred, who attempted first to gain "peaceable admission" into an evil hermit's dwelling, Cass has tried without success to talk reasonably with Flagg. Both heroes, drunk with wine, therefore, decide on new tactics. Poe's narrator reads this account from "The Mad Trist": "And Ethelred...who was now mighty withal, on account of the powerfulness of the wine which he had drunken, waited no longer to hold parley with the hermit, who, in sooth, was of an obstinate and maliceful turn" (p. 413). Ethelred splinters the hermit's door with his mace; Cass, on the other hand, flies downstairs to get a key. Both heroes gain access to the room only to find the "maliceful" personages disappeared. Ethelred discovers in the hermit's place "a dragon of a scaly and prodigious demeanor"; Cass discovers snaky Mason hiding underneath the bed. Subsequently, Ethelred with his mace "struck upon the head of the dragon, which fell before him" (p. 414). Cass, with a large stone, splits Mason's skull open, "and Mason dropped like a bag of sand" (p. 464).

After Roderick Usher's death, the story-teller concludes: "the deep and

dank tarn at my feet closed sullenly and silently over the fragments of the *House of Usher*"—and its master (p. 417). After Flagg's death, Mason is hurled over the ledge and "into the void" (pp. 463-465).

These parallels in tone and plot thus point to "The Fall of the House of Usher" as an important source for Styron's Gothic novel. The ironic and satiric contrasts develop Styron's versions of twentieth-century moral and psychic disintegration. Whereas Usher is a nice, clearcut, soundly unhealthy case of madness and evil, Mason Flagg, as one character says, is just a " 'wicked and terrible, phony creep' " (p. 40). Connecting *Set This House on Fire* with Poe's story suggests another approach toward analyzing Styron's narrator and friend, and toward understanding Styron's modern definition of evil.

## NOTES

[1] (New York, 1960), p. 445. Further references are to this edition and appear in the text.

[2] *M*. 2:392-422. Further references to this edition appear in the text.

[3] Anthony Winner, in "Adjustment, Tragic Humanism, and Italy," *SA*, 7(1961), 339-361, examines Styron's use of Gothic techniques to develop his concepts of evil. In *William Styron* (New York, 1972), pp. 71-89, Marc L. Ratner discusses the novel as "Gothic satire" and also includes brief treatment of various sources discussed in scholarly essays. Ratner is one of several critics who mention a resemblance between Styron's twosome and Fitzgerald's Nick Carraway and Jay Gatsby.

[4] Poe calls Usher "proprietor" (p. 398); and Styron calls Flagg "proprietor" of the rented palace (p. 119). Mason is also the proprietor of the family home in Virginia, an "enormous estate" described as a "renovated castle in the morning mist" (pp. 75-79).

[5] The activity in Styron's strange palace is often reminiscent of "The Haunted Palace," just as surely as certain actions and situations elsewhere recall those by Dirk Peters (whose name resonates in Peter Leverett's) in *Pym*.

[6] Despite critics' varying impressions, interpretations most consistent with Usher's other interests deal with the painting as one of Usher's concepts of Death. For a brief discussion of the painting as symbol of "Death-Madness," see Darrel Abel, "A Key to the House of Usher," *Twentieth Century Interpretations of The Fall of the House of Usher*, ed. Thomas Woodson (Englewood Cliffs, 1969), p. 51. Abel's important essay first appeared in *UTQ*, 18(1949), 176-185.

[7] For comments on the titles in Usher's library, see Mabbott's "Notes" 15-25, pp. 419-421.

[8] The young woman, of course, is not Flagg's sister, but Styron includes a Freudian-Oedipal relationship between Flagg and his mother, Gwendolyn (see pp.

72, 78-79, 94). In line with the readings of the twin sister as part of Usher's split personality, Styron develops a divided Mason (see pp. 124, 158-159).

[9] A description of Mason's ex-wife does, however, suggest Madeline's surprise appearance at Usher's door: After Peter hears "a frantic rapping at the door, the door itself flung open without a pause, and there was Celia....[H]er hand went to the back of her head, came down again, covered with blood. She said nothing at all. After a moment she stared at her red and trembling fingers, once more opened her mouth as if to say a word, and then collapsed in a heap upon the floor" (p. 160).

# "THE INSURRECTION OF SUBJUGATED KNOWLEDGE": POE AND ISHMAEL REED

*CRAIG WERNER*

Contemplating the symbolic chaos of a New Orleans Mardi Gras parade, black humorist Ishmael Reed finds "a giant black raven" rising up before him. The raven is part of a float which celebrates "The Spirit of Literature" and bears the names of Mark Twain and Edgar Allan Poe. The float also includes a "typewriter next to which a Confederate soldier held forth a bayonet." As Reed concludes, "this float was trying to tell me something."[1] Rather than speculating on the message, Reed heads off for pitchers of beer and hamburgers. Nonetheless, the apparition hovers throughout his work, pointing to a continuing fascination with the aesthetic message—at once absurd, threatening, trivial and profound—emanating from both Poe the serious artist and Poe the pop icon. In fact, Poe provides a central point of reference in three of Reed's novels: *The Free-Lance Pallbearers* (1967), *The Last Days of Louisiana Red* (1974) and *Flight to Canada* (1976). These works reflect and extend an ambivalent Afro-American tradition that alternately repudiates and endorses Poe's vision. The repudiation derives from an understandable reaction against the racism Poe shared with the vast majority of his contemporaries, northern and southern.[2] The endorsement relates to Poe's apprehension of the hidden horror of the American psyche, an apprehension fundamental to Afro-American writing. Instead of simply juxtaposing these two orientations, the encompassing ambivalence reflects a deep uncertainty concerning the relationship between Poe and parody. Frequently the pop Poe has been taken more "seriously" (and uncritically) than the "serious" Poe whom academic critics increasingly recognize as a master hoaxer. As a result, the pop Poe may seem an unwitting parody, a hoax on the memory of the hoaxer. Because of the wide currency of the pop image, this hoax transforms Poe into an extremely threatening figure embodying the very drives which he himself satirized in his best work. The juxtaposition of overblown raven and bayonet perfectly captures the ambiguity facing the Afro-American writer confronting Poe. Himself a master ironist, Reed seizes on this ambiguity to test "Reed's Law" that states: "when a parody is better than the original a mutation occurs which renders the original obsolete."[3] Poe will no doubt survive Reed's parodies of "The Raven," "The Masque of the Red Death," "The Murders in the Rue Morgue," and "Annabel Lee." Ultimately, however, the parodies may contribute to a mutation in the literary spirit that grants the Confederate soldier his bayonet and denies Charles W. Chesnutt his place on the Mardi Gras float.

Reed's response to Poe frequently demonstrates his awareness of the Afro-American attraction to Poe's vision of horror. Where Poe perceived an encompassing psychological horror, however, Afro-American writers concentrate on the social origins and implications of the horror. Evident in stories such as Chesnutt's "The Gray Wolf's Ha'nt" and Wallace Thurman's "Grist in the Mill," this response received its classic statement in the introductory essay to Richard Wright's *Native Son*. Wright wrote: "we have in the oppression of the Negro a shadow athwart our national life dense and heavy enough to satisfy even the gloomy broodings of a Hawthorne. And if Poe were alive, he would not have to invent horror; horror would invent him."[4] Similarly, James Baldwin comments on the murders of the black children in Atlanta in a passage echoing Wright: "Richard Wright once wrote that if Edgar Allan Poe had been born in 20th Century America, he would not have had to invent horror; horror would have invented him. The statement sounded perhaps a trifle excessive, like a gifted actor's extra flourish. But it does not seem even remotely excessive now. On the contrary, it seems relatively mild, even kind. Certainly nothing in Poe begins to approximate the horror now reigning."[5] Like Wright and Baldwin, Reed sees the U. S. as a haunted and horrific country. In this view, Poe is the inevitable, even the understated, spirit of a society that refuses to confront the source of its social and psychological diseases.

Reed's treatment of the horror clearly reflects his knowledge not only of Poe, but of Wright's treatment of Poe. Even while juxtaposing the apocalypse of "Usher" with that of *Native Son*, however, Reed provides a disquieting laugh-track that recalls the Afro-American tradition that finds Poe to be a fertile source of and target for parody. Although Wright's treatment of Bigger Thomas as a social version of the Ourang-Outang of "The Murders in the Rue Morgue" intimates this emphasis, Ralph Ellison is clearly Reed's most distinguished predecessor in parodying Poe. Ellison opens *Invisible Man* with a racially resonant pun: "I am an invisible man. No, I am not a spook like those who haunted Edgar Allan Poe; nor am I one of your Hollywood-movie ectoplasms."[6] The association of Poe and the movies develops into a major motif in Reed's parodies. Ellison himself parodies "The System of Dr. Tarr and Prof. Fether," itself a hoax, in the Golden Day chapter of *Invisible Man*. This image of America as a complex hoax, a place where the inmates run the madhouse, pervades *The Free-Lance Pallbearers* and much of Reed's later work. For Ellison and Reed, the madness derives partly from the corrupt heritage of racism, partly from America's unwillingness to accept the implications of its professed pluralism. Rather than embrace the cultural heritages of Africa, Native America, Asia and Egypt, Euro-American culture consigns

them to a symbolic underground. Paradoxically, this cultural hoax simultaneously consigns Euro-Americans to a static vision of reality. Clinging to the racist heritage, they embrace superficiality and deny their connection with the underground entirely. As a result, they find themselves trapped in the role of doomed madmen, all the madder for their refusal to admit they are living in an asylum. The destruction visited on Poe characters such as Roderick Usher and William Wilson can easily be seen as a mark of their inability to escape their static realities or to accept their links with the symbolic underground.

Reed refuses to accept this destruction. Accepting the pluralistic American heritage, he plunges into a world where symbols proliferate, where the raven echoes the Bible, Poe's poem, both Boris Karloff movie versions of the poem (one serious, one openly parodic), Tlinglit Indian mythology, and the highest aspirations of Mardi Gras floatmakers. Surrendering to absurdity, Reed makes no pretense of the kind of rational control invoked by Poe in "The Philosophy of Composition." Rather, he seeks to embrace the type of madness that Michel Foucault links with higher knowledge in *Madness and Civilization.* Foucault's description of madness (primarily in the pre-Classical tradition) as a form of passage relates directly to Reed's reconstruction of Poe's sensibility: "Freed from wisdom and from the teaching that organized it, the image begins to gravitate about its own madness. Paradoxically, this liberation derives from a proliferation of meaning, from a self-multiplication of significance, weaving relationships so numerous, so intertwined, so rich, that they can no longer be deciphered except in the esoterism of knowledge. Things themselves become so burdened with attributes, signs, allusions that they finally lose their own form. Meaning is no longer read in an immediate perception, the figure no longer speaks for itself; between the knowledge that animates it and the form into which it is transposed, a gap widens. It is free for the dream."[7] Both Poe and Reed clearly seek to liberate their images from the organizing principles of social wisdom; both allow the proliferation of meaning. The difference in their visions stems from Reed's determination to embrace the *gap* between form and knowledge. Since the "wisdom" of Euro-American culture denies many of the cultural traditions providing the imagery for Reed's dream, the gap—if one has the courage to plunge into it—allows access to a particularly rich range of liberating knowledge. Where Poe sought an unchanging ideal refuge from both social wisdom and from the tension between form and knowledge, Reed explores the relationships. He enters the gap protected only by a laughter that sounds with desperation, humor, irony and anger. Ultimately, Reed views all stasis—cultural or psychological—as destructive madness. In

response he promulgates a kinetic madness that employs a constantly shifting parody as its primary artistic expression. Although the kinetic madness may eventually generate insights making a kinetic sanity viable, Reed's immediate aim is simply to keep the parodic focus moving in order to deny his readers the sense of certainty which produces stasis.

Drawing with equal ease on the Euro- and Afro-American traditions of parody, Reed echoes both the masking traditions of Afro-American folk culture (used by Chesnutt and Ellison) and the consciously deceptive metafictional strategies of Samuel Beckett and John Barth. Reed also parodies serious literary forms through the conventions of pop culture and pop culture through those of "serious" art.[8] In this context Reed's fascination with Poe becomes most readily comprehensible. The Poe of Vincent Price and the Poe of Charles Baudelaire meet in *The Free-Lance Pallbearers;* the grandfather of the B detective movie and the sophisticated hoaxer are indistinguishable in *The Last Days of Louisiana Red.* Swept up in the "madness" reflected in his own words, Poe becomes a symbol of American culture far more encompassing than the Wright-Baldwin emphasis on horror would suggest. By parodying an unwanted literary master (Poe of the Confederacy) who himself has been subjected to numerous unconscious parodies (Poe of the B movies), Reed connects himself with a legitimate literary ancestor (Poe of the self-parody), thereby changing a serious parody into a camp statement complete with self-parody (Poe as Reed in whiteface).

At some point adding new levels of parody yields diminishing returns, but the presence of numerous levels highlights Reed's central strategy. The impossibility of distinguishing among parody, travesty, burlesque and camp reflects Reed's attempt to subvert the authority of hierarchical voices, to keep the revolution going—socially, artistically, psychologically. The key to Reed's revolution, and to his argument with Poe, is his rejection of the stasis that threatens to paralyze him—and his pluralistic culture—and to prevent the plunge into the gap between form and knowledge, between reality and dream. Ironically, Reed's insistence on a kinetic vision subverts his own "Law" by making it impossible to pin down a static "original" to be rendered obsolete through parody. By using Poe to motivate further revolutions, Reed guarantees Poe's continuing potency as a cultural force. Seen in this light, Reed's shifting attitude toward Poe is hardly surprising. At times he echoes Poe's imagery; at times he offers a critique of the imagination and the social ambiance which generated the images. At no time does he encourage complacent rejection of Poe as racist or acceptance of Poe as visionary. To a greater degree than the avatar of horror seen by Wright and Baldwin, Reed's Poe is as complex as the society that shaped him.

Among the most pervasive Poesque images in Reed's fiction are the asylum, the plague and the tomb. Reed's first novel, *The Free-Lance Pallbearers,* places protagonist Bukka Dopeyduk in an insane society—HARRY SAM—reminiscent of that in "The System of Dr. Tarr and Prof. Fether." Bukka finds himself playing a central role in what frequently seems a B-movie version of "The Raven" as it might have been directed by W. C. Fields and Richard Pryor: "I drunk some likker and got my head bad. At three o'clock in the morning there came a tap-dap-rapping at my door. A tit-tat-klooking at my hollow door. 'Who is dat rap-a-dap-tapping at my do' this time of night? What-cha-wont?"[9] Uncertain even whether he is summoner or summoned, Bukka is haunted by a host of "real" specters including Elijah Raven and Lenore, who provide the focus for Reed's critique of the pop Poe. In seeming contrast to Poe's raven with its one-word vocabulary, Reed's Elijah Raven constantly changes voice in an attempt to trick the white man. Although this kinetic approach parallels Reed's own parodic aesthetic, Elijah Raven manages to progress only from "What's happening, my man" (p. 9) to "Flim Flam Alakazam!" (p. 9) to "Git It On" (p. 71). Finally he rejects black power entirely and launches a new political rebellion based on saving cereal box tops (p. 109). The inmate may not be any crazier than his keepers, but he seems even less cogent than his feathered namesake.

Similarly, Lenore's relationship with a Poesque figure contributes to Reed's vision of a paralyzed society in *The Free-Lance Pallbearers.* First mentioned by Alfred, a poetic old man speaking in a "Boris Karloff voice" (p. 59), Lenore appears as the familiar Poesque emblem of lost love. Alfred, whose obsession with an idyllic past embarrasses even his friends, offers Bukka a gold watch as a "token from Lenore and the army of unalterable bores" (p. 59). Even Lenore satirizes Alfred's static obsessions which include his insistence on calling her "the second Helen of Troy" (p. 91). After the church refuses to allow the marriage of Alfred and Lenore (recasting the Poesque motif of incestuous love), Alfred's remaining friends speak to him only in French, recalling Poe's Baudelairian partisans. Though she manifests stasis differently from Alfred, Lenore shares the frenetic psychological paralysis which provides Reed's central image of American society. Slipping out of her role in the Poe movie, she emerges near the end of the novel as a porno movie star, smacking her lips and spouting advertising slogans (p. 110). Ultimately she shares both Alfred's stasis and Raven's incoherence.

This paralysis, masquerading as motion, results in an apocalypse echoing both the Poe of literature and the Poe of the movies. The final chapter of *The Free-Lance Pallbearers* occurs in a giant Victorian house complete with "eerie organ music" (p. 100), steps disappearing "into the hollow of an

abysmal throat" (p. 101), moans "coming from that oval-shaped darkness" (p. 101) and hallways lined with "human skeletons in chains" (p. 102). Reed alludes to several Poe tales in describing the destruction of the house: like that in "Usher" it "shook at its very roots" (p. 103). Ultimately a whirlpool—which Reed connects with the swirling water in a toilet bowl—sweeps away nearly everyone in the static society of HARRY SAM. The description of the flushing compresses images from *Invisible Man* (the descent into darkness following the Harlem riot), Afro-American folklore (the crossroads where the spirit Legba appears) and Poe's "Descent into the Maelstrom": "AS I RAN TOWARD THE 'FOUR CORNERS' INTERSECTION IN THE MIDDLE OF SAM WHERE VIOLENT WHIRLPOOLS OF PEOPLE SEEMED TO BE HEADING PELL-MELL INTO THE CROSSROADS" (p. 106). Bukka himself, like the protagonist of "The Pit and the Pendulum," escapes personal destruction; but his emergence from one Poe apocalypse simply brings him into the midst of another. Emerging from the underground at the end of the novel, he confronts a comic social version of the red death as he gazes on a flashing neon advertisement "WRITTEN IN CHINESE" (p. 116). Not content simply to undercut the dominant system of social wisdom, Reed emphasizes that his parodic revolution must be an on-going process. The destruction of one dominant hierarchy creates the opportunity for the emergence of another, one which incorporates some of the voices which had previously been consigned to the underground. The location of the gap shifts; stasis encroaches on kinesis; the body politic remains diseased.

The plague becomes the primary Poe allusion in Reed's novels *Mumbo Jumbo* and *The Last Days of Louisiana Red*. Where *The Free-Lance Pallbearers* parodies the Poe of the horror movies, these novels concentrate on the Poe of the detective story. Where Poe's Auguste Dupin uncovers the rational explanations for mysterious events, Reed's hoodoo detective Papa LaBas is a "jacklegged detective of the metaphysical."[10] Specifically, LaBas investigates the destructive plagues such as Louisiana Red that ravage Reed's America, discouraging movement and enforcing stasis. Reed describes the "Jes Grew" that worries the social authorities in *Mumbo Jumbo* as a kinetic anti-plague: "Some plagues caused the body to waste away; Jes Grew enlivened the host" (p. 9). Conversely, the red death in *The Last Days of Louisiana Red* threatens to destroy the "Gumbo Works," which carries on the pluralistic heritage of Jes Grew. Ultimately, LaBas and Reed trace the power of Louisiana Red to a disorder in America's collective imagination, a disorder related to fear of sexual and racial complexity. Parodying Dupin, Reed draws attention to the origins of the American horror in a simplistic and

simplifying faith in the power of reason to cope with social and psychological ambiguity.

Reed's multi-valent parody in *The Last Days of Louisiana Red* focuses on "The Murders in the Rue Morgue," showing a complex awareness of Wright's use of the same tale in *Native Son*. It has been argued that Poe's use of the ape as murderer reveals his own conscious racism, but neither Wright nor Reed seems overly concerned with the biographical issue. Rather, Wright concentrates on exploring the effects of the social acceptance of the image of black man as ape. His primary concern is with the media that portray Bigger both as a murderous gorilla and as a new incarnation of a communist red death. Reed in turn combines these motifs in order to comment on the symbolic red death plaguing America's unconscious life.[11]

Working with the Poe-Wright association between blacks and apes, Reed replaces the subhuman gorilla-Ourang-Outang with the superhuman baboon Hamadryas. Hamadryas communicates with super-rational sources of wisdom despite his incarceration in the Central Park Zoo, providing an image of the strength of underground knowledge even in bondage. He provides LaBas with important insight into the crucial lines of the mystic text "Minnie the Moocher" as sung by Cab Calloway: "Now here's a story 'bout Minnie the Moocher/ She was a low-down hoochy coocher/ She messed around wid a bloke named Smokey/ She loved him tho' he was a 'cokey."[12] Significantly the text providing the crucial knowledge appears to be entirely insane from the viewpoint of the dominant social wisdom. Hamadryas's advice, more mystical than rational, helps LaBas protect the Gumbo Works from Louisiana Red. The Poe villain becomes an anti-hero in *Native Son* and finally metamorphoses into the source of spiritual knowledge in *The Last Days of Louisiana Red.*

Even while recasting the ape in intellectual-spiritual terms, Reed endorses certain aspects of the Poe-Wright image cluster. Murderous apes do appear in *The Last Days of Louisiana Red.* Hamadryas is charged with fracturing the skull of the white zoo attendant who cuts short LaBas's visit. Reed suggests that, whatever the level of insight and achievement, any non-white person in America will have what Baldwin called his "private Bigger Thomas living in the skull."[13] Extending Baldwin's argument, Reed implies that every white person also internalizes Bigger. The crucial difference between the white and the black Bigger-ape is that the Euro-American typically refuses to acknowledge his madness and attempts to repress it by rational means. The "liberal" scholar-secret agent Maxwell Kasavubu, like Wright's Boris Max a white spokesman for black culture, is engaged in a critical study of *Native Son.* Rather than dealing with his material on an

emotional level, however, Kasavubu rejects all connection between himself and the *Native Son*/"The Murders in the Rue Morgue" myth. As a result, he suffers horrific dreams in which he becomes Mary Dalton threatened sexually by a "huge black gorilla" (p. 82). Ultimately his refusal to discuss the dreams results in his total insanity. Falling victim to the madness of Louisiana Red, he metamorphoses from Max to Mary (pp. 155-156) to Bigger himself (p. 156). Max/Bigger goes on the rampage in Berkeley Hills; when he is arrested, he is wearing a chauffeur's uniform and speaking the Mississippi/Chicago black dialect of the 1940s. As LaBas, Kasavubu has been "driven mad by his own cover" (p. 172). In *The Last Days of Louisiana Red* then, the white man becomes a black parody of a white parody of a black man/beast. Reed effectively defuses the racial implications of Poe's imaginative construct, identifying it not as a description of black reality but as an intimation of the red plague threatening the white man's cultural sanity. The culture that refuses to embrace pluralistic variety, internal and external, may find itself destroyed by the very roles it seeks to repress.

*Flight to Canada* focuses explicitly on the ways in which imaginative stasis engenders insanity. The raven motif recurs in the name of the protagonist Raven Quickskill, whose name derives from Tlinglit Indian mythology as much as it does from Poe.[14] Significantly, the Indian reference emphasizes movement and rejects hierarchical institutions: "Other slaves, however, sat at attention. They'd begun some kind of Raven cult. He didn't want to have a cult. A Raven is always on the move. A cult would tie him down."[15] Conversely, Poe has been immobilized by the paralyzed civilization that forces Raven to keep moving. Reed's analysis of Poe's place in the Southern imagination (which he sees simply as an emblem of the dominant Euro-American imagination) seems to concentrate on Poe as racist apostle of horror: "Why isn't Edgar Allan Poe recognized as the principal biographer of that strange war [the Civil War]? Fiction, you say? Where does fact begin and fiction leave off? Why does the perfectly rational, in its own time, often sound like mumbo-jumbo? Where did it leave off for Poe, prophet of a civilization buried alive, where according to witnesses, people were often whipped for no reason" (p. 10)? The phrase "no reason" demands clarification. In fact, Reed uncovers the irrational "reasons," similar to those in *The Last Days of Louisiana Red,* for the paralysis of the civilization Poe expresses. Employing an intricate complex of Poesque motifs, Reed attributes the paralysis to America's fixation on an unreal personal and social past. In addition, by connecting the "perfectly rational" with "mumbo-jumbo," the title of his own third novel, Reed suggests a buried affinity with Poe in the role of hoaxer.

Reed's use of Poe as a character in *Flight to Canada* makes it clear that he is primarily concerned with Poe as distorted by the American imagination. At times the distortions seem harmless; he gives garden party readings and sets the standards for the "dandyish, foppish, pimpish" (p. 141) element of the South. Poe, however, is also adopted by slavemasters such as Arthur Swille who acquires "opiates" from "Eddie Poe" (p. 135). The passage transforms Poe into an emblem of both psychological and social oppression. He is the Oedipal ("Eddie Poe") father-oppressor who simultaneously parodies Marxist theory by providing "opiates for the massas." The Oedipal motif recurs when Swille's murdered son returns from the grave to condemn his father as "one macabre fiend," continuing "No wonder he has Poe down here all the time" (p. 126).

Throughout the novel Swille lives in a Poesque world dominated by his sexual fixation on his dead sister Vivian. Clearly intended as a parody of numerous Poe characters, Swille repeatedly returns to the crypt to embrace his lost love's decomposed body (p. 60). His fondest memory restates "Annabel Lee": "Vivian, my disconsolate damsel, if only you...my fair pale sister. Your virgin knees and golden hair in your sepulcher by the sea. Let me creep into your mausoleum, baby. My insatiable Vivian by the sea, remember how we used to go for walks down to the levee and wait for the *Annabel Lee*. You were only fourteen years old, yet ours is a romance of the days that were" (p. 109). Beneath the romantic surface of the Old South—the South of the steamboat *Robert E. Lee*—Reed reveals an obscene and destructive fixation on a static past. His description of Vivian's return from the grave recalls the B movie Poe appropriate to Swille's psyche. Coming back to life wearing a "filmy scarf, white-death negligee, feet white and ashen, carrying some strange book of obscure lore" (p. 135), Vivian demands that Swille confront the implications of his obsession. She refuses to allow him to return to his wife. She taunts him with echoes of "Annabel Lee": "You'll never give up me, will you, brother? Out in my sepulcher by the sea" (p. 135). Returning from the grave like Madeline in "Usher," she kills her brother with a "fiery kiss." Even after his death, however, Swille's obsession haunts him. The final paragraph of his will commits him irrevocably to a static madness: " 'And my final request may sound a little odd to the Yankees who've invaded our bucolic haven, but I wish to be buried in my sister's sepulcher by the sea, joined in the Kama Sutra position below...that we may be joined together in eternal and sweet Death' " (pp. 168-169). Again, Reed portrays stasis, death and sexual madness as aspects of the same encompassing plague.

Swille's corruption parallels that of the entire slave-owning society in *Flight to Canada*. Again, Reed implicates Poe in the imaginative structure

supporting the social insanity: "He loved the sound of the screams coming from various parts of the plantation, day and night. Eddie Poe had gone bonkers over his equipment and used some of it in his short stories" (p. 108). Although the masters maintain belief in their own superior civilization—the civilization of the Confederate soldier on the Mardi Gras float—Reed clearly portrays the ante-bellum South as an asylum in the hands of the inmates. Juxtaposing Swille's death with a section of the novel titled "The Burning of Richmond," Reed asks the question concerning responsibility for the destruction: "Who pushed Swille into the fire? Some Etheric Double? The inexorable forces of history? A ghost? Thought? Or all of these? Who could have pushed him? Who?" (p. 179). Reed offers no simple answer. Focusing on either internal (etheric double), external (history) or mystical (ghost) causes reestablishes precisely the type of hierarchical "social wisdom" that encourages the complacency that doomed Swille and the South. Ultimately, as Reed comments, Poe's own imagination provides the deepest insight into the maelstrom of the Civil War: "Poe got it all down. Poe says more in a few stories than all of the volumes by historians" (p. 10).

Despite his "attacks" on Poe, there is a kind of kinetically crazy logic in Reed's decision to focus his counter-vision in *Flight to Canada* on the multi-valent image of the raven. To reject the history of the "other"—in this case of Poe the white Southerner—would be to perpetuate the Euro-American mistake. Rather than subjecting himself to the resulting destruction, Reed rejects both the denial of and the obsession with a static past. Specifically, Reed re-imagines America, land of slavery and the raven, through the kinetic figure of Raven Quickskill, who is simultaneously Southern writer and runaway slave. Raven gains his power from parodying not only Poe, but the Bible, Tlinglit mythology, and his own creator. Neither his body nor his art can be confined within a static form: "His poem flew just as his name had flown. Raven. A scavenger to some, a bringer of new light to others" (p. 13). This identification of personal identity with written text recalls Robert B. Stepto's description of the Afro-American "narrative of ascent" in which the hero can attain freedom only by becoming literate in Euro-American terms.[16] Even as he gains control over the text of his own experience, however, the "articulate survivor" (Stepto's term for the hero of the ascent narrative) risks alienation from the Afro-American culture that nurtured him. The challenge facing Reed's Raven, therefore, is to avoid picking up the static voice of Poe's raven.

Reed's Raven meets this challenge by joining in a complex parody of himself and his creator, a parody that cautions against a static reading of the critique of stasis. When Raven reaches Canada, he finds a land of fast food

stands that simply recasts the spiritual poverty of the United States and threatens him with the cultural isolation risked by the articulate survivor. Through Raven's flight, Reed parodies simplistic conceptions of freedom as a goal to be reached and then statically maintained. All stasis, in a land continually echoing "nevermore," implies death; the revolution must keep on revolving. To this end, Reed insists on the fluidity of his own text, his own identity. Raven Quickskill's magnum opus is a poem titled "Flight to Canada." The poem is part wish-fulfillment, part social criticism, part autobiography, part self-parody. Reed never stops reinterpreting "Flight to Canada" in *Flight to Canada.* Implicitly and explicitly, he challenges the reader to share the kinetic process of self and social creation. The novel's first paragraph, which applies equally well to the experience of Reed and of Raven, focuses on the reader's role in the aesthetic process: "Little did I know when I wrote the poem 'Flight to Canada' that there were so many secrets locked inside its world. It was more of a reading than a writing" (p. 7). By placing Quickskill's poem in his own novel and writing much of the novel in Quickskill's raven voice, Reed effectively forces the reader to reconstruct the text in much the same way Reed has reconstructed Poe's. He raises the possibility that his own text is a function of social illness and in fact may play a politically negative role in giving away the "secrets" of Afro-American (or any underground) cultural strategies.

This distrust of even his own text reflects Reed's concern with what Foucault calls "global" or "totalitarian" theories that subsume individual perceptions within their own alien structures. Therefore, even an immediately valid perception may contribute to the oppression or repression of further perceptions. Today's motion is tomorrow's stasis. Recommending a "non-centralised" criticism "whose validity is not dependent on the approval of the established regimes of thought," Foucault endorses an "insurrection of subjugated knowledges."[17] Reed's parodies contribute immediately to this insurrection, which by its very nature cannot provide a "wisdom" capable of organizing the subjugated knowledges into a "sane" structure. The very presence of a global wisdom forces the subjugated knowledges to return to the symbolic underground or to become part of the totalitarian regime. Faced with this desperate circumstance, Reed determines to keep one revolution ahead of the hierarchy, to keep seeking and releasing the pluralistic knowledge in Afro-American culture, in Tlinglit mythology. Finally he seeks to disrupt the hierarchy itself by releasing the subjugated knowledge buried by and within the Euro-American imagination, the knowledge flickering through the smile of the B-movie Poe.

No text can be any more sacred than another in this radically pluralistic

vision. Poe remains valuable for his insights, whether or not he recognized their implications. Similarly, Reed takes himself seriously only insofar as he can laugh at Raven—his own and Poe's—and then move on. Providing an analog within his texts for the complex process of parody and self-parody that supports the insurrection of subjugated knowledge, Reed challenges his readers to join in their own underground revolution, to rescue Poe from the stasis of his own vision and enlist him in the revolution against the Confederate Soldier on the Mardi Gras float.

## NOTES

[1] Ishmael Reed, *Shrovetide in Old New Orleans* (Garden City, 1978), p. 23.

[2] For the basic argument on Poe's racism, see *Race and the American Romantics,* ed. Vincent Freimarck and Bernard Rosenthal (New York, 1971), pp. 2-4. The same volume includes the "Paulding-Drayton Review," on which much of the case rests. Although there has been much discussion of Poe's authorship of the review, there seems little reason to doubt the general conclusion drawn by Freimarck and Rosenthal.

[3] Reed, *Shrovetide,* p. 248. For a full-scale discussion of Poe's use of the ironic mode, see G. R. Thompson, *Poe's Fiction: Romantic Irony in the Gothic Tales* (Madison, WI, 1973). Other valuable contributions to our understanding of Poe's ability to employ irony in subtle fashion include Benjamin Franklin Fisher IV, "Poe's 'Tarr and Fether': Hoaxing in the Blackwood Mode," *Topic* 31(1977), 30-40, and James M. Cox, "Edgar Poe: Style as Pose," *VQR* 44(1968), 67-89.

[4] Richard Wright, *Native Son* (New York, 1940), p. xxxiv.

[5] James Baldwin, "Atlanta: The Evidence of Things Not Seen," *Playboy* 28, no. 12 (December 1981), p. 142.

[6] Ralph Ellison, *Invisible Man* (New York, 1952), p. 3.

[7] Michel Foucault, *Madness and Civilization* (New York, 1973), pp. 18-19.

[8] My argument concerning Reed's use of parody has been profoundly influenced by Leslie Fiedler's essay "The Dream of the New," *American Dreams, American Nightmares,* ed. David Madden (Carbondale and Edwardsville, 1970), pp. 19-27. Fiedler views Poe as the exemplar of the American relationship to the parodic mode and establishes the framework which supports a reading of Reed as a "true" literary descendant of at least one aspect of Poe.

[9] Reed, *The Free-Lance Pallbearers* (New York, 1969), p. 26.

[10] Reed, *Mumbo Jumbo* (New York, 1972), p. 241.

[11] The Poe-Wright connection has been discussed at length in Michel Fabre, "Black Cat and White Cat: Richard Wright's Debt to Edgar Allan Poe," *PoeS,* 4 (1971), 17-20; Linda T. Prior, "A Further Word on Richard Wright's Use of Poe

in Native Son," *PoeS*, 5 (1972), 52-53; and Seymour Gross, "*Native Son* and "The Murders in the Rue Morgue': An Addendum," *PoeS*, 8 (1975), 23.

[12] Reed, *The Last Days of Louisiana Red* (New York, 1974), p. 34.

[13] Baldwin, *Notes of a Native Son* (New York, 1964), p. 33.

[14] Reed, *Shrovetide*, pp. 228-229.

[15] Reed, *Flight to Canada* (New York, 1976), p. 144.

[16] Robert B. Stepto, *From Behind the Veil: A Study of Afro-American Narrative* (Urbana, 1979), p. 167.

[17] Michel Foucault, *Power/Knowledge* (New York, 1980), pp. 80-83.

PRINTED BY
THE COVINGTON PUBLISHING COMPANY,
COVINGTON, TN.